Praise for *The Power Principle*

"I wish that this book had been published when I became CEO! In *The Power Principle: Influence with Honor,* Blaine Lee reminds leaders that the attribute of character, which includes honor, integrity, and deep respect for others, will ultimately make the greatest impact on an organization and inspire the most people to extraordinary results."
—Archie W. Dunham, President and CEO, Conoco, Inc.

"In a society too often focused on short-term results and gratification, we need leaders who remind us that conducting ourselves with honor, with patience, with love, and with care undoubtedly will produce relationships that bear great fruit in the long run. *The Power Principle* offers a workable theory of leadership and power based on principles of fundamental human decency. It holds out great hope for shaping leaders today and in the future. I applaud this insightful work and recommend it to people in every walk of life."
—Reverend Edward A. Malloy, C.S.C., President,
University of Notre Dame

"Dr. Lee brings us some clear principles for living a life of hope, aspiration, and service—and for relationships that can change lives."
—Frances Hesselbein, President and CEO, Peter F. Drucker Foundation

"*The Power Principle* sheds new light on where power comes from and how it should be used. Lee's insights are critical for those trying to lead organizational change."
—Philip J. Carroll, President and CEO, Shell Oil Company

"Blaine Lee is a truly gifted individual who, without question, will be a major catalyst of change in people's lives. His life and his dedication to mankind (and womankind) is reflected in *The Power Principle*. It is a wonderful book!"
—Stedman Graham, President and CEO, S. Graham & Associates;
author of *You Can Make It Happen: A Nine-Step Plan for Success*

"What poeple think they want is power. But what they really need is heart-centered visionary leadership which *The Power Principle* so aptly teaches!"
—Mark Victor Hansen, coauthor of *Chicken Soup for the Soul*

"The theory of principle-centered relationships is an extraordinary concept. Blaine Lee's insights into the connection points between work success and life success may be the most important ideas we can learn as we prepare for living in the next millennium."

—John Sculley, President and CEO, Sculley Associates;
author of *Odyssey: Pepsi to Apple . . .*

"In a power-hungry world, power is, ironically, poorly understood, especially by those who lust after it most. Blaine Lee understands the essence of power. He tells how to obtain it and how to wield it wisely in this highly readable and deeply profound work."

—Michael O. Leavitt, Govenor of Utah,
Former President of the Council of State Governments

"Blaine Lee's exploration of personal power *is* powerful. *The Power Principle* is so full of real stories that all can find themselves in it. Hierarchy in business, families, and communities has traditionally been the ladder of power and the source of much misuse and abuse. The bottom line is that a principle-based orientation drives self-esteem, achievement, relationships, and personal fulfillment."

—Jack Linkletter

"*The Power Principle* teaches us how to develop the self-confidence and inner strength to choose power over powerlessness and survival over victimization. This is a book for everyone who wants to reach his or her highest potential."

—Candace Lightner, Founder, M.A.D.D.
(Mothers Against Drunk Driving)

"*The Power Principle* is the most insightful and inspirational study of power and how to use it that I have read in years. There is a Native-American concept of knowledge that claims that people do not really 'know' something until it falls from their heads to their hearts. This is a book from 'the heart' for 'the head.'"

—Douglas R. Conant, President, Nabisco U.S. Foods Group

"Successful school administrators spend their professional lives creating challenging and meaningful learning experiences for students. Focusing on the strategies from *The Power Principle* enables these leaders to free individuals to reach their highest potentials with 'honor' and commitment."

—Judy J. Nash, Ph.D., Former Director, NASE Programming,
American Association of School Administrators

"Years ago a wise man taught me a profound but difficult to comprehend and apply truth: the only way a leader has power is to give it away. *The Power Principle* helps all of us who wish to exercise power with integrity and honor to grapple with this mystery, shedding light and insight on how we can gain more power by giving it to others."

—Kirk L. Stromberg, Director, Strategic Planning,
American Association of Retired Persons (AARP)

"An enlightening insight into the essence of leadership for today's interdependent business climate. *The Power Principle* is a catalyst for sincere introspection with a road map for paradigm shifts. It is a must read for the pragmatic leader of the next millennium."

—Clyde Fessler, Vice President of Business Development,
Harley-Davidson Motor Company

"Blaine Lee has captured the essence of living a life of integrity with principle-centered power. *The Power Principle* teaches you how to connect with your inner conscience, to live by it, and to truly influence with honor the lives of all those you come in contact with."

—Robert Schuller, author of *If You Can Dream It, You Can Do It;*
Reverend of Crystal Cathedral and *Hour of Power*

"In my experience with the NFL, I have found that those with the most power are those who balance both 'character and competence.' *The Power Principle* offers us numerous real-life examples of how to influence with honor no matter what team we're on!"

—Steve Young, Quarterback, San Francisco Forty-Niners

"In this readable and lively masterpiece, Blaine Lee carefully illuminates the truths that unleash dormant power, rechannel misdirected power, and are the only meaningful antidote to corrupting power. You will not see power again through the same lens after experiencing this book."

—Bob Goodwin, President and CEO, Points of Light Foundation

"*The Power Principle* reminds me of a line spoken by William Wallace in the movie *BraveHeart* explaining why people follow him: 'Men don't follow titles,' he says. 'They follow courage.' All of Blaine Lee's stories and examples describe the courage of leadership, as well as principle-driven leadership. It's one thing to have convictions, it's quite another to act on them. Living the Power Principle will ensure long-lasting success."

—James E. Ferrell, Chairman and CEO, Ferrellgas

THE
POWER
PRINCIPLE

INFLUENCE WITH HONOR

Blaine Lee
COVEY LEADERSHIP CENTER

Simon & Schuster

SIMON & SCHUSTER
Rockefeller Center
1230 Avenue of the Americas
New York, NY 10020

SIMON & SCHUSTER and colophon are registered trademarks
of Simon & Schuster Inc.

Designed by Irving Perkins Associates

Manufactured in the United States of America

10   9   8   7   6   5   4

Library of Congress Cataloging-in-Publication Data
ISBN 0-684-81058-1

ACKNOWLEDGMENTS

To:

My wife, Shawny, for her partnership, her belief, her example, and her love, which made this book worth writing.

My children, Blaine Christian, Benjamin, Adam, Michal, Joseph, Joshua, Casey, Abraham, Eliza, Gabriel, and Celeste—who made me want to live what I was learning and patiently lived with me while I experienced what I needed to learn.

My mother, Thelma Reeder, for her encouragement and a lifetime legacy of learning and teaching.

My assistant, Karen, who was patient and persistent, who found sources when no one else could, and who believed in the value of this book before it was a book.

My editor, Dominick Anfuso, whose expertise was as great as his heart, and whose seasoned blend of courage and consideration confidently orchestrated the conversion of a manuscript into a book.

Bob Asahina, who helped me understand the importance of dealing with powerlessness.

Greg Link, for his professionalism, perspective, wisdom, tireless efforts, and sustained friendship.

Stephen M.R. Covey, President, Covey Leadership Center, for seeing the need for this book, adjusting my schedule, and making resources available to make the writing possible.

Stephen R. Covey, for his affirmation that principles are supreme, that the Power Principle is the fundamental foundation of all successful human influence, and for his confidence in me.

Mike Taylor, a one-man computer coalition who graciously made technology my servant throughout the project.

Anne Andrus, whose clarity of thought, congenial availability, quick but deep understanding, editing skills, and ability to work all night kept the project on track.

The hundreds of managers, leaders, and teachers who read the manuscript in an early stage and offered helpful feedback.

My Heavenly Father, without whose inspiration this book could never have been written.

CONTENTS

FOREWORD

by Stephen R. Covey

THIS IS A MARVELOUS, LIFE-CHANGING BOOK. IT REPRESENTS A LIFE-time of learning on a subject that is as vital in life and relationships as air is to our bodies. *The Power Principle* will transform our personal lives and our careers. It significantly impacts all our relationships, organizations, businesses, families, and society as a whole when we learn to influence with honor.

Carl Rogers once taught, "That which is most personal is most general." Power and influence are literally as personal and as general as breathing air. It surrounds us. We are all in the business of influence. Whether we're dealing with clients, employees, employers, colleagues, and particularly in our own home, there are no exceptions. Influence is the most basic, most universal, and yet the most personal activity in life. But like "fish who discover water last," we often are unaware of how we use power and why the most common approaches seem to work in the short run, but fail in the long run. We can consciously choose far superior approaches.

To understand the principle which ultimately governs power and influence with others is more important than to learn a thousand techniques of influence. This book teaches this principle. Understanding this principle, *really* understanding it, will affect every relationship you have. Within these pages, Dr. Blaine Lee gives a brilliant analysis of the three fundamental power strategies that are used in life, the paradigms they are based upon, and the consequences that result from their use. Blaine, my friend and longtime business colleague, is one of the finest teachers I have ever known and has become a world authority on leadership and organizational development, particularly in the development and use of power and influence.

The two most commonly used strategies for influencing others are socially acceptable but are not in alignment with universal principles. That is why they don't work over time. These popular approaches focus on efficiency and control and are based on either a fairness-exchange approach or a forced-compliance one. But when you're working with people and building relationships, fast is slow and slow is fast. Efficiency doesn't cut it. Have you ever tried to be efficient with your spouse on a tough issue? How did it go? Or with your teenager on an emotionally charged issue? How did that one go? How about with your employees or business associates? Efficiency is just not effective. *The Power Principle* represents a third strategy, a third alternative—the Buddhists call it the middle way—not a compromise middle, rather a higher middle way like the apex of a triangle. If people don't learn this third alternative early on by the force of their conscience, they will ultimately learn it by the force of circumstance!

Let me also mention what this book is not, when examined through the lens of Henry David Thoreau's profound statement, "For every thousand hacking at the leaves of evil, there is one striking at the root." This book is not a quick-fix, success-recipe book which hacks at the leaves. This book is not a "feel good" book which attacks the twigs. Neither is it a heavy academic report. There are many stories and much appealing inspiration here, but it is far more than an organized series of lessons tied to inspirational stories. This book strikes at the very roots in developing a deep understanding of the fundamental key to power and human influence over time. The only "problem" with this understanding is that it requires us to grow, to challenge our assumptions, to often change our whole orientations in life and in relationships. Its focus is character, not technique.

Oliver Wendell Holmes once said, "I wouldn't give a fig for the simplicity on this side of complexity, but I would give my right arm for the simplicity on the far side of complexity." This book will take you from the simple to the complex and then back again to the simple. Deep soaking in the complexity of the power versus powerlessness challenge is necessary or there can be no deep understanding, and without deep understanding, the new paradigm won't "take" and the sustained energy to act on it won't be created.

After a decade of working together, I thought I knew Blaine Lee's thinking, but all I can say after studying his book is that I didn't. There is so much depth to him, so many dimensions. This book is the work of an entire lifetime—as student, teacher, scholar, consultant, husband, father, and leader. This work is comprehensive, extremely well illustrated, and bristles with insight and wisdom.

Blaine has paid the price and earned the right to talk about power and influence because he has honed his communication skills in a free and open market by training executives who choose to come to listen to him. Captive-market teachers usually begin with their own minds, not the mind of the learner. But for those who compete in the free marketplace, and in an open workplace, they have to produce what works. Sometimes, however, they go too far and "sell out," to become popular by telling others what they want to hear, not what they need to hear. Blaine neither popularizes nor theorizes, but takes the higher-influence road, which explains his power and influence.

This very book illustrates the main point it contains. Blaine starts with the minds of the learners, and then introduces them to the principles, and most of the illustrations come from the learners themselves. This has given Blaine a real feeling of the pulse of a person or group. He has also become a student and a scholar of the literature (which becomes evident as you read this material), so that you have a sense he is a cutting-edge-thought leader on the subject of power and influence. Thus, when you're dealing with an author who combines the pulse of the learner with the best thinking on the subject, something magical begins to happen that is truly synergistic—new ideas, new insights, new alternatives are created that are far superior to any yet advanced.

He also beautifully identifies the struggle we all have in applying the principles, for he's deep into the struggle himself, and when he stands apart and observes his own struggle, insights flow which are so general because they are so personal. As you read, you can feel it. You feel you are not just listening to someone giving autobiographical stories and then extrapolating to their life, but that you are dealing with a scholar in the field, an expert on the subject, who has also struggled like you and me to internalize and apply. That's why the insights and wisdom he shares have a profound ring of truth and relevance and excitement. It is in the blending of the mind, the heart, and the spirit that the highest, the deepest, and the most personal universal wisdom is produced.

Perhaps a story might illustrate such wisdom: A desperate man once appealed to a wise leader on behalf of his wayward son. The boy had been into drugs and addiction and lacked any kind of motivation to change. This father emotionally pleaded for help and advice, "What can I do about this boy, for I have exhausted all my influence with him?" Sensing the strict and distant manner with which this father had raised this boy, the wise man replied, "You must return to his first year and begin again." Although this was obviously not physically possible, this father needed to realize that his problems couldn't be fixed overnight with a new red convertible or a camping and fishing outing. They couldn't be masked by a forced treatment program or a parole officer's watchful eye. The Bible tells us that old wine must be removed from a bottle before fresh wine is dispensed, else the bottle will break. So too with this boy. A new approach was required, one in which this father needed to take the time to plant young, fresh seeds into soil that had been neglected for years. He needed to build what I call an "emotional bank account" with this child and it could not happen overnight.

It is only when we understand the importance of these universal principles that we can begin to understand the kind of power Blaine is talking about in this book. For example, although medication and surgery may mask physical pain and help delay the onset of poor health, only prevention and preparation through nutrition, stress management, and exercise will have a lasting effect. Similarly, honor, love, respect, integrity—these all have enduring significance and they always will be the foundation for creating sustained influence and cultivating relationships.

The Power Principle is also beautifully illustrated within a societal and historical context in explaining the steady decline of confidence in our social institutions. Several years ago, I made a comprehensive review of the success literature published since 1776. I observed that, up until around World War I, organizations as well as people were strongly concerned with what I like to call the "character ethic." In other words, character traits such as integrity, industry, civility, cooperation, service, modesty, and honor were highly valued. Yet, particularly after the Second World War, this emphasis on character became less and less significant as cosmetic strategies began to emerge. Personality values took center stage and organizations shifted toward exterior rather than interior concerns. Appearances, public images, and attitudes became pivotal and prosperity was primarily seen through quarterly reports. Acute problems were often addressed, leaving the underlying chronic problems to fester and resurface.

However, today the global marketplace and world-class realities make it apparent that this focus on image and status rather than content and quality erodes trust, diminishes the merit of the products and the involved relationships. Shortcuts became the norm and inevitably revenues and profits started to dwindle as customers and employees became disillusioned and wary of quick-fix ideas and results. Then, as cynicism congeals, institutionalized dependency grows, control strategies and hidden agendas multiply, and the cycle feeds on itself. Thus, confidence in almost all institutions has slowly eroded. (Cotton candy looks appealing and tastes delicious, but has no substance to fill a hungry body and no vital nutrients to build bones and healthy blood.) In the same way, this country began to starve, and still is starving for the character ethic of our past.

The Agricultural Age was rooted in nature, in principles. The Industrial Age became abstracted from nature and the new efficient techniques started to eclipse human values. The Information Age is removed from nature by several orders of magnitude with new technologies embodying unbelievable power for good or ill depending on the driving values. If our families, businesses, government, churches, and schools don't return to the fundamental needs of the people and to universal principles our whole civilization is in peril.

Adam Smith, who wrote *The Wealth of Nations* and who many consider to be the father of modern capitalism, wrote an earlier book, *The Theory of Moral Sentiments* (1759), wherein he laid out the necessary moral philosophy by which his later economic work was to be understood. In short, he taught that a free market economic system, like our constitutional democratic political system, is based upon intentional good will, or upon the essential morality of the people, and that when that is gone, ultimately, both of those systems will be compromised and eventually destroyed. Dr. Kirk Hart, educator, writes, "The future of America seems problematic. . . . These heightened times call for the highest qualities of civic character from both leaders and citizens."

In the last analysis, however, it's still an inside-out approach. The welfare of society ultimately returns to the honorable actions of each person. Helen Keller beautifully describes the impact of such a person:

> There are red letter days in our lives when we meet people who thrill us like a fine poem, people whose handshake is a brimful of unspoken sympathy and whose sweet, rich nature imparts to our eager impatient spirits a wonderful restfulness. . . . Perhaps we never saw them before and they may never cross our life's path again; but the influence of their

calm, mellow nature is a libation poured out upon our discontent, and we feel its healing touch as the ocean feels the mountain stream freshening its brine. . . .

You will feel this healing, hopeful touch as you read this book. *The Power Principle* teaches that we should never in the slightest violate the unique agency of an individual despite the position we may have over them. Whatever power that can be gained through manipulation and control will eventually fail. This has been apparent in Third World dictatorships where a ruler will use fear and deception to keep his subjects in line for decades yet eventually is overthrown by these same "maliciously obedient" people. True power and influence never come through fear, deception, or even compromise. A parent may continually insist upon strict adherence to curfew yet may never come to understand the inner concerns and feelings of his or her own child. We should always treat our own employees as we want them to treat our finest customers—as volunteers—because that is what they really are. I can buy your hand but not the deepest loyalty and devotion of your heart. I can buy your back but not the finest and most creative thinking of your mind. Loyalty must be earned, not demanded. Power and influence with honor take time and must be earned. We can't keep pulling up the flowers to see how the roots are coming.

How you deal with other people will, to a great extent, determine the quality and happiness of your life. You are a source of influence; how will you handle that privilege? This book is a hope-filled manual that will help us all influence others more effectively for the rest of our lives.

INTRODUCTION

THE ANSWER IS IN YOU

The sole advantage of power is that you can do more good.

BALTASAR GRACIAN

THE PRINCIPLES YOU LIVE BY CREATE THE WORLD YOU LIVE IN; IF you change the principles you live by, you will change your world.

We all want power. We may not want to rule nations or run corporations, but we do want to get results in our lives. We want our children to listen to us; we want our co-workers to work with us rather than against us; we want our friends to respect us. Many will tell you the keys to power reside in forcefulness, negotiation, compulsion, or compromise. They're wrong! Though these tactics can help you get what you want in the short term, they do not create power that endures. True and lasting power doesn't stem from maneuvers or tactics, negotiation or intimidation. It is at once more subtle and more complex than that. The key to power is something we all know and recognize. It is honor. That's right! Honor is power! When others honor you, you have sustained, long-term influence with them. This is the Power Principle.

A BETTER WAY

Unlike other books about power, this one will show you how to develop principle-centered power in your life. Principle-centered power

1

is the type of power possessed by Mahatma Gandhi and Nelson Mandela; power that inspires loyalty and devotion and that transcends time and place. It is based on trust and respect and survives long after the death of the one possessing it. It uplifts and motivates those affected by it. It is a higher form of power—a better way.

As you read this book, you will find encouragement and hope. You will receive much so that you will have much more to give to others. Each of us is surrounded by people who look to us, count on us, and depend on us to make a difference. The need for change in the world is great, and I believe you have greatness in you. But to change the world, we must start with ourselves. Gandhi challenged us to *become* the change we seek in the world. This book can help you change, to become more powerful, to influence others with honor so that you can do more good.

NINE POSITIVE PREMISES

This book is based on the following positive premises:

1. You already understand much about power because you have experienced its many forms as others have influenced you.
2. Power and influence can be acquired and developed.
3. You choose to be powerless or powerful every day.
4. Powerlessness and each of the three paths to power have different foundations.
5. Depending on the situation, you may attempt to influence others with honor, with fairness, with fear, or you may sometimes doubt your ability to influence at all.
6. The results you get with each approach are absolutely predictable.
7. Whatever your official title or position, ultimately your ability to influence others is a result of what you are, as well as what you do.
8. You can change.
9. You can make a difference, for good, and the world needs what you can do.

AN UNCOMMON APPROACH TO POWER

The Power Principle takes an uncommon approach to power. It is based on principles, not practices. If you understand principles, you can create effective practices. Your understanding and ability to apply what you are learning can transcend specific situations, people, and problems. If you underestimate your power, you get inaction; if you overestimate it, you get conflict and antagonism. If you are clear about your power, you can increase it. You can literally do more good.

When you understand the Power Principle, you become more careful what you ask of others; this happens because you are more likely to check your own motive before you ask someone to do something. You can be more confident when dealing with others, because you stop trying to control them and instead ask them to act according to their conscience. When you understand the relationship between this kind of power and influence, you will be able to influence others without forcing them. Learning and living the Power Principle can help you become a more effective, wiser, and happier person. And along the way, you will discover that it is better to win with love, even though force sometimes seems so easy.

We honor the people who live by the Power Principle, and we remember them all of our lives. Their influence stays with us, whether or not we are in their presence. We feel honored by them. This principle-centered power encourages self-control and ethical, proactive behavior in us. By studying these powerful personal models we can increase our principle-centered power and become principle-centered leaders. By increasing our awareness of how we interact with others, and by believing that this kind of leadership is valuable and achievable, we can influence with honor.

LESSONS FROM THE AIR FORCE ACADEMY

You may doubt your ability to build this kind of power in your life. You shouldn't. We are all capable of change and growth; we just need to know where to begin. I had an experience many years ago that shaped my beliefs about our capacity to grow, about how that growth starts, and about where we find the ultimate answers. This experience will help you understand why I wrote this book and also what it can do for you.

Many years ago I taught at the United States Air Force Academy in Colorado Springs, Colorado. I was there during the Vietnam War and my job as a captain in the Department of Behavioral Sciences and Leadership was to prepare the young men at the academy for their participation in the war. Many would become pilots, and some would end up on the ground in enemy territory.

The cadets followed an intensive academic regimen during the fall, winter, and spring. During the summer, however, we took them out of the classroom and into the mountains to train them in more practical matters, namely survival techniques. We taught them valuable lessons such as identifying potable water and edible plants, and setting broken bones. We also touched on more difficult topics such as how to evade capture if they were shot down, and how to resist if they were captured.

During their second summer, I warned the cadets they might be "captured." Few believed me, but after I issued a second warning they asked me how they could prepare. My advice at that point was vague. After all, how do you prepare when you're not sure what to prepare for?

Some made their own special preparations such as grabbing an extra apple from the cafeteria before going out on patrol or sticking a Swiss army knife in the toe of their boot. But as time wore on, they forgot the warnings and slipped into a state of contentment—they were glad to be out of the classroom. Midway through the summer, when they least expected it, we physically captured the cadets. One by one we took them into a field tent and did a strip search—a rather unpleasant experience. We confiscated everything they had with them, including any hidden supplies. Then we escorted them to a simulated POW compound we had constructed. It was similar to camps they might encounter should they ever be captured in Southeast Asia. For three days, the compound was their home.

Though we didn't hurt the cadets physically, we rattled them emotionally. We subjected them to tremendous psychological pressure, hoping that it would prepare them for what they might confront later in their military careers. In a word, this training could save their lives.

Most of the cadets did pretty well in the compound; at least they "survived." We didn't give them much to eat, and we didn't let them sleep. They became fatigued—first physically, then emotionally, then psychologically. If they started to crack, my job as the training officer was to take them aside and give them just enough food and encouragement so they could make it through their ordeal.

After three days, we flung open the doors to the compound and liberated the cadets. Without fail, they came out confident, assuring us they were now ready for anything Vietnam could throw their way. We then fed them a huge meal in celebration of their success.

SOMEONE WHO HAS BEEN THERE

As their bellies filled and the bragging died down, I introduced an academy grad who had been shot down in Vietnam. He had been captured, but managed to escape. The cadets were impressed. Here was someone, not much older than they were, who had really been through it. They pumped him for information. They wanted to know everything.

One cadet asked him, "In case I get sent over there, what kind of knife should I take?" Somehow, even after his recent experience, this young man felt a knife could ensure his survival. Dispelling any such notion, the lieutenant answered, "It's not about knives." Then he told his story.

He explained he had been through the same training at the academy that the cadets had. He had gone on to survive pilot training and jungle school in the Philippines, and had eventually been assigned to an aircraft. During pilot training he had been issued a vest to wear under his flight suit. It held a pistol, ammunition, antibiotic tablets, and all the gear he would ever need for survival on the ground.

After many successful missions, one day he was hit by enemy fire. He described how he had clutched his chest to feel the reassuring outline of his survival vest as he ejected. He was hurt badly on impact and immediately captured by enemy forces. What do you suppose they took away first? The vest, with everything he had brought for survival. The lieutenant concluded his story by telling the cadets that despite terrible circumstances, he eventually managed to escape his captors.

WHAT'S IN YOU MAKES THE DIFFERENCE

Amazed at the story they had just heard, the cadets barraged him with questions, "How did you do it? What did you use to break free? What was your secret?" Expecting to learn of some new high-tech weapon or device, they were surprised by his reply, "I survived all right, but it wasn't because of what I had *on* me. It was what I had *in* me that made the difference."

These powerful words have been a guide to me as I have taught over the last twenty years. What is in you is much more important than some gimmick or technique you may read in a book. The keys to principle-centered power aren't found on these pages—they are inside me and they are inside you.

This fact is reflected in the comments made by some who have read *The Seven Habits of Highly Effective People* by my business partner and friend, Stephen R. Covey. We hear sometimes that his book "merely reflects common sense." We agree—it is the kind of common sense that begins to resemble the wisdom found in traditional cultures and ancient writings, rather than something "new." The problem is, common sense is not always common practice. The answers are never "in the book," as they were in your high school math class. The answers are *in you.*

There are few secrets here. But you will likely come across many examples, stories and phrases that will remind you of some important principles you already know. My intention in writing was to create an experience to help you know what you know, to link what you think with what you feel and believe, to connect your heart and your head. For some, the few inches between the two represent a long, long journey, the journey of a lifetime. The answers are not here—the answers are already in you. You already know.

CHAPTER 1

POWER AND INFLUENCE

The measure of a man is what he does with power.

PITTACUS

POWER IS NOT A NEW PHENOMENON. IT FORMS THE FOUNDATIONS
of government, sociology, psychology, history, religion, and the many
disciplines that study how people live and work together, influencing
each other. It can be intriguing, because power can be surprisingly
complex. It can be enticing, because power can be seductive. But it can
also inspire and uplift and exalt, because power can be used to help
people accomplish marvelous things.

What feelings do you have when you think about power? To some,
power means control. To be powerful may feel heady, exhilarating, exciting. Some feel strong with it and impotent without it; invincible
with it and vulnerable without it; comfortable with it or scared by it.
Some feel that to have power is bad, that power itself is bad. Didn't
Lord Acton insightfully observe that power corrupts and absolute
power corrupts absolutely? Others feel it is desirable or even essential
for successful living. But power is not really good or bad; it is neutral.
Power itself is not negative or positive, although our feelings about it
may be. Power is the potential to influence others for good or evil, to
be a blessing or a scourge. Like nuclear energy, it can provide the elec-
tricity to light a city, or it can fuel the bomb that destroys it.

You might not think of it as such, but power pervades every aspect
of your life. You wield it and are subject to it. This is because we are all

7

interconnected. We live together, work together, shop together, worship together, and play together. In all these settings, we are with other people whose feelings, views, desires, goals, and values may be different from ours. When we come together, it is natural that we influence and are influenced by each other. Power is our ability to influence one another.

WHO IS POWERFUL?

So who among us is powerful? How do we define power between individuals? If you're like most people, you know power when you see it, but you can't really define it. We seem to have an innate ability to measure power in our fellow man. An exercise I often perform with organizations illustrates this point. I've gone into companies and other groups with this request, "Here's a personnel roster—rank these people in terms of their power." With no more than this single instruction, people have no difficulty completing the task. Although there is some disagreement about the ranking of those in the middle, most people readily agree on who really has power. In fact, what I often find is that everyone agrees who's at the top and bottom of the list. People seem to sense who is powerful. I find this agreement whether I am asking about power at work, power in politics, power in the community, or power in families—wherever people are together.

A group of automotive engineers testing the horsepower of an engine would be expected to concur on how powerful the engine is. Since we don't have physical instruments for measuring interpersonal power, what is it that causes this agreement when people are asked to rank the more powerful and less powerful people they associate with? I believe it is our perceptions, based on our experiences—we feel it. When I ask people about those they know who they consider to be powerful, they often explain the source of their power in terms of an instance in which the powerful person played a significant role. This frequently includes some reference to the kind of relationships the powerful person has. For example, one might say, "Enrico is so powerful—he gets anything he wants because people are afraid of him." Or, "Suzanne is pretty powerful—she has what others want, and the only way they can get it is to go through her." Or, "I'd say that Chris has power with other people and they choose to follow him because they trust him—they believe in what he is trying to accomplish."

Reflect on your own experience. Do you know a powerful person? This might be someone you have worked with, someone you have lived with, or some historical or current public figure you have read about. However you define power, this person has it. What makes others choose to follow this person?

THREE PATHS TO POWER

There are three options you should consider. First, is it because they are afraid not to? Perhaps this person has the capacity, authority, or ability to intimidate or bully people, to do something unpleasant or uncomfortable *to* other people. Is this person powerful because they can hurt others in some way, or embarrass them, humiliate them, impose sanctions against them, fire them, or take something away from them? If they are afraid that this powerful person can do something they don't like, others might comply just to avoid the problem. With fear as a source of this person's power, others might go along to get along.

Consider a second option. This person might be influential with others because of what they can do *for* them. This person has the capacity to do something that other people want. For example, they might offer one of the following: "I will pay you if you'll do what I want. I have something to exchange for your time and effort. I can give you information. I can give you opportunity. I can give you resources. I can give you power. I've got something you want, you've got something I want. Let's make a deal." This person has power because they can provide things that other people want, in order to get what they want in return. This is different from the first kind of power. There is no threat or force involved. Ask yourself, Is this second option the reason why people choose to follow the individual that I was thinking about? Is there something valuable they offer to do *for* them in exchange?

A third option represents an entirely different approach and a different kind of power. This category suggests that the person you believe is powerful is someone others believe in, someone they honor, someone they respect. They comply with this person's wishes because they want what she wants. Whether she is there or checking up on them or paying them does not matter. She believes in them and they believe in her. As a consequence, people willingly and wholeheartedly give themselves to what she asks of them. This person has power *with* others, not over them.

It may seem artificial to divide your analysis this way. Perhaps the reasons people choose to follow the person you are thinking about fall into more than one category. Or perhaps the reasons people choose for following or listening or paying attention vary over time. The important thing is that you think about a real person and the possible reasons why they are powerful, why others choose to follow them.

WHEN ARE YOU POWERFUL?

Now consider a different situation. We all recognize power in others, but are you prepared to recognize it in yourself? Think about a situation in which *you* were the powerful person, where your influence was significant with a group of people during the past year in your personal life or your professional life. Whether formally or informally, you were recognized as the leader—they chose to follow you.

Recall a time in your life when you felt particularly powerful. Maybe you made a brilliant presentation or closed a major deal. Maybe you got a group of Boy Scouts to behave on a camping trip, solved a family dispute, or talked your way out of a potential problem. Maybe you were initiating a new activity or product, installing a new system at work, collecting money for a worthy cause in your own neighborhood, changing a program or policy at your children's school, or working to accomplish something for your community.

Think of a specific setting, and a specific group of people that you influenced. In relation to that group, particular project, or endeavor, why did they choose to follow you? Why did they listen to you? Why were you influential with them? Consider the same three options for this analysis as you did for the person you recalled earlier.*

Which of the three types of power was most characteristic of you in the situation you recalled? It is possible that there was some combination. There seems to be a continuum of power, from feeling that we can do anything, to compromising, to demanding, to feeling that there

---

*If you would like to receive a complimentary, self-scoring personal feedback profile to help you evaluate your power, please call toll-free 1-888-7-POWER-9 or visit our Internet home page at www.covey.com.

is nothing we can do. But it is also likely that one of the three dominates the others in your interpersonal dealings, whether at work or at home. When you ask yourself these questions, you might realize that the way you handled a particular situation was not the only way available to you. In some instances, you might explore your options and move from one type of power to the next. Perhaps you use love and kindness, but when that falls short, you resort to bargaining. If bargaining fails, you might be reduced to threats. Maybe you even give up.

What parent hasn't experienced this cycle with a child? A friend told me of such an instance that occurred when she was toilet training her son. Her first attempts at persuasion entailed kindness and understanding. She explained how proud she and his father would be if he managed to fill the toilet rather than his diaper. He refused to listen. In a second futile attempt, she explained to him how the earth would move and the angels would sing if he could only achieve this goal. All the child could say was, "No, no, no."

She thought his smug two-year-old grin of self-amusement and satisfaction would drive her to the brink, but she maintained her composure. "How about you go on the potty, and I'll give you three marshmallows!" His response was laughable. "I don't want to go on the potty. Give me some marshmallows!" His demands continued for a matter of minutes, drowning out her pleas, and she finally broke. "All right, mister. You go on the potty or I'm going to lock you in your room and you'll never have another marshmallow as long as you live." Needless to say, this approach failed as dismally as had the first two, and the child ended up running into the bedroom, where he screamed, with the door closed.

Though many of the situations we face may seem more important at the time than a confrontation with a temperamental two-year-old, we can learn some valuable lessons from this woman's experience. First, we always have a choice. Second, crisis plus time equals humor. It may be funny to look at this situation from a distance of miles and years. Most of us manage to arrive at adulthood having been potty trained somewhere along the way. But at the time, the confrontation between what we want and what another person wants can feel pretty intense.

HOW DO YOU FEEL ABOUT POWER?

If you feel that you could have more influence with others, that you could be more effective, whether it be with a child or a boss, you are not alone. Here are some revealing comments from participants in a public seminar I recently conducted. I asked the question "How do you feel about the power and influence you have with the people in your life?"[1]

> A career executive with two preschoolers at home agonizes, "I don't feel like I am raising my own children. My influence with them is minimal. I try, and we have the best help we can get, but my kids don't seem to want to do anything I want them to do."

> A manager in a small company protests, "All these new hires have such high expectations of us, but they are unwilling to commit, unwilling to learn, unwilling to get on board. They don't seem interested in doing the job that has to be done. In the old days, it was easy—'No work, no job.' But now there are threats of litigation. Everybody has more rights than we do, yet we are somehow supposed to achieve quality, continuous improvement, and reduced costs. What can I do?"

Each of the comments you just read describes a dilemma. The individual is stuck and feels they do not have the power and influence they want. Although their concerns are legitimate, their beliefs are preventing them from seeing a way out.

THERE IS ALWAYS A PATH TO POWER

No matter how frustrated you may feel, there is always a way out. In every situation that arises, we choose to be powerful or powerless. It may not always feel like it, but it is a choice. And there are consequences for these choices in terms of the results that we get, and the subsequent increase or decrease in our power and influence. If we choose powerlessness, it is often because we doubt there is any other option. Powerless choices can lead to lose/win relationships, irresponsibility, stagnation, immobility, and despair. In this book I will show you that powerlessness need not be a part of your life. Even those among us who seem to have no power can become very powerful.

Based on interviews and my own research, I've characterized what I call the power process, which describes the dynamic relationship between people as they attempt to influence each other.

IT ALL STARTS WITH YOU

The power process starts with you. From my perspective, when I look at power and the choices that people make, it seems like it *all* starts with you. When I say you, I'm thinking about you in some very specific ways—your skills, your future, your past, and your character. When you encounter a new situation, you've got a certain skill set. You may have sought out that situation or it may have come to you unsolicited. The skills that you have enable you to do the job. Your skills are the things that you can do right now in the present.

In addition to the skills that you have, you have a capacity to develop or acquire new talents and gifts. Your capacity has to do with the skills that you will have in the future. You have a lot of potential, a lot of possibilities within you.

You also have a history. Your history is a record of where you have been and what you have done. You have dealt with people in certain ways, ways that have resulted in various outcomes with them in the past. You may have found that even with new assignments people already have feelings and ideas about you. Perhaps they've heard something about you; your history has preceded you. You may carry that history and its effects with you for a long time. Sometimes our history feels like ankle irons. It keeps us from being effective right now because of something that happened in the past.

Sometimes we have to outlive our history. You might have read *The Scarlet Letter* by Nathaniel Hawthorne. The heroine of the book, Hester Prynne, was caught in adultery and confessed without naming her partner. Beyond her public humiliation and ostracism, as a part of her punishment she had to sew a large letter "A," to represent the word "Adulteress," on all her clothing. She was made to do this so that everyone in the community would know what kind of person she was. Well, she outlived it. She raised her daughter as a single parent. She lived a quiet life as best she could, working for others and giving back to the community in small ways. Because of the service she rendered, the compassionate giving that she came to be known for, little children growing up a decade later in that community asked their parents if the prominent "A" on her clothing stood for "Angel."

In addition to our history, we also have character. Character is what we are. You have an internal set of beliefs, motivations, desires, and principles that are manifested by your behavior. Together they comprise your character. Leadership, power, and influence are about what you are and what you can do, your capabilities and your character. They're both important. But what you are speaks so loudly, the saying goes, others often can't hear what you are saying.

Your character, your present skill, your capacity to develop and acquire new skills in the future, and your history of living all combine to make up what you bring to new situations. Periodically you will find yourself in a situation that requires you, with your present and future capabilities, character, and history, to influence other people to accomplish something. When you come to such a situation and especially when other people are involved, you have a choice. A problem is looming large, an opportunity is on the horizon, and you have a choice. "Problems are opportunities in work clothes," Henry Kaiser said. Perhaps most opportunities come disguised as problems.

WHAT POWER BASE CAN YOU OPERATE FROM?

Whatever the challenge, we have a choice. Will we choose one of the three types of power, or will we choose to be powerless? Powerful or powerless? That is the fundamental choice we make over and over and over again in life. Will we choose to act or be acted upon? If we choose to be powerful, which path to power will get us the results we want most? You might ask yourself, "What power base will I operate from, or will I choose to be powerless?" If other people are involved, you may be a formal or informal leader, or just a member of a group. In any case, you are in a position to determine and select a base to operate from to accomplish your purposes. The wise leader recognizes that a real leadership choice is made when you choose a power base. "Which power base will I operate from?" The more accurate question is, "What power base *can* I operate from?"

When we doubt our ability to affect others or make things happen the way we want, we back away from situations assuming there is nothing we can do. We choose to be powerless. There are many reasons we may feel this way. We might be ignorant of possibilities and alternatives. We may be frozen emotionally, unable to respond. We might get trapped in our circumstances genuinely believing there is no other way. If, however, we choose to act, even if we are acting in less than optimal ways, we choose to be powerful rather than powerless.

When we are afraid that nothing else will work, or that we won't make the deadline, or that others might not respond, we often resort to *coercive power,* or the power to do something to someone. We're afraid of failure, so we scare others into cooperating with us. We may threaten them, punch them, punish them, or do anything necessary to achieve immediate compliance.

When we use coercive power, we are able to control others' behavior, but only as long as we force them. If we remove the threat, they no longer need to follow our wishes. Though we might get the immediate result we desire, the long-term result can only be negative. Those we force may become unable to act on their own, and instead wait for direction from us. They may also resent us for our methods and seek to sabotage or undermine our efforts.

Sometimes we move beyond force and use bargaining to get what we want. *Utility power* is based on what you can do for me and what I can do for you. It is the power to do something for someone. Together we decide what is fair and we make a deal. The deal may be that you pay me to do a job for you, or that I trade you something I have for something I want. Our deal is constantly up for grabs as we check to see what other options we have. Maybe you find someone better qualified to do the job, maybe I decide I no longer need what you have.

I believe that the majority of adult interactions fall into this category. Utility power works. It gets short-term results. The downside is that utility power disappears when you no longer have what I want. As long as I am getting what I want from you, and I think what I have to give in exchange is fair, we have a deal. When it is no longer fair, according to either party, the relationship ends or may revert to coercive power. Utility power dissipates. If the scales are tipped, an otherwise honest person might decide to do something against the other person (or company or country) to "even the score." Utility power is centered on independence as each person tends to look out for their own interests.

PRINCIPLE-CENTERED POWER

Principle-centered power is based on honor extended to you from others and by you to others. This leads to influence that lasts over extended periods of time and can even outlive the person from whom it emanates. Principle-centered power leads to the wonderful relationships we experience with close associates, family members, and friends. When people honor each other, there is a trust established that leads to synergy, interdependence, and deep respect. Both parties make decisions and choices based on what is right, what is best, what is valued most highly. There is control with principle-centered power, but it is internal; it is self-control. Principle-centered power encourages ethical behavior because followers feel free to choose based on what they want most, what they want in the long term, rather than what they merely want now.

THE POWER PROCESS

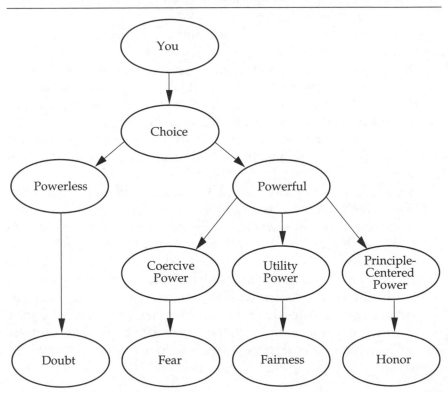

You can develop principle-centered power in your life. With it you can become more influential than you may have thought possible. In ways that will endure and perhaps extend beyond your lifetime, you can be as powerful and influential in the lives of others as the most important people in your life have been in yours. Good and important things may happen as your influence spreads. But you may be surprised at who needs to change to make this happen, and how these changes occur. It is a puzzle to some people that their influence increases as their honor increases. But it does. Honor is power. It is not appearance or manipulation, clever words or egotistical desires that bring about this change. It is something deeper.

MAKING A DIFFERENCE IN THE LIVES OF OTHERS

You can probably think of someone who had this type of power in your own life, someone who had a positive, significant influence on you. I ask participants in my seminars to identify someone like this. I ask them to report who it was, what this person had done, how this person made them feel about themselves, and how they feel about this person today. Here are typical responses:

My first boss treated me in such an honest, respectful, caring way I felt valuable, as if I was making an important contribution. I felt I was worth something, that I was important to the operation of things. He showed me how to do things that I had never done before and acknowledged my efforts and accomplishments. I would have done anything for him.

My mother was always interested and supportive. She gave advice carefully and without judgment. She encouraged my creative endeavors and cared about my well-being. I felt I could do anything I set out to do. She consistently gave me unconditional love—that was her greatest gift.

My mentor gave me freedom to manage, showed respect for my opinions, encouraged my creativity, and gave me opportunities. She made me feel positive about myself, more confident. I ended up feeling that I made major contributions to our company's success. I had great respect for her integrity. Because of her confidence in me, and her respect for my opinions, I took on more responsibility and she ended up with more time to do the things she wanted to do.

My grandmother loved me. She cared for me, taught me her values, encouraged me, and raised me. I felt cared for. Her willingness, love, and hard work to help me through a very difficult time in my young life was given freely, without question, with no strings attached.

FOOTPRINTS ON THE SANDS OF TIME . . .

I have file drawers filled with positive, grateful personal comments like these. I am no longer surprised when I hear people describe this incredible power that exists because of how someone treated them at some time in their life. In "A Psalm of Life," the poet Henry Wadsworth Longfellow teaches us, "Lives of great men all remind us we can make our lives sublime, and, departing, leave behind us footprints on the sands of time." These men and women left an influence that could last well beyond their lifetimes and will not be erased or diminished with time.

I want you to believe that you can achieve what you want most by creating principle-centered power with other people. I want you to cultivate the hope that by conducting your life with honor, you can get long-term results that are worth achieving. I have that hope in me. I have shared the principles in this book with thousands of people, with couples and companies, in live seminars, conferences, workshops, and retreats all over the world. And I have learned from those I have taught. I have not mastered these principles—mastery is a lifelong quest and I am still on the journey. I am learning, as a consequence, that we can do better and be better in our interactions with the people we care about.

The world has many needs, causes, projects, and problems. Our families, our companies, our communities, and our nations need building. People who operate from a base of principle-centered power can make a tremendous positive difference. Today, more than ever, we need to influence with honor.

CHAPTER 2

POWERLESSNESS—WHY DON'T THEY LISTEN TO ME?

> On the brink of the ocean of life and truth we are miserably dying. . . . Sometimes we are furthest away when we are closest by. We stand on the brink of an ocean of power, but each must take the steps that would bring him there.
>
> RALPH WALDO EMERSON

NOBODY LISTENS TO ME

Most of us have experienced the frustration of not getting our message across, of being ignored, of not being listened to. Maybe your teenager doesn't heed your advice on dating. Maybe your boss repeatedly dismisses your suggestions without really considering them. Maybe your employees won't complete their work in the way you request. After a while, you may begin to feel there is nothing you can do to get the results you want, so you just stop trying. Once you stop, you've given in to powerlessness.

Powerlessness touches us all in one way or another. Most of us choose to play the victim in some aspect of our lives. Sometimes we feel our government, our communities, our companies, and even our families are bigger or stronger than we are—that our single voice cannot make a difference. Believing we will not be heard, we choose not to speak. We become resigned to passivity, committed to indifference.

Powerlessness erodes our self-esteem and our effectiveness in dealing with others. In our families, it breaks down communication and fosters misunderstanding. We may feel helpless to control our children. Our children may feel powerless to get us to listen to their changing wants and needs. We decide we can't change, even though change may be required to salvage our marriages or other close relationships. Sometimes we'd rather just give up where we are and start over somewhere else with some other spouse or company or neighbor or country, rather than try to preserve something we once had but are gradually losing.

If we feel powerless at work, those feelings may lead us to suppress our ideas, be less productive, and betray our capabilities. Study after study reveals that most people don't even begin to develop their full potential in their jobs. If you're a supervisor, maybe you feel powerless with those who report to you. You may be in charge on the organization chart, and your title may even be prominently displayed, but those who report to you actually run the show. Maybe you feel your boss doesn't respect your opinions and you retreat into a shell, accepting what you're given, yet not really excelling as maybe you could.

If you feel powerless in any of these ways, you're not alone. As a guest on a recent talk show, I listened carefully to the nature of the concerns expressed by those who called in. The consistent message was not that everyone has problems—that is obvious. It was the helplessness that I heard in their voices that troubled me.

Though people may have power in some aspects of their lives, there always seem to be areas where they feel there is little or nothing they can do.

CHOOSING TO BE POWERLESS

Each of the callers was stuck in his or her present dilemma. And being stuck, they made a choice to be powerless. They were probably doing the best they knew how to do.

Often it is a crisis that leads people to choose powerlessness. Think

CHOOSING TO BE POWERLESS

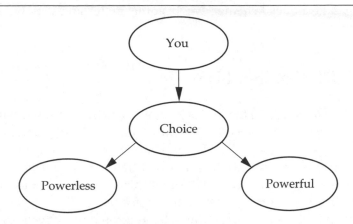

of the expectations you might have if you were struck by a significant loss, such as loss of your job, health, home, or a loved one. Where would you look for solace or answers? For most of us, our response reveals a natural human tendency for expecting somebody to do something, for expecting someone to listen to us and pay attention to us and provide for us. And when what we expect does not happen, the conclusions we draw cause a kind of learning that affects our beliefs and our future expectations.

We may learn, under such trying and difficult circumstances, that organizations and institutions will fail us. This in turn could lead to the conclusion that we must look out for ourselves because no one else cares or is going to help. If we are the leaders of these organizations, *we* may feel a kind of powerlessness. A CEO recently told me that he cannot guarantee employment for his employees anymore. In fact he said he wasn't sure he would be around a year from now. In the place of such uncertainty, we could sit back and hope for the best, or decide that the best place to find a helping hand is at the end of our own arm.

When we have difficulty and run into roadblocks in our attempts to get help, we might conclude that life is tough, and then you die, as a popular bumper sticker proclaims. But we might also learn that we have a lot more friends than we thought. We may learn that we can survive hardship, adversity, even tragedy beyond what we thought we could bear. What we actually learn, from any given set of circumstances, determines whether we become increasingly powerless or more powerful.

THE VICTIM MENTALITY

Many of us have begun to view ourselves as victims in some aspects of our lives. We may exercise power in certain situations, but play the role of recipient in others. We feel we have to accept things we do not like because we cannot control them. Others are responsible for our failures as well as our successes. Sometimes it seems the only way we can get ahead is if somebody else does it for us.

Unfortunately, our modern lifestyles reinforce these feelings rather than weaken them. Television lets us view the world without participating in it. It presents the joy and the suffering, the beauty and the ugliness in compact thirty-minute segments. Whatever the issue, however serious or trivial, it is presented, explained, debated, and resolved all before the next commercial.

Once we become accustomed to such speedy resolutions, we feel frustrated if we can't fix our own problems quickly and easily. I know a woman who was abandoned by her husband, and left to raise three teenage children without any financial support. One of her daughters suffers from anorexia and bulimia and recently tried to commit suicide. The daughter is an attractive, talented young woman, but has problems deep enough that they cannot be solved in thirty minutes or thirty days. Her mother is already working three jobs in an effort to support her family, but in the face of such a crisis, cannot figure out what to do to help her daughter. After being told she can be a millionaire by Saturday or lose thirty pounds in two weeks by drinking milkshakes, she feels like a failure when she cannot just fix her daughter's problems.

Another source of powerlessness for many of us is the "busy-ness" that we impose in our lives. We fill our lives with activities that keep us so absorbed, we have little opportunity to step back and see what is really happening. We rush to work, to community meetings, to our children's activities, but don't slow down long enough to notice the things that might otherwise demand our attention. Sometimes we simply become numb to what is really important.

This was the case with a man I know who was by all external appearances a successful, faithful family man. He secretly had an affair that lasted ten years, but it came to an abrupt end when the other woman's husband learned of his wife's infidelity. The husband came after this man with a gun and threatened to kill him. In the aftermath of this incident, the man left his family in search of his soul. After a time he returned and saw a therapist who treated him with counseling and medication.

Today this man has rebuilt his life and filled it with all sorts of activities. He is involved in his community, and has a rich and productive professional life. From the outside, it looks as though things are in perfect order. The tragedy is that his wife, the woman he hurt and betrayed, who is still wounded and hurting, does not fit into his new life. He has no time for her pain or to help her heal. His problems have been "fixed," but he has not addressed hers. He denies that they exist. The drug has temporarily filled the hole in his soul and made life bearable, but has not helped him overcome his own feelings of powerlessness. His world has provided him with diversions, countless ways to fill his public life without having to take part in the intimate, private life of his own family.

HOW WE BECOME POWERLESS

In the face of such distractions, we might forget that we can make a difference, that we can do things. We have a hundred channels on TV to lure us in. We can flip channels for hours and still not cover everything available to us. Everything we need to know, everything we need to buy, everything we can imagine is accessible through the click of a button. We don't need to talk to our neighbors or friends to find out what's going on: we can watch the news. We don't need to go out and have fun ourselves: we can let characters on sitcoms and talk shows do it for us.

When we become absorbed by such diversions, whether we acknowledge it or not, we lose the ability to do things for ourselves. We might not seek out our own answers or try to make things happen.[1] We might accept the life we are offered rather than make our own decisions: it is the convenient choice.

A colleague told me of a client who described the powerlessness he felt because of the complacency convenience inspires. He explained, "I thought everything in my life was great. My family was happy and healthy, I was successful and had enough money to do the things I wanted to do. But one day when I was at the country club, it hit me. I felt like life was going on outside, and I could see it—just barely—through the hedges around the country club. I was in a protective bubble, insulated by the patterns of my life and my affluence." His powerlessness came from the feeling that everything was fine. There was nothing he needed to do. It wasn't that he felt he couldn't do anything; he just didn't think there was anything he ought to do.

Part of this paralysis arises when we are confronted with too many options. A friend told me recently that he was flipping through the channels he picked up on his satellite dish and found that seven different channels were offering similar exercise machines at the same time. Each program claimed that its machine was the best, that its machine could save your life while reducing your waistline. Each disparaged the competitors and tried to make the case that it was the one to buy. How can we expect to make a clear decision in the face of such multiple, simultaneous, differing, and contentious stimuli? How are we supposed to make sense of it all? Often we feel overwhelmed and become immobilized—we are powerless to form an opinion or make a decision.

Not only have we become indecisive in the face of too many options, we've also grown wary of doing things for ourselves. Our powerlessness extends into our homes when we convince ourselves we are incapable of performing even the most basic tasks. A young couple I know rented the upper half of a small duplex and took care of the yard to receive a reduction in their rent. When the wife noticed a small dip in the lawn, she called the landlord and asked whom she should call to fix the problem. It never occurred to her that she could make a trip to the local nursery, purchase two square feet of sod, and patch the hole herself. Instead her automatic response was, "Let's get someone out here to take care of this."

When we start thinking we cannot do things ourselves, we stop our creative processes. The early pioneer settlers repeated to their children a couplet that expressed this self-reliant orientation:

> *Fix it up, wear it out;*
> *Make it do, or do without.*

We might reinstate the values underlying that couplet today. Perhaps if our resources are limited and we cannot afford to hire a professional, we devise a way, but often we look to someone else. Once we expect someone else to do it for us, we stop searching for ways to do it ourselves. After a while, we forget how to figure things out, how to find solutions. We always have a reason why we can't do it, and why someone older, richer, or more skilled can. A friend shared with me her experience playing a party game when she would think of an answer but not say it. The next player in the game would give the same answer and be correct. She learned a valuable lesson—speak up! She said an emotional response from when she was a youngster in grade school—worrying about her answer being right or wrong—kept her from speaking up before. The irony is that the reason practitioners, technicians, and professionals are good at solving problems is that they have faced a lot of problems and have *had* to learn how to solve them.

POWERLESSNESS AT HOME

Our doubt that we can solve our problems, or that getting involved will help, is not limited to minor tasks—we've also come to believe that we cannot face the tougher social issues. I have a friend who lived in a Northwest coast community that had become dominated by gangs. One day one of his children came home and had obviously been in a fight. When he and his wife asked the boy what had happened, he said, "I can't tell you. If they find out I told, it'll just get worse." The parents continued to question him, and finally he explained his predicament: "Here's the way it is. You're either in a gang, or you get beat up by a gang. Everybody has to belong somewhere, and if you're not part of a particular group, then you're going to get beat up." This teenager saw no way out.

Certain that they could do little to minimize or eliminate the gang influence in their community, this family moved to another state. They determined that staying might lead to painful or dangerous consequences. Doubting that they could make a difference, they fled to a more rural setting. Unfortunately, they did not get away from the problem—gang action followed them to the new state, where their son joined another gang. And, tragically, the story ended with a fight, a bullet, and the death of their son.

You might ask what other options did they have? How could one family take on a group of gangs? There is no simple answer to these questions. After the funeral I was amazed, humbled, and inspired as I watched my friend plead with the gang members to stop the fighting, change the lifestyle, to not retaliate for his son's death.

I don't know the outcome of this series of events; it is not over yet. Many youths join gangs to find something they are not getting anywhere else. It may be acceptance. It may be a sense of family and belonging. It may be camaraderie or a sense of adventure. Too many are alone. Others, doubting that they are of value to anyone, just drift. Some seem separate and detached, aware of others' problems but alone and disconnected, doubting that anyone is really interested in them. Rather than join others, they isolate themselves. A person in this condition can attend a football game in a stadium with fifty thousand people, and still feel alone. He doesn't talk to the people around him, and he hopes they won't try to talk to him. He is united with his fellow fans in a common cause—cheering for the home team—but does not interact with them. Even in a crowd, he is lonely.[2]

WHO IS POWERLESS?

If powerlessness affects most of us in these subtle ways, perhaps without our awareness, are any of us exempt from its pressures? While we all grapple with issues of powerlessness at some point, there are certain groups that feel more powerless than others. You might be surprised to learn that there are times in our lives when we have more power than others, when we choose to be powerful rather than powerless.

As children, we feel invincible. When we go to elementary school, we will do anything, try anything. We'll sing, we'll dance, we'll write poetry—all because we have not yet learned to be inhibited or self-conscious. If we want to be superheroes, we tie towels around our necks and jump off the bed. If we want to paint a masterpiece, we get out our crayons. We are not self-conscious or worried about what others might think.

The power that we feel in our childhood is too often squelched by the adults in our lives—our parents, our teachers, and other authority figures. We hear things such as, "What a lousy poem." "What a stupid thing to say." "Flowers have green leaves and red buds, not the other way around." We start to think maybe everybody else is right, that we can't do the things we thought we could. In this way, we are taught to assume a powerless stance. We learn to say I can't. We learn to doubt ourselves, our capacities, our possibilities.

We experience another period of invincibility somewhere around the time we enter high school and get our driver's license. Our hormones are flowing, we can drive, we can go out at night—without our parents—and do things they don't know about or might not approve. We have endless energy and feel compelled to attend every football or basketball game and every party, even if it means we get just enough sleep to stay alive.

This second power surge comes to a grinding halt as graduation approaches. Will I fulfill all the requirements to graduate? Where will I go to college? Will I even be accepted by a college? I can't afford another speeding ticket; they'll cancel my insurance. Where am I going to get the money for a car of my own? So we learn once again that we cannot do everything we want to do. There are rules and restrictions and norms and highway signs that tell us what the limits are.

Perhaps the most ironic element of these periods of power is that all the time we are going through them, we think the adults are the ones who have the power. They can stay up as late as they want. They can watch the movies they want, take the day off from work if they want. They can go where they want, when they want. Adults, on the other hand, envy children for the freedom they enjoy. They aren't burdened by innumerable responsibilities. They can go out and play for hours on end. They can be astronauts, explorers, cowboys—whatever they want to be. Does anybody really have power, or do we just think they do? The paradox is that we always believe it is someone else. Regardless of our situation, we find ways to justify why everybody but us is powerful.

POWERLESS AND POWER LOSS

What happens to us to convince us that we are powerless? It is strange that as we get older, we can grow more doubtful and insecure rather than more confident. There are many things that we face as adults that challenge our belief in ourselves and lead us to lose feelings of power.

Powerlessness can begin in the simplest way, with the smallest incident. Starting with a little thing, it can snowball to avalanche proportions. Disappointment over an unwelcome response or unexpected outcome can grow into discouragement. Lacking confidence and

REACTIONS TO DISAPPOINTMENT

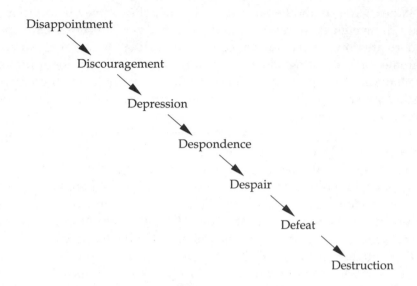

Disappointment

Discouragement

Depression

Despondence

Despair

Defeat

Destruction

courage, we may take actions that we otherwise would not. We figure we've "lost it" anyway, so there is nothing else to lose. Such actions betray our character, belie our intentions, and can lead to a loss of self-esteem. When we no longer value ourselves, we may sink into the depths of depression. If the negative feelings continue, we continue the downward spiral until we believe we can do nothing. We feel defeated and lose hope. Unless something stops this emotional slide, destruction awaits. This could be the loss of an opportunity, the loss of a job, the loss of a relationship, or in extreme cases even the loss of a life.

George Bernard Shaw has observed, "When we are discouraged we use our reason to support our fears and our prejudices. We have some unwholesome doubts, and doubt is the first step on the road to betrayal and surrender."[3] That betrayal and surrender may be to another person, commitment, or cause. Or it may be a betrayal of our better selves. It occurs when we unwittingly sell out to lesser possibilities in ourselves.

The general sense of powerlessness we feel when we are faced with a painful situation for which there is no apparent way out comes to a climax in the decision to take one's own life. This decision is frequently precipitated by some sort of loss, such as loss of power, loss of a loved one, loss of a career, or significant loss of status. Even a strong fear of such a loss can trigger such feelings of powerlessness. These feelings lead the individual to the conclusion that the only way to regain a sense of power is through one final, desperate act, which affirms their ability to do something. The paradox is that the energy and planning which go into the suicidal act could, if channeled in more positive ways, become a path out of the depressive, dark emotional cave in which these people feel they are trapped.

Seeking out or being responsive to another person is often the key to emerging from the severely depressed state. In fact, the most reliable preventive measures include being with someone who is trusted, who will listen and understand; engaging in some diversion; or losing oneself in some worthwhile or challenging enterprise or activity.[4] In an interesting study, the National Institute of Mental Health compared four types of therapy for depressed patients. As expected, all methods helped some patients. The surprise was that when patients were seen regularly by a physician who gave them only a placebo and a listening ear, there was as much improvement as was observed in the other approaches. These physicians merely listened attentively, were curious and sympathetic, and continued to patiently watch and wait. That is a prescription any of us could administer.[5]

WHEN DO YOU FEEL YOU DON'T HAVE POWER?

On another recent talk show, the host, a priest, introduced me as the author of a new book on power. He asked the listeners this question, "When do you feel that you don't have power?" Their responses were varied, yet consistent. All of the callers explained situations in which they felt alone, confused, and discouraged. They emerged from each experience with less power than they had before they encountered it.

One caller had lost his job almost two years earlier. He had collected unemployment for a while, but eventually had lost his home, his car, and his status in the community. In retrospect, he realized that he had defined himself through his work. Without it, he felt he was nothing—his life had no meaning. When he lost his job, he lost himself. He did not know how to carry on.

Another caller explained that her mother had recently undergone a hip replacement, and in the wake of a difficult recovery had decided to give up on life. Though she was still alive, she did nothing for herself. She had her meals brought in to her. She would not leave her house, even though she was able to. In her mind, her physical limitations became a justification for the mental and emotional limitations she placed on herself. Because of her decline in health, she convinced herself she was powerless.

The reason callers cited most often as a source of powerlessness was loss of a loved one. Many described their inability to go on after someone close to them had died. They could not approach life—or death—without sinking into the depths of emotional despair. Some could not make decisions on their own. Others could not go out in public. Many would not let themselves care for other people—the risk of losing another loved one seemed too great. Some said they could not bear the thought of purchasing a burial plot or taking out a life insurance policy, because their experience had been too painful.

A number of the younger callers reported their unwillingness to commit to long-term relationships as a source of great frustration. They explained that they are not afraid of relationships, per se, only the commitment that tends to accompany them. They want companionship, intimacy, sharing, bonding—all the characteristics of a serious relationship—but none of the accountability that is required to make it durable. The result is that they move from one superficial relationship to the next, retaining a few memories and all their loneliness. Because they are not willing to give what someone else wants, they cannot get what they want.

HOW IGNORANCE ROBS OUR POWER

The pride these young people display is not the only emotion that can impede our progress in life. Sometimes it is our ignorance that cripples us. I read about a woman who didn't have much money to spend on personal indulgences, yet, more than anything else, she dreamed of taking a Caribbean cruise. After seeing a television commercial for one of the major cruise lines, she had decided that a cruise would be the single best experience she could ever have. She saved her money and scrimped on extras for two years, and finally had enough to purchase a ticket.

She chose a cruise that circled the Caribbean, but did not dock at any islands. The entire trip would be spent at sea. She prepared for months for the eagerly awaited date of departure. The day finally arrived. After embarking, she found her way to her cabin and unpacked her belongings. Walking up and down the ship's passages, she noticed that many of the passengers were getting dressed for dinner and going to the upper deck to dine.

Embarrassed by her modest wardrobe, she returned to her cabin and made a meal of some crackers and canned meat she had brought along. She repeated this ritual every evening, until the last night on the ship, when she decided she would venture above and treat herself to a gourmet dinner. She knew there was going to be a big farewell party, so she donned the best dress she had packed and made her way to the dining room.

Over the course of the night, she thoroughly enjoyed herself. She ordered from the menu, sampled from the sumptuous buffet lines, and watched some of the other passengers revel on the dance floor. "So this is what they've been doing up here all week," she mused to herself. "This is what I have been missing. . . ."

When she was ready to return to her cabin for the evening, the woman waited for the steward to bring her check. He never came, so she signaled across the room to him. When he arrived, she said, "I'm ready for my check." He chuckled and smiled curiously. "What are you talking about?" he questioned. "My bill for the meal. I know I have not been up here before, but I'm prepared to pay." The steward couldn't believe what he was hearing. "Of course you are joking, ma'am. All of your meals were included with this trip. They're already paid for."

As we go through life, many of the "meals" are included. Sometimes we settle for less than we could, simply because we don't know what is possible. In this way, we become powerless through ignorance. Even if others tell us what is possible, we tend not to believe them—we doubt that what they say is true. Or if it is true, it does not apply to us.

NEGATIVE FEEDBACK STRIPS AWAY POWER

We also deprive ourselves of power when we convince ourselves we lack the skill, talent, or knowledge to do something. Sometimes we forget that as children we drew pictures, sang songs, danced, played, without instruction and without inhibition. And then someone somewhere along the line gave us feedback, well-intentioned often, mean-spirited sometimes, that caused us to doubt ourselves and our capacities. A client told me about such an incident in her life. She recalled in the sixth grade working on an art project for her parents for Christmas. She could hardly wait for the teacher to come around so she could show her the masterpiece. When she finally came, her only comment was, "Well, it's obvious you'll never be an artist." The girl was crushed. She never gave her cardboard, string, and foil reindeer to her parents. She threw it away, convinced that it was really bad. The pathos was evident in her voice as she told me about this experience, then added this significant postscript—for the next twenty-five years, she avoided any kind of art classes or projects, claiming, "I'm just not an artist."

Enrico Caruso was told as a young man by one of his teachers that he had no voice, and that he should become an engineer. What loss the world might have had, if he had listened to this criticism. I love music and have enjoyed singing in and directing choruses for church groups. I sang in musicals and operas during my college years and had the opportunity to play the part of Mayor Shinn when our family participated in our community theater production of *The Music Man*. I was in the chorus with the San Antonio Chordsmen when this group of over 150 nonprofessionals sang our way into the national championships of the Society for the Preservation and Encouragement of Barber Shop Quartet Singing in America.

It has always seemed a needless tragedy to me that although *most* of us sang in kindergarten—loudly, confidently, and proudly—by the time we had reached the sixth or seventh grade, when we could try out for the school chorus, something had happened. Maybe someone exclaimed, "What are you doing here? You can't sing." From that moment on, we were convinced we could not sing. We internalized the criticism and believed it. We let a single person (who may know little about music or our potential) determine our future for us. Once the doubts set in, we began to believe them. Our roles shifted from participant to spectator, from volunteer to victim. We seldom get better as long as we define ourselves as victims.

Doubt is most often the source of our powerlessness. To doubt is to be faithless, to be without hope or belief. When we doubt, our self-talk sounds like this: "I don't think I can. I don't think I will." It implies failure to adhere to promises or allegiances, because we believe they will do no good, or that we cannot fulfill them. To doubt is to have faith in the worst possible outcome. It is to believe in the perverseness of the universe, that even if I do well, something I don't know about will get in the way, sabotage me, or get me in the end. To be faithless means to not be true to duty or obligation, to be unworthy of faith or trust, to be unreliable, because something else has intervened. We excuse ourselves because we don't think we can come through for someone or something we have committed to. It is to be undecided, unresolved, unsettled, or skeptical, to disbelieve or distrust or regard as unlikely. This is the emotional overlay of doubt. It is pervasive. It often spreads beyond a certain incident or experience, but may have had its beginning in a single incident.

ESCAPE CONDITIONING

When we let a single emotional incident affect our behavior permanently, we engage in a behavior psychologists have termed escape conditioning. If we are placed in difficult circumstances, with the threat of terrible things about to happen to us, and we suddenly, perhaps accidentally, stumble upon a way out, we might choose that same way out the next time we're in trouble. This is exactly what happens when a laboratory animal encounters the escape box. In this routine psychology experiment, an animal is placed in a box, presented with an unpleasant stimulus, like a noxious but harmless electrical shock, and allowed to escape. If the animal is returned to the box, it immediately escapes again. Why? One theory holds that escaping "ensures" that the bad thing will not happen. In fact, some laboratory animals have been observed to "escape" the potentially unpleasant experience over a hundred times, even though the electrical current is never turned on again. Never mind that nothing unpleasant may ever happen again in the box. The animal has been conditioned to escape, because escape leads to avoidance of the unpleasant consequence. This behavior is very strong—the animal will continue to escape, even if you *never* use the unpleasant stimulus again.

Emotional learning in humans is quite similar. Bad, unpleasant, uncomfortable things happen to everyone sooner or later. We sometimes base our feelings and behaviors on a single traumatic experience.

Something bad happens once, and, determined to not have it happen again, we do whatever it takes to avoid the problem and potential pain. We continue to escape rather than face a potentially hurtful situation. By responding out of fear, we never know whether another outcome might have been possible. Mark Twain once observed, "A cat that steps on a hot stove once will never step on a hot stove again . . . but neither will it step on a cold one." It isn't hard to see that similar behaviors hold true for humans. Often, when we have a very strong emotional experience, we overlearn. We overgeneralize. We read too much into the experience. We choose to be powerless. Our doubts, solidified by misinterpreted later experiences, betray us. As Shakespeare said in *Measure for Measure*, "Our doubts are traitors and make us lose the good we oft might win by fearing to attempt."

If you have been traumatized by a painful experience in your life, making a leap of faith is the only way you can overcome the powerlessness it created. With a lot of courage and a little hope, you can do things you never thought possible.

LEARNED HELPLESSNESS

Whether our challenges are personal or professional, we may end up feeling there is little we can do to improve the situation. In this instance we might be displaying a behavior known as learned helplessness.[6] Like escape conditioning, learned helplessness was first observed as an interesting side reaction in studies with laboratory animals.

In these experiments, animals who had learned to escape from unpleasant stimuli were later harnessed to prevent them from escaping. What scientists observed after they removed the harness surprised them. Even though the animals were physically able, they would no longer try to escape. It was as though the animals had learned to be helpless.[7]

Though this experiment involved laboratory animals, it is reminiscent of everyday human experience. How often do we fail to stand up for ourselves, or let someone else define our options, assuming we can do nothing because in some early experience, we really could do nothing? Yes, there may be a very explainable rationale why as a child or teenager or as a new husband or employee we really were doing the best we knew how to do, and whatever we did or chose was not quite adequate. We can, from the present perspective of better educated understanding, look with new ideas at our old selves and see possibilities that were genuinely beyond our grasp at the time.

In the new situation, our doubts, born of our earlier experience, may still predominate. Even though the doubts may be irrational, their power to immobilize us is real. Whether it is an animal whimpering in a laboratory experiment or us, standing paralyzed by events we feel we cannot control, escape, or change, we are observing the frustration of powerlessness.

Helplessness occurs when someone does nothing because they perceive, incorrectly, that trying harder or trying something different will *not* help. When we refuse to take action that we might otherwise take, we may be demonstrating helplessness because we feel powerless. We doubt that we can make a difference. Perhaps we've tried and failed. Perhaps our attempts in the past to take action have been condemned or punished or, even worse, ignored. In such cases, we might be guilty of projecting our old frustrations into these new situations when they don't actually apply.

You are helpless when you believe you can do nothing, and that belief keeps you from trying. You escape when you have learned to do something to avoid pain, and you refuse to try anything else. The very thing you have learned to do is the thing that keeps you from learning that something else is possible, that things have changed, that things could change for you. Actually, both phenomena are variations of the same thing. Helplessness generally results when we face a number of situations that we cannot control. Escape learning generally results from one or two dramatic incidents. In each case, prior learning influences later learning and both kinds of behavior are difficult to eliminate.

What you have learned in the one case is to do nothing, and "doing nothing" keeps you from learning that things could be different. In the other case, you have learned to do something, and "doing something" which appears to work prevents any new learning from taking place.

THE RESULTS OF CHOOSING TO BE POWERLESS

This chapter has illustrated many of the ways we learn to choose to be powerless. Doubt is often at the root of the problem. The results include unresponsiveness, when we stop acting and wait for something else to happen or someone else to do something; irrationality, when we persist in believing words and ideas (even if they are only expressed internally) to be true that are false; and immobility, when we get stuck emotionally or intellectually and are unable to consider new options.

THE RESULTS OF CHOOSING TO BE POWERLESS

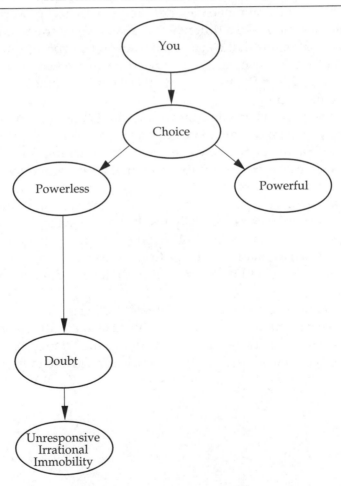

What we *do* when we choose to be powerless is:

Ignore
Disregard
Wait
Delay
Take no action
Despair
Become indifferent
Neglect
Become apathetic

What we *get* when we feel powerless is:

Status quo
Lose/win relationships
Helplessness
Unpredictable/unknown results
Uncertainty
Wishes and fantasies
Diminished capacity

There *are* other possibilities. Marcel Proust has suggested that the journey of discovery consists not in going to new lands but in having new eyes. Perhaps we can learn something about overcoming powerlessness by seeing, with new eyes, how learned helplessness is transformed into helpfulness.

The next chapter will show you how to move from helpless to helpful, from powerless to powerful. The remainder of the book addresses the reality that we can influence others, through three different paths to power. In each case, the approach we take will determine the results we get. We can be encouraged by the research that suggests that there are specific things we can do today to overcome feelings of powerlessness or helplessness in our own lives. Although we may have chosen to be powerless in the past, we can make a different choice now.

CHAPTER 3

POWER SHIFT—
FROM POWERLESS
TO POWERFUL

New infantryman to commanding officer: "Sir, where is my fox-hole?" The officer's quick reply: "You are standing on it: just throw the dirt out!"

AUTHOR UNKNOWN

IF YOU'RE FEELING POWERLESS IN ANY ASPECT OF YOUR LIFE, YOU can change! You can move beyond powerlessness and regain the power you feel you have lost or never had. The lab animals who were taught to be helpless were later taught to be resourceful in any situation, to keep trying until they found a way out of their problems. People can be the same way. Once we realize there is always something we can do—that we always have a choice—we can begin to fortify our power base and build power in our lives.

POWERLESS EXECUTIVES

Perhaps the first step in moving past powerlessness is to examine just how powerless we really are. We may feel we can't get the results we want in our lives, but our concerns can seem trivial when compared to the challenges faced by those who have limitations greater than our own, namely physical and mental handicaps. I had an experience a few years ago which led me to reexamine the roots of my own power-lessness and to discover the true power of the so-called powerless.

I had been invited to conduct a five-day leadership development training workshop with the senior members of a large financial group in the Northeast. This group included some of the original employees who had, over a period of twenty years, become the leaders of the cur-rent company. All the senior executives for their largest division were in the workshop.

We spent two days establishing rapport, developing the team, and getting grounded in the fundamental principles of leadership, such as developing integrity, respect, dignity, living with honor, establishing a common vision, and building the problem-solving capacity of other people. On the third day, we spent the afternoon in a primitive setting in the woods near the training facility, where participants had to solve simulated survival problems. This pushed these leaders to drop their facades and defenses and create a true spirit of learning, sharing, and teamwork around common goals. It was a wonderful group and one of those learning experiences when everything seemed to be going right.

Our discussions of principle-centered living, which stressed exercis-ing integrity in moments of choice, striving for a dynamic balance with all of the real-time demands on these busy executives, and con-verting values to actions, had brought the group to a new level of acceptance and understanding. A spirit of unity, an unusual apprecia-tion for the differences represented in the group and the commonality that connected them, and a sense of hopeful destiny characterized by a shared vision of a successful future prevailed.

As we returned from the woods late in the day, tired and dirty but hanging on to one another and feeling like a team, we were met by a courier who had an urgent message. The CEO and his aides would be joining us for dinner and would be making an important announce-ment! How thoughtful, I supposed, to be willing to make the effort to affirm the value of the training by flying in the corporate plane to our meeting site and spending the evening with us. We all agreed to stay in casual clothes, anticipating that the good feelings of the afternoon would spill over into the evening's activities.

A short time later everyone was enjoying refreshments outside the dining room when the CEO strode in, dressed in expensive formal attire, with a drink in one hand, a broad smile across his bronzed face. He was flanked by two other executives, similarly dressed. The happy chatter came to a halt as he moved to the center of the room and asked for everyone's attention. Jim,[1] the director of this group, rose to acknowledge the CEO, but was waved off. The CEO then made the following brief announcement; I've never forgotten the words, nor their effect on everyone present. "Just wanted to let you know that Jim is being let go. Fred here will take over the group. The change will take place Monday morning. Hope you are all having a good time. Now, drinks for everyone and let's eat!" and he turned to the bar with his free arm around Fred, the new director.

Those few words could not have been any more devastating to the group. An emotional bomb had been dropped for no apparent reason, with no provocation, and no explanation. The room was silent, except for the loud bantering of the CEO and those at his side over near the bar. Jim, the now former director, stood and weakly asked, "Could I say something to my friends?" The CEO turned back and shrugged his shoulders. Jim then said something about his twenty-two years of service, his appreciation for the people in the room and gratitude for being a part of the building years, said good-bye, and left the room.

I followed him down the hall and into the rest room, where he just leaned against the wall, eyes closed, tears streaming down his face. He had some intimation that a leadership change was coming, he said, but had not expected this. There had been no wrongdoing, no huge financial loss or embarrassing failure, no negative performance reviews. He was as shocked as the rest of us. We talked briefly, then I returned to the group. A few others had left the dining room. The majority stayed and ate in relative silence. Dinner broke up early and the room cleared.

I was the consultant who was shepherding this workshop. I was the facilitator who had come in from out of town to help the group conceptualize a new vision for the next decade. I was the expert who could show them the way, sharing success stories of how it was being done in other places. But I was at a total loss for words. I didn't know whether to convene the group, to counsel Jim privately, to have an open meeting that night, to cancel the next two days, or to confront the CEO. I didn't know what to do. The situation demanded wisdom, and wisdom eluded me.

I ended up getting in my rental car later that evening and driving, no place in particular, with my brain on automatic pilot, thinking, trying to make sense of the events of the day. I felt helpless in the face of genuine emotional turmoil, sorrow, grief, and, perhaps, injustice. I found myself in front of a large bookstore, the kind of place where I have often gotten an idea or had my thinking stretched. I love books. In a book, the author comes to you with their best clothes on, presenting their finest thinking fine-tuned and honed for clarity.

My eyes wandered from shelf to shelf, book to book as I browsed aimlessly. Then a title caught my attention. The word "power" in large letters jumped off the cover. *The Power of the Powerless,* the title read, by Christopher De Vinck. I grabbed the book and tucked it under my arm.

Back at the hotel, I idly flipped through the pages of the book. Suddenly my eye caught a change in print. An essay, a few pages long, near the front of the book, was set off by a different typeface. "I grew up in a house where my brother was on his back in his bed for thirty-two years. . . ." I read silently. I thought this was a book about power.

Intrigued, I continued reading. "He was blind, he was mute. His legs were twisted. He didn't have the strength to lift his head or the intelligence to learn anything." I read on, riveted by the words, the story, the personal sharing. A few minutes later I had finished the essay. I was transfixed. And I knew what I was going to share with the group the next morning when we met together.

THE POWER OF THE POWERLESS—OLIVER'S STORY

Here is the essay in its entirety, as it had been originally published in the *Wall Street Journal,* April 10, 1985:

> I grew up in a house where my brother was on his back in his bed for thirty-two years; the same corner of his room, under the same window, beside the same yellow walls. He was blind, he was mute. His legs were twisted. He didn't have the strength to lift his head or the intelligence to learn anything. Oliver was born with severe brain damage, which left him and his body in a permanent state of helplessness.
>
> Today I'm an English teacher. Each time I introduce my class to the play about Helen Keller, *The Miracle Worker,* I tell my students the story of Oliver. One day, during my first year of teaching, I was trying to describe Oliver's lack of response, how he'd been spoon-fed every morsel

he ever ate, how he never spoke. A boy in the last row raised his hand and said, "Oh, Mr. De Vinck, you mean he was a vegetable." I stammered for a few seconds. My family and I fed Oliver, we changed his diapers, hung his clothes and bed linens on the basement line in winter, and spread them out white and clean to dry on the lawn in the summer. I always liked to watch the grasshoppers jump on the pillowcases. We bathed Oliver, tickled his chest to make him laugh. Sometimes we left the radio on in his room, but would pull the shade down on the window over his bed in the morning to keep the sun from burning his tender skin. We listened to him laugh as we watched television downstairs. We listened to him rock his arms up and down to make the bed squeak. We listened to him cough in the middle of the night. "Well, I guess you could call him a vegetable. I called him Oliver, my brother. You would have loved him."

One October day in 1946 while my mother was pregnant with Oliver, her second son, my father rose from bed, shaved, dressed, and went to work. At the train station, he realized he'd forgotten something, so he returned to the house and discovered the smell of gas leaking from our coal-burning stove. My mother was unconscious in her bed. My oldest brother was sleeping in his crib, which was quite high off the ground, so the gas did not affect him. My father pulled them out of the room, through the hall, and outside where Mother revived quickly, and that was that.

Six months later, April 20, 1947, Oliver was born: a healthy-looking, plump, beautiful boy. Oliver seemed like any other new-born, my mother and father told my brothers and sisters. There was no sign that anything was amiss. But one afternoon, a few months after he was born, my mother brought Oliver to a window. She held him there in the sun, and there Oliver rested in his mother's arms and there Oliver looked and looked directly into the sun, which was the first moment my mother realized that he was blind.

My parents, the true heroes of this story, learned with the passing months Oliver could not hold up his head or crawl or walk or anything. He couldn't hold anything in his hand, he couldn't speak. So they brought him to Mt. Sinai Hospital in New York for a full series of tests, just to see how bad the condition was. The only explanation anyone could agree on was that the gas which my mother inhaled in her sleep during that third month of her pregnancy had reached Oliver and caused the severe incurable hopeless condition before he was born. At the end of a long week of waiting, my parents returned to the hospital and met with the doctor, Dr. Samuel De Lange. When our children are in pain, we try to heal them. When they are hungry, we feed them. When they're lonely, we comfort them. "What can we do for our son?" my parents wanted to know. Dr. De Lange said he wanted to make it very clear to both my mother and father there was absolutely nothing that could be done for Oliver. He didn't want my parents to grasp at any false hope. "You could place him in an institution." But my parents answered, "He's our son. We will take Oliver home, of course." The good doctor said, "Then take him home and love him." And I guess that was sound medical advice. Dr. De Lange speculated Oliver would probably not live beyond the age of seven, maybe eight. He also suggested Oliver be taken to another neurosurgeon to confirm the diagnosis, and this is what my parents did. Yes, the second doctor repeated the first verdict. Oliver's case was hopeless. While he scanned the forms my parents filled out, the second doctor noticed that my mother and father were born in Brussels, which led him to say, "You know, during World War II, my parents were taken in and fed and protected by a Belgian family, for we are Jews. Now I guess it's my turn to help a Belgian family." And the doctor didn't charge my parents for the tests or the care or the medication. I never met these two doctors, but I loved them all my life as the child loves the heroes in a fairy tale.

Oliver grew to the size of a ten-year-old. He had a big chest, a large head. His hands and feet were those of a five-year-old, however, soft and small. We'd wrap a box of baby cereal for him at Christmas and place it under the tree. We'd pat his head with a damp cloth in the middle of a July heat wave. Oliver still remains the most helpless human being I ever met. The weakest human being I ever met, and yet, he was one of the most powerful human beings I ever met.

As a teacher, I spend many hours preparing lessons, hoping I can influence my students in some small, but significant way. Each year thousands of books are printed with the hopes that the authors can move people to action. We all labor at the task of raising children or teaching them values, hoping something gets through, after all of our efforts. Oliver could do absolutely nothing except breathe and sleep and eat and yet, he was responsible for action, for love, for courage, for insight. For me, to have been brought up in a house where a tragedy was turned into a joy explains to a great degree why I'm the type of husband and father and writer and teacher that I have become.

I remember my mother saying when I was small, "Isn't it wonderful that you can see?" And once she said, "When you get to Heaven I bet Oliver will run to you and embrace you, and the first thing he'll say is 'thank you.'" It leaves quite an impression on a young boy. Of course it is I who must thank Oliver and my parents for defining for me the boundaries of love, which were the house and the yard and the woods where we ran and played. And all of the time Oliver laughed and slept between his fresh sheets under the window day after day.

I remember too, my mother explaining to me that we were blessed with Oliver in ways that were not clear to her, at first. We were fortunate that Oliver's case was so severe. The best we could do for him was feed him three times a day and bathe him and keep him warm. He didn't need us to be there in the room all day. He never knew what his condition was. So often parents are faced with a child who's severely retarded or is hyperactive, demanding or wild, who needs constant care. So many people have little choice but to place their child in an institution. Each circumstance is different. No one can judge another. But I've come to believe we're here to tend to these lilies of the field. We do the best we can. If you have a boy or girl like Oliver in your home, you'll know what's best for him or her, for your family. The decision is never easy. I asked my father, "How did you care for Oliver for thirty-two years?" He said, "It was not thirty-two years, I just asked myself, 'Can I feed Oliver today?' And the answer was always, 'Yes, I can.'"

I remember once I was a little boy sitting down beside my brother. I was alone, beside my brother. I was alone in the house and I wanted to see if Oliver was really blind. You know, if he was faking it. So I spread my hand over his face and shook my fingers close to his open eyes. Of course, he did not blink or move. His eyes were brown like mine, yet so different. Often it was my job to feed Oliver supper—a poached egg mixed with cereal, warm milk, sugar, a banana. "Yuck," I often thought, "I wouldn't eat this stuff." But feeding Oliver throughout his life was like feeding an eight-month-old child. His head was always propped up to a slight incline on pillows. A teaspoon of food was brought to his lips, he'd feel the spoon, open his mouth, close his mouth, then swallow. I still, today, can hear the sound of the spoon ticking and tapping against that red bowl in the silence of his room. "Oh, Mr. De Vinck, you mean he was a vegetable."

When I was a child I was afraid of the dark and shared a room with my younger brother. Our room was separated from Oliver's by a single wall. Five inches of wood and plaster divided us from each other during the night. We breathed the same night air, listened to the same wind. Slowly, without our knowing, Oliver created a certain power around us which changed all of our lives. I cannot explain Oliver's influence, except to say that the powerless in this world do hold great power; and sometimes the weak do confound the mighty.

Postscript: When I was in my early twenties, I met a girl, we fell in love. After a few months, I brought her home for dinner and to meet my family. After the introductions, the small talk, my mother went to the kitchen to check the meal and I asked the girl, "Would, would you like to see Oliver?" For I had, of course, told her about my brother. "No," she answered. She did not want to see him. It was as if she had slapped me in the face. Yet I just said something polite and walked to the dining room.

Soon after I met Roe, Rosemary. A dark haired, dark-eyed, lovely girl. She asked me the names of my brothers and sisters, she bought me a copy of *The Little Prince*, she loved children. I thought she was wonderful. I brought her home after a few months to meet my family. Introductions, small talk, dinner. Then it was time to feed Oliver. I walked into the kitchen, reached for the red bowl and the egg and the cereal and milk and banana and prepared his meal. Then I remember I sheepishly asked Roe if she'd like to come upstairs and see Oliver. "Sure," she said, and up the stairs we went. I sat at Oliver's bedside as Roe stood and watched over my shoulder. I gave him his first spoonful, his second . . . "Can I do that?" she asked, with ease and freedom and compassion. So I gave her the bowl and she fed Oliver, one spoonful at a time. The power of the powerless. Which girl would you marry? Today Roe and I have three children.

LEARNING FROM OLIVER

I shared this essay the next morning with the group of executives. Somehow it added a clarifying dimension, about the size and scope of their problems, about the nature of power, about gratitude for life and the simple, but taken-for-granted privileges of sight and speech and learning and movement. I have shared Chris De Vinck's poignant prose with many audiences as I have taught seminars all over the world. I am as moved as I write his words today as I was that first evening far from home, perplexed and at a loss for how to make sense of the powerlessness we all felt that night.

I have talked to Chris about his brother. Chris went on to become a writer for the *Wall Street Journal*. He published other books and made a huge difference as the Language Arts supervisor for a large school district in the East. He and his family gave me a gift when he shared his brother's story. The essay, its publication, and how one source after another picked up the essay until it finally crossed the desk of the president of the United States and Chris spent time with him, is another story.[2] But I will be forever grateful to Chris and his brother Oliver, to his wise parents who one day at a time exerted tremendous influence and were influenced in turn, and to the truth Chris taught, as captured by an editor at the *Wall Street Journal* in the title "The Power of the Powerless."

Oliver teaches us that we all can make a difference. If he, so severely lacking in physical and mental capabilities, could make such an impact—have so much power—so can you. Sometimes we feel that we've got to climb a mountain or raise a monument to leave our mark on the world. What we fail to recognize is that often we make a difference simply by existing, by handling what life gives us. Maybe the way we deal with our challenges and our rewards inspires someone else to achieve worthwhile things in their own life.

I came away from that teaching experience empowered because of what I had learned from Chris and Oliver. What happened to the leaders who heard the story of Oliver? The executives I taught spent the rest of the workshop on personal work. They more clearly defined their personal missions and worked to align their personal lives with those visions. In the years since that training took place, other leaders have come and gone in their business. Some of the leaders have been more sensitive than others. Some are more competent than others. Life is not fair. But each of the participants in that workshop was able to dig deeper, find security from within, identify their own personal resources, and declare their independence from the inequities imposed upon them by the arbitrary leadership changes in their own organization. They learned a lesson that many are just now learning—there is no security in a job. Any change, any loss, does not make us victims. Others can shake you, surprise you, disappoint you, but they can't prevent you from acting, from taking the situation you're presented with and moving on. No matter where you are in life, no matter what your situation, you can always do something. You always have a choice and the choice can be power.

Mother Teresa has taught this concept wherever she serves. A woman who had been successful in business and had amassed a small fortune once approached her, wanting to know what she could possibly do that would matter, feeling inadequate in comparison to the famous Mother Teresa who had devoted a lifetime of service and compassion to the untouchables of India and the poor of the world. Her answer: "What I do you cannot do." The woman was devastated. Her intent was genuine, her desire was real; why was she being turned away? But Mother Teresa rekindled her enthusiasm and lifted her sights when she continued: "What I do you cannot do; but what *you* do, I cannot do. The needs are great, and none of us, including me, ever do great things. But we can all do small things, with great love, and together we can do something wonderful." And so we can. With these words and through her actions, we learn there is always something we can do. We can diminish our doubts. A little doing dispels a lot of doubt. We can choose, even in those small ways, to be powerful rather than powerless.

WHAT CAN I DO?

The capacity to move from a position of powerlessness comes as we realize that we always have a choice. Though we may feel trapped or helpless, we can choose the attitude with which we face our challenges. If we take on the victim mentality and assume there is nothing we can do, we will never gain power. We will live what Henry David Thoreau termed "lives of quiet desperation."

I learned just how crucial our attitude can be when I met Candace. She managed to find hope where there might only have been pain, immobility, and dysfunction. Candace was a divorced mother of three—twin girls and a younger boy. Her daughters were thirteen when the tragedy entered their lives. Cari, one of the twins, was walking to a school carnival just a few blocks from their home when she was struck and killed by a drunk driver. Candace's grief was profound. She had survived a terrible loss with the death of her mother a few years earlier. She had been through the rehabilitation following another accident involving her young son. But this death, this needless death? Why? She said that for days she could hardly look at her other daughter without seeing and thinking of Cari. She was overcome by grief. She refused to leave her home. A few days later, on the evening the driver was arrested (he had fled the scene of the accident), Candace reluctantly went out to a restaurant with a few friends. On the way to the restaurant, they encountered highway patrol officers taking measurements at the scene of the accident. Not knowing she was Cari's mother, the officers informed her that the driver had been arrested on four previous occasions. That he had been drunk each time. And that he would probably not even see jail time for what he had done.

DO SOMETHING!

Candace was furious. She could only keep repeating, "What am I going to do? What am I going to do?" As they continued on to the restaurant, her sister said, "I know you are not going to let this go. I know you are going to do something." Her friend said that, knowing Candace, she would not let Cari's death be in vain. She would take her tragedy and turn it into something positive. She would fight back. "I'm going to start an organization because people need to know about this!" Candace reportedly told the women who were with her that night. And she did. It was named at the suggestion of another friend. And you and I have been affected because that one mother, out of her grief and the power in her soul, made a decision that grief-stricken night in Sacramento, California, to *do something*.

The result was MADD—Mothers Against Drunk Drivers. Within a short time, Candace Lightner came to the conclusion that she was not against individuals, but deplored the behavior that had caused the death of her daughter, so the name was changed to Mothers Against Drunk Driving. Candace mobilized her frustration rather than being paralyzed by it. She founded an organization that would work with the federal government, state and local governments, parents, and children to prevent the deaths of other people's sons and daughters. She did this even though, as she told me, she had never before been active as a voter or been involved in political organizations. Her ignorance of the political and legislative processes did not stop her. She was not daunted by her inexperience or lack of expertise.

Though Candace was angry, her message was not. She did not condemn the people who drove drunk, but rather their behavior. And with the support of the police, of bar and liquor store owners, of the people who loved them, their behavior could be changed. After all, they had choices, and at any point, they could choose not to—not to enter the bar, not to order the first drink or the fourth, not to get behind the wheel of the car.

Under Candace's leadership MADD grew into an organization of national prominence. She left after a number of years at the helm to pursue other worthy causes, including rebuilding her own personal life. The effects of her decision, made so many years ago in that restaurant, are widespread and have outlived her involvement in the organization she founded. Although Candace found the process agonizingly painful—she eventually found ways of dealing with the challenge through friends, therapy, and the writing of a book about the grieving process[3]—she was able to address the anger she felt both toward the driver and the system that had made it so easy for him to get into his car and kill her daughter. Since MADD's inception, over 1,200 laws have been enacted, fatalities from drunk driving have diminished markedly, and existing legislation in forty-seven states has been changed—all because of one woman's choice to be powerful, not powerless.

WILL A POWER SHIFT WORK FOR EVERYONE?

Though Candace is an extraordinary woman, her experience is not. Tragedies, accidents, and difficulties strike many of us. Like Candace, most of us are capable of a paradigm shift—of changing our perspective on the way things are, and on the way things can be. Sometimes the easiest way to accomplish this is to observe someone we admire, or someone who is getting the effects we want to get, and make an effort to see things the way they do. In time, we truly begin to see things differently.

For others, however, a shift in attitude may not be sufficient or possible. If you suffer from severe depression or other mental illness, the material this book presents is not going to solve your problems. Some of us, as much as we might want to turn our lives around on our own, need therapy with a professional, whether priest, counselor, or psychiatrist.

STARTING WHERE YOU ARE

Even if things seem completely unchangeable, *you can change* starting where you are.

As you challenge your doubts with growing faith, take heart from the following words written by my good friend and professional associate David Whyte. David has a keen sensitivity to the spiritual struggles common to the human condition and has written wisely about them in his bestseller.[4] He was struggling at a certain time in his life with his own inadequacies, doubts, and misgivings. Inspired by the appearance of the moon, which was at the time in a waning cycle moving from the full-moon stage to near darkness, he drew a parallel that has often reassured me.

Faith

I want to write about faith,
  about the way the moon rises
    over cold snow, night after night,

faithful even as it fades from fullness,
  slowly becoming that last curving and impossible
    sliver of light before the final darkness.

But I have no faith myself
  I refuse it the smallest entry.

Let this then, my small poem,
  like a new moon, slender and barely open,
    be the first prayer that opens me to faith.[5]

   You can be open to faith. You can consider the possibility of change. You can, with growing awareness, choose power over powerlessness. Where are you now? Below is a brief self-assessment designed to help you determine where you are in your personal journey to increase your own power. Such assessments are provided at the end of each of the remaining chapters. Consider each question carefully. Reflect on the answers that come to mind. Be honest with yourself.

SELF-ASSESSMENT

1. Under what circumstances are you likely to become immobilized by doubt or lack of faith?

2. What triggers this reaction in you? Can you describe your doubts?

3. In these situations, what better alternatives have you not chosen that seem at first unlikely or improbable?

4. What is one thing you could do that would challenge the irrational thought that the best thing to do is nothing?

5. Is there another way? What is another alternative?

CHAPTER 4

COERCIVE POWER— CONTROLLING OTHERS THROUGH FEAR

Wherever did we get the idea that we could get people to do better by making them feel bad?

SEMINAR PARTICIPANT

THOUGH POWER CAN BE A POSITIVE FORCE IN OUR LIVES, IT CAN also be destructive and demoralizing. This is true not only for those subject to power, but also for those wielding it. Coercive power relies on the premise of control and uses fear as its instrument. When we use coercive power, we do it not to influence others but to force them to obey. We achieve compliance through threats, cajolery, bullying, or physical force—whatever is necessary to cause fear in those we are seeking to control.

The coercive person can make our lives unpleasant. He induces pain and makes us feel bad about ourselves. We end up complying with his demands, even temporarily, because we are afraid of what might happen if we don't. We might lose something important to us, such as our job or possessions. We might even be punished or publicly humiliated for our failure to adhere to the rules.

THE POWER PROCESS

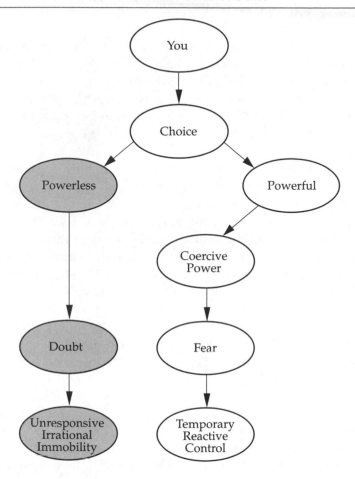

When we choose coercive power as the path to power, we have decided to "make them do it." How do we make them do it? By eliciting fear in them. If they are afraid, they will comply. Why do governments or businesses use force? Why as individuals do we use force? Why do we try to make other people do things? What is in us or in them that precipitates such action and causes us to justify in our own minds the actions we take?

MAKING OTHERS DO WHAT YOU WANT

I often ask seminar participants, "When do you feel comfortable making other people do what you want?" I have asked thousands of people and come to expect a predictable range of answers. These include enforcing safety measures, meeting deadlines, averting potential or present threat to life or property, preventing moral or ethical violations, and dealing with someone who has limited or impaired ability to function.

Sometimes we believe force is necessary in the interest of safety or disaster prevention. If, for example, we see a small child chase a ball into the road, into the path of an oncoming car, we might yell at the child, demanding she stop. Or we might grab her to avoid almost certain disaster. After the crisis has been averted, we might then threaten and intimidate her to prevent her from repeating the act. We feel that in some circumstances, when danger is imminent or likely, it is justifiable to do whatever is necessary to prevent an accident. There are railings along the edge of the World Trade Towers in New York City to keep observers, both careless and careful alike, from falling from the top. Someone made the decision to implement this safety measure to forcibly prevent accidents, rather than give visitors the opportunity to fall.

There are other times when we use coercive power because it is expedient; it is the quick solution. We do the thing that seems the most direct, or that requires the least additional energy, planning, or preparation. Frequently, the expediency we feel results from a genuine urgency. We force someone to do what we want, whether they want to or not, because there is little time for dialogue and the consequences of doing nothing are too great. Sometimes we use force because we can; we can pull it off, we can get away with it. If there are no adverse consequences, some will resort to bullying and intimidation just because they can. Consider Daddy Warbucks's confession in the musical *Annie:* "You don't have to be nice to the people you meet on the way up if you're not coming back down![1]"

Sometimes we justify force because we feel so much is at stake, whether it is urgent or not. This is true in the case of national security. The threat of retaliation makes deterrence an acceptable military posture. In times of war, we cannot afford the luxury of willing performance or democratic decision making under fire, so "make 'em do it," "use force if necessary," even "threaten their lives if you have to" become rules of thumb. These measures ensure that the necessary actions are taken by both leaders and their followers.

Outside of war, genuine emergency, or reasonable expectation of danger, we sometimes feel expediency that is not a matter of reasoned judgment. If you had visited my home one Sunday morning recently, you would have laughed. Picture this: Dad, six feet one and two hundred plus pounds, is verbally pushing the kids around, barking orders, and being generally oppressive. "Find those shoes! Change that diaper! What do you mean, you can't find your pants? I told you to get in the car, now get. I don't care if you haven't had breakfast. Stop teasing your brother! Do you want a spanking? This is the last time I am telling you . . . Come on! Do you want to be left behind? (Swat) And something worse will happen if you don't hurry faster!"

The justification for this barrage? Is the house on fire? Have we discovered a terrorist in the basement? No, we are just getting ready to go to church, where we will learn about love. And kindness. And gentleness. And respect. And patience, which I will probably consider once the pressure I feel to get everyone ready—to be there on time—has dissipated. A little forethought, a little Saturday night preparation, might prevent this kind of expediency.

FORCE AS A LIFESTYLE

But what about force as a lifestyle? What about intimidation as a way of routinely dealing with others? Dilemmas around our use of coercion do not usually stem from actions that are intended to save lives. They usually come when those we are trying to force do not want to submit to our wishes. Perhaps they are too stubborn, too tired, too reluctant, or just don't care. How do you respond in this situation? The easy path, often, is to use force. To coerce. To threaten or intimidate or pressure. We elicit fear in others as we tell them what will happen if they don't comply. We tell with our words and with our actions and our body language. Our countenance may be used as a weapon to control someone. We do it *to* someone. We do it to teach them a lesson. We make an example of someone so that everyone else knows we mean business!

This was the case with Rachel, a brand manager for a major consumer products company. She was told to meet financial forecasts.

Though her efforts included some innovative cooperation with other departments, she fell short 18 percent. Her career, for all practical purposes, was over. She was assigned a dead-end position. The new brand manager was then invited to take the challenge of exploring creative alliances with other departments. But having heard tales about the fate of the previous brand manager, he refused to get others involved, and proposed an extremely conservative forecast and marketing plan.

In our daily lives this drama is played out regularly in similar, though less severe terms. We threaten with our words and actions. In organizations I work with, managers talk about being unable to suggest new ideas, new ways, new approaches, because it is not safe to do so. There exists an unwillingness to take risks, even if the risk involves telling the truth. Why? Because once upon a time someone like Rachel tried, or risked, or went out on a limb, and was cut off or cut down. Risk-takers are ridiculed, belittled, transferred, and eliminated. An incident becomes a part of folklore that is carefully repeated and passed on to new employees as evidence of the "way things are" and as justification for safe behavior.

Sometimes I will ask a group of employees to tell me some stories about heroes and villains, folklore that is told, especially to new employees, to illustrate the values of the culture. I can tell a lot about an organization by listening to this undocumented but deeply believed folklore. If I hear a horrendous, oft-told story, I ask to interview the person who actually had the experience. Seldom are they around. Often the stories end with some moral, to carry a myth and cause adherence to the mores it represents. But it never ceases to amaze me how people will cling to an incident from the far distant past as justification for current behavior. Social learning has taken place, and the myth gets strengthened with each new telling.

Warren Bennis has documented how executives are afraid to be candid in giving feedback to the people who report to them because of fear that advice won't be followed or will be perceived as criticism, leading to hostility. As a consequence, "Management turns into a manipulative art, where deception, spin, maneuvering, guided ambiguity and other small deceits and sleights of the tongue replace straightforward communication."[2] On the other hand, 70 percent of the people who directly reported to these executives also withheld advice and found it difficult to give accurate and timely information if it was at odds with the norms and preferences of the boss. Information was not shared even when employees knew that certain disaster, otherwise preventable, would be the result.

In one large multinational consumer products company, there existed a well-known threshold of research-and-development investment beyond which a new product could not be criticized openly. After this point, the project was perceived as the "pet" of a particular senior executive, and any criticism was viewed as disloyalty or sabotage. So, even though market testing demonstrated that the new product was going to fail, no one would speak up, and hundreds of thousands of dollars would be spent and lost in a full market release of the product. Ultimately, heads would roll, positions would be shaken up, jobs and titles would be sacrificed, and money would be unnecessarily lost. Why? Because employees were afraid to speak up at the stage when alternative actions might have been considered.

WHAT ARE YOU AFRAID OF?

What happens when we become afraid? When we operate out of fear, we become guarded. We are careful with what we disclose, what we share, what we reveal, what we attempt. We don't want to be labeled. We want to stay on safe ground. We become tentative, and our capacities stay buried beneath what might have been or could have been. We are frightened. We are protective. We are dependent, emotionally, on how others treat us.

The fear resides not only in the terrified followers. Fear is elicited in them primarily because of the fear that exists first in the heart of the leader. The leader is afraid? Yes! Of what? Of what might happen. Of the possibility that followers will not follow. That no one will do as they are supposed to. Something significant or important must be accomplished, and the consequences demand compliance. The leader may be afraid of those consequences because they affect him. He might look bad, be judged, be held accountable, or worst of all, lose his power!

The fear we see in the world, in our families, and in our organizations is possibly an extension of the fear that is in us. The leader may spell fear *f-e-a-r*, fear of *failure*, fear of being *embarrassed*, the *anxiety* of uncertain fears, and fear of being *rejected*. I remember reading a historical account about Stalin, at the height of his power. He stayed in a huge castle, buried deep within the inner recesses of the fortress, barricaded in a small, bombproof room, with walls made of concrete three feet thick, with only one tiny window protected by thick, yellowed glass. His self-imposed incarceration, with only a few amenities each night, and a military cot for his bed, was his fortress within a fortress. He would sleep fitfully, then leap to his feet to check at the yellowed glass, to make certain that the dark moving objects on the other side of the glass, his personal guards, were on duty protecting him. He was one of the most powerful men in the world, living in total fear. With fear rampant, the apparent recourse is to "make 'em do it."

IMITATIONS OF POWER

Often rudeness is the insecure person's imitation of power. How does a spouse, parent, teacher, leader, or supervisor get that way? Sometimes simple conditioning has taken place. If you are not getting the results with someone that you want, and you approach them menacingly with a threat, with the intent of making them do it, chances are they will respond in a compliant way, at least in your presence and in that moment.

But examine the dynamics of that interchange. If you threaten and they comply, whose behavior just got reinforced? Yours! And what then becomes the likelihood that given a similar situation you will use the same weapon again? Pretty high. Even though you could try a different approach, why should you? Coercion and fear worked before, didn't it? Abraham Maslow coined an expression to communicate this phenomenon. He said, "He that is good with a hammer tends to see *everything* as a nail." I might paraphrase to say, "he sees *everyone* as a nail." Even though there are other management and leadership tools in his bag, he continues to resort to this one because there is an illusion of efficacy. It appears to work. Like the daredevil who jumped off the ten-story building replied when someone at the fifth-floor level asked how he was doing—"Everything's okay so farrrrrrrr." For the daredevil and for us, whether we are managers, parents, or neighbors, spouses, leaders, or customers, there is eventually a sudden stop that changes everything. The sudden stop may come in the form of a closed door, a pink slip, a divorce notice, a subpoena.

LEARNING ABOUT POWER AT WORK

When I got my first job out of college, I had a boss who let me know right away just how things would work. He sat me down and said, "Blaine, I need to explain something to you. When two people ride on a horse, somebody's got to ride in front." It didn't take me long to realize which part of the horse I got—and it wasn't the front.

What he was telling me was that I was always going to take a back seat. He was the one who had the important view, who had control of the reins. After that whenever he wanted my opinion he would either have to give it to me or beat it out of me. The fear I felt in response to his overbearing approach prevented me from contributing much. I was hesitant to make my true opinion known, and instead, always deferred to his view, *even when I knew he was wrong*.

My response represents the behavior of many people when they feel fear. In high school, we learn in biology that in the face of danger animals experience a fight-or-flight reaction. Most of us are no different in this regard. When presented with a threatening situation, we either face it and do something about it (approach), or avoid it, sometimes simply by running away (avoidance).

Both approach and avoidance behaviors are learned and can be unlearned. If we react a certain way and somehow a desirable result follows, our response is reinforced. In subsequent situations, we repeat the behavior to get the effect we want. For those who turn on their attackers and win, force becomes a valuable tool. For those who turn away from their challengers, the sense of relief that accompanies escape becomes an incentive to flee emotionally or physically from difficult situations.

Though these behaviors can sometimes produce the result we would like, often we fail to realize we have other options. We settle into the role of bullying or being bullied rather than seeking another alternative. When we feel a threat, we revert to one of these two basic emotional responses.

POWER AT HOME

Some years ago I had an experience with one of my sons that taught me how vulnerable I am to this type of response, and also how important it is to check your motives before confronting another person. It occurred one night after I arrived home from a business trip. I had been on the road for a number of days and was exhausted. It had been a very tiring trip and I just wanted to put my feet up and relax.

On this particular evening, a mechanical problem with the airplane had delayed my flight by an hour and a half. By the time I arrived in Salt Lake City, found my car, made the trek home, and pulled into the driveway, I was about two and a half hours later than I had planned.

As I lugged my bags toward the front door, I felt physically and emotionally spent. Absorbed in my own frustration and fatigue, I was unaware that on the other side of the door a drama had been unfolding. Hours before, Shawny, my sweetheart and companion, had asked our twelve-year-old son to straighten up his room and take a shower before dinner. He had refused. When she repeated her request, he said something to the effect of "No, I don't have to, and you can't make me!"

Apparently he had reached that pivotal moment in adolescence when defiance seems imperative. Despite Shawny's insistence, he had decided to make a stand. I was due home momentarily. Shawny and I have an agreement that we handle difficult child-raising problems as a team. So she told him the three of us would discuss this little problem in a few minutes, upon my arrival.

Well, the few minutes slowly became two and a half hours. Meanwhile, my son went upstairs into the bedroom, feeling all the power that a twelve-year-old can feel. I can just hear the thoughts racing through his head, "I took on Mom. I fought the law and the law didn't win. I won!"

But as I approached the door to my home, I had no idea any of this was happening. Imagine my dismay when I opened the door, so glad to finally be home, and the first thing my sweetheart said was, "*Where* have you been? You said you were going to be here two and a half hours ago. Your son is up in his room, and he won't do anything I say. He won't even take a shower! Would you please do something about *your* boy?"

It occurred to me that she was upset. After all, I am a professional. It also occurred to me not to point out my observation at that moment. Instead I mumbled something about how glad I was to be home and asked her to repeat her complaint.

Now Shawny is an excellent manager, usually handling with dignity and finesse problems that bog me down. But her frustration had been building for over two hours, and she was ready for some help.

"I just told you, *your* boy is up in his room. He won't take a shower. He won't do anything I say. Will you please do something about your son!" I really wasn't up for this, but she needed help, so I would rise to the occasion.

I set down my suitcase, but picked up some emotional baggage as I headed up the stairs. I thought to myself, "I don't need this. I didn't come home for this." I didn't have much left to give. "Okay, I'll talk to him," I barked at Shawny. "Is that what you want? I'll get him in the shower!" By the time I reached the second floor, I was stomping and fuming. I loved my wife, but I was mad at her for dumping this on me just as I arrived home.

As I plodded down the hallway, I considered what approach to take with the boy. We had already had the obligatory talk about puberty, hormones, and body odor, so I knew he understood the importance of preteen hygiene. Having had this "quality time" recently, I thought, I would get right to the point.

I entered the room and found him sitting on his bed, headphones on, listening to music. His eyes were closed. I reached across the bed, grabbed the headphones, and yanked them off his head. How's that for an opening move? You know, get their attention first, right? Then I began my no-nonsense attack. "Hey what's this problem with you and Mom and not taking a shower? Get in there and take a shower! Now!" I turned to leave the room.

I wasn't thinking at the time that these were the first words my son had heard from me in nearly a week. I didn't offer a greeting or ask him how he was; I just laid into him. I wasn't through the doorway when I heard him say in a soft voice, "No, Dad." Whoops. He was on a roll. He had Mom going and now he was going to take on Dad.

I turned in disbelief. "What did you say? You know, your mom is really mad at you. Do you want me mad at you too? Now get in there and take a shower." What style of management is it when they don't "get it," so you repeat yourself a little louder, and add a threat. I glared at him as I issued my directive. He looked me straight in the eye and said, "No, Dad."

I could feel I was starting to lose it, so I took a deep breath and tried to calm myself. I *was* a professional and had been taught to handle difficult situations, I had learned ten different theories of child development in graduate school, and back then they had all made sense, since I didn't have any kids. Now I have many children and *no* theories.

I decided to take the rational approach. I would be calm, cool, and take control. I would make him understand why he needed to shower—after all, the sanitation of our home was at stake. I forced a smile and said, "Son, remember the other day we had a little talk about your body and changes. Well, guess what? This room stinks! You stink! Now take a shower."

So much for the rational approach. Again, he looked up at me, unfazed by my demands. I was furious he could remain so calm while I was losing my cool. "*No*, Dad," he threw the words at me.

That was it! I reached down and picked up my son. "Oh yeah, we'll see who's going to take a shower." He started yelling, kicking, his arms and legs flailing in all directions.

I carried him down the hall, into the bathroom, and dumped him in the shower stall. I grabbed a bar of soap, threw it into the stall, and turned on the water. "*Now, you take a shower!*" I demanded. I left the bathroom feeling a rush of adrenaline. I had won. What was the objective? Get the boy in the shower. Where was the boy? In the shower. I had won.

I went back downstairs to my wife, who, hearing all the commotion, looked up at me and asked, "What happened?" I announced that our son was in the shower. I could see the awe and reverence on her face. Smiling, she asked, "How'd you do it?"

As I searched for an answer, the reality of what I had done began to settle in on me. I muttered a thing or two and finally mustered up the courage to confess. "Shawny, I threw him in the shower." "You did what?" she exclaimed in disbelief.

I repeated my answer. She was incredulous. "You threw *our* son in the shower? You teach this stuff, Blaine. You're supposed to do it right." She threw her arms into the air and stormed off in the opposite direction.

I asked her to wait while I went upstairs to talk to the boy and hopefully undo some of the damage I had done. When I reached the bathroom, I found my son standing right where I had left him, fully clothed and now drenched. He was steaming, and it wasn't from the hot water.

CROSSING THE SENSITIVE LINE

I took a towel and handed it to him as a gesture of good will. He knocked the towel out of my hand and just glared at me. I apologized, but it was too little too late. It was as if we had an emotional bank account with my son, and I had made this little five-cent deposit to try to make up for a ten-thousand-dollar withdrawal. In every relationship there is a critical, sensitive line. It is invisible but it is real. You cannot cross it with impunity. If you cross it, you might not be able to extricate yourself. I had crossed that line with my son. He was silent. He would not look at me. Finally, I left the room.

All that evening he remained silent, offering only an icy stare. The next morning was not much better—a little grunt in the hallway as we passed. He never said the words, but I knew what he was thinking. "You talk about choice and freedom and valuing people, but when it comes right down to it, you're going to make me do what you want. Aren't you, Dad? You don't really value me. You don't really care about me or my feelings." It was as if in one moment I had undermined the trust I had worked a long time to develop with him.

It was about a week later when my son approached me and said, "Dad, do you remember that problem with the shower?" "Yeah. Do you want to talk about it?" I asked. "No, I don't. But, don't you think I'm old enough now that I can choose to do that myself?" I agreed that he was and promised never to use force again with him in that way. I have worked hard to live up to that promise.

I was so struck by his maturity I went to Shawny and told her what he had said. Her response surprised me a little. "You know, I've been thinking of something. You came home, flew off the handle, and went stomping up the stairs like a wild man. I didn't need that. I needed a little help right then. I expected something from you. Couldn't you tell I was upset? Maybe if you had stayed downstairs, we could have sat down and talked, maybe calmed down a little bit. You never know, he might have taken a shower while we were downstairs talking." I thanked her for her wisdom. Family living can be a marvelous laboratory for life.

WHAT ARE YOU TEACHING AND LEARNING AT HOME?

I apologized to my son, genuinely. I realized that I had crossed a very tender and delicate line in our relationship. It was a long time before he could comfortably trust me again, because he had learned something about me. Under pressure, what was Dad going to do? In a difficult emotional time, what was Dad going to do? I had revealed myself to him. Following that incident, I had to react differently in difficult situations many times before he began to really trust me again.

Under certain pressures every one of us might gravitate toward coercive power even when the house is not on fire, it is not wartime, nor are OSHA safety standards being violated. This is unfortunate because when we lean on our size or position, it weakens our relationships and legitimate power. We can force another person if we have more credentials, more status, more possessions, and so on. But we no longer have the same power or influence. We can only slowly rebuild it as we overcome our nature and our history by making significant deposits in the relationship, by apologizing and taking responsibility without rationalizing. There are no shortcuts to building trust.

Today, I try to take each of my older children on the road with me at least once each year, to spend time with them and let them see what I do for a living. In a seminar, my son has heard me tell this story, and he confirmed that I actually threw him in the shower. I'm not very proud of my behavior that day, but I chose to share it with you so you would have a backdrop for asking yourself a few key questions. What causes *you* to cross the line with those you love or work with? When life is not at stake and there are no moral or ethical infractions involved, what pushes *you* to use coercive power? Do you have the awareness and self-insight to realize where you are in this critical area? What causes you to cross that sensitive line?

In the following chart I have summarized what hundreds of people have told me in response to this question. See if some of your habits are listed here.

EMOTIONAL FACTORS THAT TRIGGER CONTROL

Here are some things that we might be thinking, feeling, or experiencing that cause us to attempt to force others:

    impatient
    tired
    lonely
    angry
    emotional scripting—how you were treated as a child

expedient—feeling pressure (insufficient time, too many things going
    on)

any other approach requires too much (effort, time, patience)

feels good—something perverse in human nature that delights in
    controlling or having power over others

lack skill—can't do anything else

lack desire—don't want to do anything else

lack information—unaware of alternatives or possibilities

ignorance—unaware of immediate effects; unaware of long-term re-
    sults; don't have the answer

mentally ill

medical malfunction—hormone or chemical imbalance, PMS

substance abuse—side effects of drugs, alcohol

psychopathology—mental dysfunction with psychological roots
    manifested by delusions of grandeur, misperceptions, schizo-
    phrenia, paranoia

sociopathology—distrust, hate, mistrust, antisocial feelings, see so-
    ciety in general and other people as adversaries

lack hope

don't believe anything else will work

it's expected; feel you are supposed to deal with subordinates, oth-
    ers, in that way

are afraid of what might happen if you don't—in this litigious soci-
    ety we are afraid others may come after us if we don't go after
    them first

it's quick

only way, you think

only way you can think of at the moment

seems appropriate

ego is threatened

insecurity

just want to do it at the moment—stubborn, cantankerous

frustrated by other things and the frustration is manifested here

system rewards it

expectations from others that it is acceptable or the norm

it works

it's easy

needs are superficially met

short-term effectiveness

limited repertoire, skills; he that is good with a hammer . . .
what we've seen others do
what has been done to us
what was rewarded in the past
nothing fails like success—because it worked before, why change?
autobiography—that is all I have experienced myself
protective of myself
requires little from us
avoids the vulnerability of interaction and disclosure

SOCIAL FACTORS THAT TRIGGER CONTROL

Here are some things that may be going on *around* us that cause us to
try to control other people:

peer approval—others we want to be liked by do it
peer consensus—others we are like do it
social sanctions—society rewards or approves us, macho image
social modeling—others we admire do it
mob psychology—lack of individual accountability, responsibility
mentoring—others we want to be like do it
seems to work, and there's no immediate downside
illusion of control
illusion of effectiveness
it does work—for a while
others do what we want
it gets the job done
immediate effects—we get results right now
short-term payoffs seem worth it
systems and structures prevail over individuals and values unless
    those values are truly shared

KNOWING WHEN TO HALT

A man once told me at one of my seminars, "Blaine, at age fifty, I'm finally getting some insights into my behavior. Every single time I find
myself hungry, angry, lonely, or tired, I'm vulnerable. I remind myself

by using the word HALT to pause for a monent, to determine if I am about to do something I will feel bad about later—something I did, not because I really thought it was best, but because I was *hungry* or *angry* or *lonely* or *tired*. Hunger can be psychological, a big desire or need for something. Anger is a secondary emotion. Something else is usually going on, and the anger is a manifestation that there is an imbalance somewhere else. Lonely means I am cut off from other people, isolated from them. My isolation can be geographical or psychological. Fatigue can be such an enemy, so when we get tired, worn out, or just fatigued, we become impatient, sometimes we lash out irrationally, sometimes without provocation. When that's going on inside of me, I'm liable to do something stupid, something that I might regret." He continued, "When I feel that way, it's a trigger for me to push the pause button, just like you have on a VCR, catch my breath and do a reality check." Given this man's experience, think again about what causes you to do something that you'll regret later, to cross the line from reason to force. What could you do to trigger a pause, a temporary halt, to consider what you are about to do, and what alternative might be better?

Perhaps we are tired, exhausted, or spent. Or perhaps we are under a pressure of time or perceived scarce resources. We feel that there isn't enough of something—time, energy, money, materials—so we have to intervene to solve the problem, deal with the issue, make something happen.

Perhaps the coercive person has grown up in an oppressive, top-driven, autocratic culture. Perhaps fear has been modeled as a tool that is appropriate. After all, it appears to work. It is immediate. It can be called on instantly. Everyone understands intimidation—it needs no explanation or translation. Perhaps their own mentors and models have been rewarded by the system or by their leaders for compliance, for imposition, for ensuring that certain results are "guaranteed or else."

The price of coercive power, without fail, is great. In his book *Coercion and Its Fallout*,[3] Murray Sidman laments the pervasiveness of coercion and notes the detrimental effects it spawns:

Why is coercion so universal? Punishment poisons relationships, pushes children out of the family, subverts learning, generates violence, and makes us ill. Negative reinforcement produces lives of desperation, stamps out ingenuity and productivity, turns joy into suffering, trust into fear, and love into hatred. Coercion is responsible for so much misery; why does it persist?

THE RESULTS OF COERCION

In a scene from the movie *Ben-Hur*, the new Roman governor assigned to Jerusalem enters the city on horseback with pomp, ceremony, and a military escort. He notices, however, that none of the local Jewish leaders have come to greet him. His general acknowledges that the Jewish people are resentful and resistant. They don't want to be ruled by Rome. In an effort to control the crowd and intimidate the Jews, the general has positioned armed guards along the main road. "This will not be a friendly welcome. But I guarantee it will be a quiet one," he assures the governor as he rests his hand on his sword. The general knows the Jews will not willingly accept their new governor. So he settles for grudging compliance, for reluctant obedience. He is actually afraid. He knows he is outnumbered. He knows he is not on home turf. He knows he is hated at the same time he is feared. He knows he cannot leave his back unprotected.

Dick Grote traced the current progressive discipline practices operating in many organizations to the 1930s and unions' influence with management.[4] At that time it was normal for an employee to be summarily dismissed without prior notice. As a hedge for the employer, the practice developed to give increasingly severe warnings to an employee who was not measuring up. Then would come a period of probation and eventually a "final warning." These systems invariably led to adversarialism, separation, isolationism, conflict, and sabotage. Grote summarized five primary problems with punishment as a management tool in the workplace:

1. Supervisors allow some people more leeway than others.
2. Supervisors, uncomfortable with what they have to do, often hesitate until there is no alternative.
3. Over time, punishment loses its power.
4. Since people avoid the things they are hit with, punishment produces avoidance.
5. Although short-term consequences include immediate improvement, long-term results are disastrous.

He concluded, "The quickest and simplest way to reduce the frequency of an undesired behavior is to apply some form of punishing consequence. But the reduction in the frequency of misbehavior is the short-term consequence. The use of punishment produces side effects and long-term consequences—anger, apathy, resentment, frustration—that end up being far more costly than whatever the original misbehavior might have been."[5]

Not only are painful consequences created in the long term, but it is a tremendous burden for the person in charge to manage or lead with coercive power. It is obviously a burden to the followers who might be manipulated and pushed into compliance. But it is also a burden to the leader. It is a huge task to control others. There is no reprieve. As Booker T. Washington noted, "You can't hold a man down without staying down with him." So you are constantly on guard. You can never relax. The coercive person carries all the weight, all the responsibility. He is the only one worried about getting the job done or done right. He alone must constantly consider how to ensure obedience. He cannot let up, because great forces are pushing back against him. When he is not around to make sure things go right, then he must have a second in command, or those he can directly control, standing in place of him as a symbol and carrier of the threats. The cat cannot be away, because he cannot allow the possibility that the mice will play. Once a pattern of coercive power is set, the leader is in a no-win situation. If he is absent, anything can happen. If he is present and persists in using coercive power, all of the creativity, innovation, invention, group spirit, enthusiasm, and drive that people possess will eventually be used against him.

THE PRICE OF COERCION

The coercive leader must not only manage for performance, but he must also manage for failure avoidance. There are many things that must be done right and done in concert to achieve success. But just one thing gone awry can bring disaster, undo results, or impede success. Hundreds of operations must function harmoniously to make an assembly line run properly. But someone who wants to disrupt the process need only throw a monkey wrench into the system and the whole line grinds to a halt. The coercive leader must be all-seeing, because his eyes alone are committed to success. The responsibility for accomplishing the task is his alone. Others only do what they are told, what they are forced to do, what they are made to do. They only do it when someone is standing over them, physically or figuratively. They comply because they have no other option.

What happens when the coercive leader lets up, turns his back, or reduces the pressure? It depends on the followers. Sometimes sabotage results, if anonymity is possible. Sometimes retaliation follows. Resentment has a thousand manifestations. Work is slowed down or stopped. Accidents occur. No one knows how or why it happened or who did it. Mass retribution by the leader, group punishment, or group confrontation only bonds the followers, as they unite against a common enemy—you. If what they share is their dislike of you, what results can you expect?

I was consulting with an organization when a supervisor asked me to help with an employee dilemma. The problem was actually that the atmosphere in the workplace had become adversarial and a "war" had begun. Employees were taking turns staying home from work, but they had their friends punching in for them daily, as though they were on the job. They were "stealing" time from their employer. Productivity was down. Management finally caught on to the problem. Apparently, employees didn't like some policy that had been instituted, so this was their way of getting back. I inquired what had been done to combat the problem thus far. Management had purchased a new time clock! Then they took everybody's picture, got some ID cards with a magnetic stripe on the back, and issued one of the new time cards to each employee. They positioned one of their people near the new time clock each morning. An employee would enter the building, get out their ID card, and hold it up next to their face. If it matched, the manager would let the employee run the card through the machine.

I wondered, thinking, "How would I feel knowing as I drive into work that someone is going to be standing at the entrance waiting to check me out. That seems a little extreme." And, frankly, it felt like an invitation to retaliate. I asked if the new process had worked. He said, "Yeah, it worked great—for two weeks." What happened after two weeks? They paid off the manager. He said the employees took up a collection, made a petty cash pool, and paid the guy more than management was paying him. The manager was letting them run the new ID cards through for each other again. Then what did they do? Well, they put one of their senior people near the entrance to monitor the time cards in the morning. Once in the morning and twice in the afternoon the senior manager would walk through the building with a computer printout in hand, looking for everyone who had used their time card that day. He would compare each line item entry on the printout with an actual person at work. You may be wondering if that worked. It did. For two months. And then, they got even. There was another retaliation, followed by another and another.

HOW DO EMPLOYEES USE THEIR CREATIVITY?

How long can that go on? People are enormously creative and they will use that creativity for you or against you. As soon as the slightest opportunity is available, resistance emerges. It is natural. It can be counted on. It is hurtful and harmful and a problem for the leader. But it will occur. Some will say, "We don't get mad, we get even." All these forces are unleashed and people feel justified when the leader or parent or teacher chooses to control through coercion.

In an automotive sheet metal stamping plant, the assembly line grinds to a stop. Giant presses go silent. Hours later, workers find a shovel jamming a belt. Where did it come from? How did a shovel get in the plant? No one could explain it. But everyone knew the new foreman was arrogant and dictatorial and had pushed the workers too far. The cost? Thousands of dollars, a safety violation, work stoppage.

It happens commonly, but the results of the coercive leader are disguised in bottom-line reports of attrition, missing inventory, and unreported losses. People feel justified in stealing from or hurting an employer if they are treated poorly. If they are not trusted, they cannot trust. If they cannot trust, they do not feel loyalty. After all, what has the employer done for them but make them feel scared, hurt, and angry?

So can you really control others through fear? The answer is a qualified yes. You can control their behavior, but you cannot control their emotions or the actions those emotions might spark. Control of behavior through fear has been demonstrated in families and companies, in cultures and countries. But what is the nature of the control? It is negative, reactive, and hurtful to everyone involved. More importantly, it is temporary. In the case of a company, if a single, coercive leader is at the helm, things will simply fall apart or turn to chaos upon the leader's demise. Without the leader's control, and in the absence of the fear he instilled, there is nothing to keep people tied to the organization that is the source of their pain. If the leader is in control for a long period, eventually people will resist. Ultimately, he and his power will be undermined.

FREE AGAIN

To control behavior is not to control hearts or minds or spirits. The human spirit cannot be permanently subdued through oppression and fear. As Aleksandr Solzhenitsyn has observed: "You only have power over people so long as you don't take everything away from them. But when you've robbed a man of everything, he's no longer in your power—he's free again."

To be "free again," children end up fighting their parents, leaving home, and choosing lifestyles their parents don't accept. To be "free again," employees leave companies. They take trade secrets and marketing plans, customer lists, equipment, and other employees with them. They look for a place where they can work more freely, and do what they value. To be "free again," citizens leave countries. They become immigrants in a land where they believe they can control their own fate. They risk their lives to hide, to escape, to fight overwhelming forces to be free.

So where is the coercive leader left when others break free, or even when they stick around? He walks a tenuous line. He holds no legitimate power because those he controls will leave or betray him when given the right opportunity. Ironically, these same people may reinforce the leader's destructive behavior. When they are punished, or "kept in line," they generalize the punishment to the punisher. In other words, they transfer the negative feelings associated with the punishment to the person inflicting it. Those being punished are willing to undergo the pain of punishment because it allows them to temporarily feel more powerful than the leader. By defying his wishes, they can get the momentary satisfaction of arousing his anger and frustration. They might choose to delay their gratification and get back at him later. In their minds they think, "You might be able to stop me now, but just you wait. I'll get you later." Sooner or later, what goes around comes around.

When we assume a coercive posture, we are probably acting out of fear within ourselves. We may fear that we will look bad if the outcome is anything less than perfect. We may worry that others will reject us if things do not go according to plan. Perhaps we feel anxious and uncertain about the future and what's going to happen—both to us and to others.

THE CONSEQUENCES OF FEAR

The consequences of basing your power on fear are numerous. Sometimes the behavior just goes underground. People still do things you don't want, but they don't do it when you are around. If people's negative feelings are elicited and then suppressed, they do not die; they hide. One of the invisible effects of suppression is that people hate you. They hold grudges, they resent you, they have all kinds of feelings as you attempt to push them in a direction they don't want to go or to do something they don't want to do, or to prevent them from doing something they do want to do. But if they feel threatened and if they feel fully justified, those feelings may not be manifested publicly. People go inside, people go underground, people don't talk about it except to others that they're colluding with or they feel safe with, but those feelings are still there and they may last for weeks or months, even years. People will look for a chance to get even, or to get back at you.

The problem is that there is an illusion created for the manager who is being coercive. Someone might comply out of fear while you're there, but when you leave, you don't have any assurance anything will happen, so you have to put something else in place. It might be a system, or a monitoring device, or a video camera, or a person checking up. When you're not there or the system is not working, people can do what they want and what they might want to do is somehow get back at you. So the problem is exacerbated by the very method that you're using to control it. People aren't doing what you want; then you apply force and pressure and there's an illusion that it's working. But the feelings that are also generated, which are not visible, will materialize when you can least afford it. All of a sudden you have a sickout when there's a big project that's due. Somebody has found a way to express those feelings that you caused to go underground.

This same kind of thing can happen in a family. I know a family in which the parents were very strict as to the kind of dress their two daughters could wear during their teen years. What they wore to school and what they wore when they went out with friends was determined by the parents. The parents were so unreasonable, so dogmatic, and so unwilling to listen to their daughters that the daughters just finally caved in and agreed to wear whatever their mother chose for them. Without their parents' knowledge, however, the daughters stored some of their clothes at their girlfriend's house. After they left home, they'd go to their girlfriend's home, change clothes, and then go to school. After school, they went back to their girlfriend's, changed out of the clothes they'd worn all day and into the clothes they'd worn as they left home that morning. As they reentered their home, the parents smiled as they observed what they thought was compliant behavior.

In fact, the daughters were complying, but the parents weren't getting the results they wanted and they were really teaching their daughters to be deceptive. The charade came crashing down one day when the mother was at a mall and one of the daughters was skipping school and they ran into each other. What a surprise! Part of the learning from this for the parents could have been that if you don't deal with the problems, they'll just go underground. That is true whether the setting is home or business. The parents ultimately had to come to grips with the fact that the capacity of their daughters to choose was something that was as important as enforcement of the dress code they wanted to impose. One of the daughters finally came to grips with this whole issue, and matured into self-regulation. The other daughter is still living in defiance today. She's married and has her own children, but she still has a terrible relationship with her mother. She feels her mother is still trying to tell her what to do even though she is a grown woman. She still disagrees and her mother persists in using the same coercive tactics. Nothing really has changed for them in fifteen or twenty years.

Can you control others through fear? Yes. Does it get you what you want? Sometimes, in the short term, it seems to. There is the illusion that everything is okay; that your approach is working. But control is always an illusion. When we are primarily self-centered, rather than principle-centered, and we fear, we will become coercive. Our approach may be soft or hard. Compare the two lists that follow:

What we *do* when we are coercive:

In the hard approach:	In the soft approach:
Suppress	Mislead
Force	Beguile
Control	Deceive
Intimidate	Seduce
Bully	Deter
Threaten	Divert
Scare	Sadden
Belittle	Discourage
Prohibit	Inhibit
Disparage	Trick
Emasculate	
Disenfranchise	

Whether our particular style is soft or hard, the net result is the same. While the soft approach may feel kinder, it leads us to the same place in our relationships as the hard approach. In either case, here is what we *get* when we are coercive:

An adversary
A fight
Compliance
Opposition
Dependence
High risk
Revenge
Negative external control
Sabotage
Malicious compliance
Distrust
Win/lose relationships
Quick fixes
Transitory results
Revolt

WHAT'S THE ALTERNATIVE?

We can learn to change our coercive behaviors. If we are committed to improvement, we can find other methods for influencing others and achieving desired results. A number of the Baldrige Award* winners have approached the Covey Leadership Center after winning the award and in our conversations with them have underscored this reality. They tell us the hardest part of their journey toward quality is giving up control. Even though they are the best at what they do, they are constantly striving to improve. Over the years, they have learned that their greatest challenge is dealing not with their customers, but with their own people. It's dealing with their employees and learning to see them differently. It's letting go of control in a way that empowers them rather than abandons them.

Do we have the courage to let go of the behaviors we so readily turn to, that seem to produce the quickest results? Can we find a way to discipline without punishment? If we can, we will not be disappointed by the results. W. Edwards Deming, a pioneer in the field of quality control, maintained it would be impossible to achieve success in the workplace without first driving fear out of it. Why? Because of all the problems we have examined in this chapter. He knew that fear in workers inhibits creativity, innovation, and commitment to quality; moreover, it fuels dangerous tendencies in its victims, namely sabotage and retaliation. Quality is impossible when people are afraid to tell the truth.[6] Deming's work has inspired many to seek more harmonious methods of management in the business world.

Coercive power is based on fear in the leader and in the followers, and leads to external, temporary, negative control; resistance; and sabotage. If you choose to use coercive power because it seems warranted or justified at the time, consider carefully what you are about to do. Count the cost before you proceed. Perhaps there is another way.

The first step in moving beyond coercive power is to evaluate yourself and determine when and how you try to force others to do what you want. Is this part of your style? Is it pretty rare for you to become

---

*Each year the United States government presents the Baldrige Award (named after former Secretary of State Malcolm Baldrige) to the manufacturing and service enterprise that best meets an extremely demanding set of criteria. The award represents the highest recognition of quality given by the United States of America.

coercive? Answer the questions in the following self-assessment to get a feel for the impact coercive power has in your life.

COERCIVE POWER SELF-ASSESSMENT

1. Under what circumstances are you likely to invoke coercive power?

2. What triggers this reaction in you? What are you afraid of?

3. In these situations, what do you do that creates fear in others?

4. What results are you getting that cause you to continue approaching others in this way?

5. What is another alternative?

6. What potential results would be worth a change in your approach?

CHAPTER 5

UTILITY POWER—
LET'S MAKE A DEAL

> Let us never negotiate out of fear. But never let us fear to
> negotiate.
>
> JOHN F. KENNEDY, INAUGURAL ADDRESS

IF YOU'RE LIKE MOST ADULTS, YOU DON'T RELY ON COERCION AS
your primary source of power. You leave the despair of powerlessness
and move away from the fear of coercive power. While force might
seem an easy, if temporary, solution to our problems, bargaining can
be an even more effective tool. Rather than bullying and frightening
each other, we most often use negotiation to get what we want. We
give and take, barter and trade, and strive to do what seems fair. We
make deals—with our children, our spouses, our friends, and our co-
workers—and we get results. When we engage in this type of power
brokering, we are in the world of utility power. I call it utility power
because it works. It works so well, in fact, that most of us use it most of
the time to get the results we want. Bear in mind, however, while it is
efficient, it is not without its problems.

The world of utility power feels very different from the limbo of uncertainty or the tyranny of oppression we find with powerlessness and
coercive power. Utility power is based on the potential for exchange. I
have something you want, and you have something I want. We make

The Utility Power Process

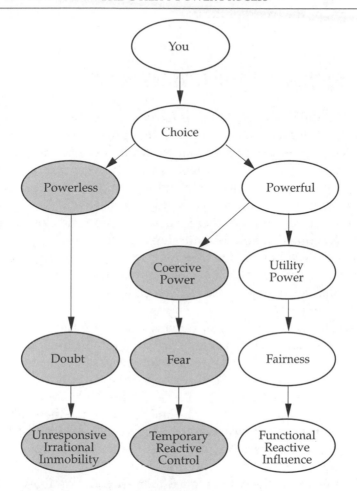

a deal. We trade. I get what I want, and you get what you want. It's fair. We both feel good about the transaction because it is reasonable. It makes sense. And most of the time, in the end, we get most of what we want. There may be a desire or condition left hanging, and we may feel that there was something left "on the table" after we are done negotiating, but—it works.

I believe that much adult functioning occurs as we operate with utility power. It is useful, straightforward, and appears rational. I can enter into a relationship with my eyes open. I can leave the relationship when I no longer get what I want. Does it sound simple? It can be.

Does it sound efficient? It often is. Does it work? Well, that depends. Let us examine the world of the deal.

THE FOUNDATION FOR UTILITY POWER

The foundation for utility power is fairness. Fairness means we both feel that the transaction was worth it. It is a basic, though low-level form of win/win. We each get what we want out of the deal; we each get what we bargained for. If I feel I'm getting less than I'm giving, then I can renegotiate. I can dicker and deal and deliberate until I get what I want from you or you convince me that what I'm getting is worthwhile, or I can go elsewhere. There is an ebb and flow in the interaction. A sequential kind of courtship or dance takes place, with an awareness of need or desire, a search for fulfillment, a review of what is available, an invitation to engage, an interaction, a conclusion, an assessment, and a disengagement. If we cannot reach a conclusion, we part.

We use utility power every day, many times in settings we take for granted. If, for example, you enter a fast food establishment, you have high expectations that they have what you need and you can get what you want. What do you do? You don't have to pull a gun on the cashier and demand a burger, shake, and fries. Nor do you sit down with him and compare life histories and mission statements. No. You walk up to the counter, place your order, and pay. If you have the money, they've got the food. The exchange is simple. You both get what you want.

If for some reason the cashier failed to meet your wants—your food was cold, or you received incorrect change—you could do something about it. You could demand different food, your money back, or to speak to the manager. You might even go so far as to write to the president of the chain, or advise your friends to eat elsewhere. You also might dismiss the incident as trivial and not worth worrying about. After all, it was only a fast food meal. What can you expect? Sometimes it's good, sometimes it's not. That's the way it goes. In other words, you would have given enough energy to balance the mental scales represented by the exchange. Did you get what you paid for? Were your expectations realized? If you didn't expect much, then you weren't disappointed. If you expected more than what you got, you might continue to act until you felt the scales had come level again. The scales are level when you feel you have been dealt with fairly.

This everyday interaction is a simplified example of the way we use utility power to get results. As you will read later, most of our interactions are more complicated than buying a meal, but the basic premises remain the same. Both parties are free to end or continue the transaction. Either person can walk away at any time. There are consequences, of course: if you leave, you will still be hungry and may have to look elsewhere for your meal; and if the cashier declines your order, the chain might lose you as a customer, or worse yet, the cashier might lose his or her job. If everything works out to your satisfaction, there is another kind of consequence—you will likely return for another meal another day.

THE POWER OF INDEPENDENCE

Independence is the hallmark of utility power. While coercive power relies on dependence and submission, utility power relies on freedom. Those involved in a transaction are independent—they can walk away from the deal if they don't like what's happening. And just as they are free to leave, they are also free to stay. In fact, if you are not free to walk away, you are not free to choose to stay. In that case, you are operating in the world of coercive power.

We learn to use utility power early in our lives. As children, we see our parents use it with other adults. Many times they use it with us to get us to comply with their wishes. How many of us ate our vegetables so we could watch TV or endured a trip to the dentist so we could receive a special toy as a reward for our bravery? We were experiencing the utility value of this exchange. We gave up something we had or we gave in to something someone else wanted, to get what we wanted. Tom Sawyer's clever bargaining with all the kids in the neighborhood to exchange the brass door knocker, the apple, and other similar children's treasures for the "privilege" of whitewashing Aunt Polly's fence is a classic example. I have something you want; you have something I want; let's make a deal. And we both get to decide if it is a good deal.

TYPES OF UTILITY POWER

What is it you have that others want, and that you might therefore trade to get what you want from them? Money? Information? Some special expertise? Access to resources that are appealing to them? There are many types of utility power. Even though we're comfortable using utility power on a daily basis, we aren't always aware of the different types that are available to us. I have described ten of them below. What they all have in common is that they represent something you might have that others find useful or appealing. Read through the list, thinking of the kinds of power you have.

REWARD POWER. You can reward others if they do what you want. The reward can be social, monetary, plaques, trophies, or anything the person prizes. Reward power is based on others' expectation of receiving praise, recognition, or income for complying with your wishes and functions as a reinforcer for the behavior or actions you want.

POSITIONAL POWER. You have the job title or the informal position that causes others to listen to and take direction from you. Positional power is derived from your position in the group or organizational hierarchy. If you are the boss or parent or leader or big kahuna, you can demand more from others than if you do not have a recognized position in the organization. New managers and parents tend to overestimate their position power; old-timers often do not fully utilize it.

EXPERT POWER. When you have a special skill, expertise, or knowledge and others believe that expertise is relevant to their needs and exceeds their own, they do what you want to get it. You are a specialist, an expert, and what you are good at is not something that is readily available. You may have great knowledge in one particular area that causes others to regard you more highly, but only when that particular expertise is needed.

CHARISMA POWER. Although somewhat intangible, charisma is almost universally recognized. People are drawn to you. It is not just one thing, but the unique combination of personal traits you display. Sometimes referred to as natural leadership, it is based on the appeal of attractiveness or other traits you possess. Followers admire and are attracted to you. Strangers find themselves watching you and being intrigued by you. Your charm almost has a magnetic appeal to some people. You are charismatic.

INFORMATIONAL POWER. When you know something others need to know, you have informational power. Perhaps you know when a certain decision is going to be made, or who is going to take action, or where the fish are biting, or where the sale is going to be held. This is not expertise as much as information, perhaps fragile or transitory in nature, and your power, which may also be temporary, is based on knowing or having access to this information because it has high potential value to the others. Maybe people need to know what you know before they can proceed, or to determine whether they are on track. Information can be power.

OPPORTUNITY POWER. When a crisis occurs, you have an opportunity to be observed by many people if you can take appropriate, helpful action. Based on emergency or nonroutine situations, opportunity power can be demonstrated when a natural or man-made dilemma creates anxiety and uncertainty in other people. If you are projected into the spotlight temporarily due to some circumstance, your choice determines your future. If you perform well, the attention you receive can lead to additional opportunities and increased influence long after the crisis has passed.

RESOURCE POWER. If you have access to key persons, commodities, goods, and services valued by others, even though the things you have access to are not necessarily yours, you may become very powerful. This gatekeeper, or keeper-of-the-keys, role is often seen in organizations when an assistant or second in command regulates who gets to see the boss. You may not have what they want, but if you can help them get it, your utility power can be great.

INSTRUMENTAL POWER. Perhaps you are a can-do person, who has the capacity to get things done, mobilize others, get a group moving, or take needed action when there is an impasse. Based on your ability to make these important things happen, you may find yourself with instrumental power.

APPRAISAL POWER. Appraisal power is based on your capacity to give informative or corrective feedback about the quality of an effort or performance. This feedback can be critical to the members of the group because it allows them to improve their performance, become more effective, or attain important goals. If your appraisal encourages as well as informs them about how they are doing, you may become very important to them, and they may agree to your requests just so they can get this feedback.

RELATION POWER. When you know someone who is powerful, you may by association borrow some of their power. Relation power exists as long as you maintain that relationship with someone (family member, executive, celebrity) who is powerful. The other person may be powerful for any number of reasons. But your power comes from your proximity to them. Others can access them through you.

   In the chart below, check off each of the types of utility power that you have. Ask yourself, "Is this something I have or can get? Do other people want it? How badly? Will they do what I want to get what I have without being threatened or intimidated?" If it applies to you—if it is something you have—check it off.
   Once you have checked off the types of power you have, add up the ones marked, and enter the total at the bottom of the column. You

HOW POWERFUL ARE YOU?

At Work	At Home	Types of Utility Power
☐	☐	Reward Power
☐	☐	Positional Power
☐	☐	Expert Power
☐	☐	Charisma Power
☐	☐	Informational Power
☐	☐	Opportunity Power
☐	☐	Resource Power
☐	☐	Instrumental Power
☐	☐	Appraisal Power
☐	☐	Relation Power
☐	☐	TOTAL

might be surprised by the variety of power sources available to you. There are many things we can draw on to influence people. Sometimes we get trapped into thinking we have only one option, when in reality we have many.

UTILITY POWER AT WORK AND HOME

If you went through the list with only one setting in mind, you might find it worthwhile to go through the list a second time and change the setting. Take yourself away from work to home—where you live, where you love, where you fight with the neighbors. Or move from the home to work, with the pressures of budgets and work deadlines. Which types of power do you have access to in this other setting?

Where do you have the most options? Work or home? Most people see themselves functioning differently away from the job. We tend to compartmentalize our lives that way, even though we may have similar opportunities in both settings. Most of us do not act the same way in the comfort of our homes as we do in the formal setting of the office. That is normal. We have different expectations and different behaviors for different social situations. We don't behave the same way in church as we do at a sporting event. Though we may think certain options are not open to us in these different situations, we might be surprised at the sources of power we possess.

One of my sons taught me an interesting lesson in this regard. If I had gone through the checklist ten years ago, I would not have chosen expert power as one of the types of utility power I had at home. I was a father and a husband, but my area of expertise and professional training was education and psychology. The places I was an expert were in the office and at the university. My thinking on this changed one day when my teenage son asked me what "cosine" meant. I told him it was a trigonometry term, but it soon became obvious he meant "co-sign," not "cosine." He said, "No, Dad. I went down to the credit union and talked to them about this '69 Volkswagen I found for $900. They said I need someone to co-sign. What does that mean, Dad?" At that moment I realized I had some expertise after all. His simple question led to a longer discussion than he had anticipated, and, no, I did not end up co-signing anything!

WHY WE USE UTILITY POWER

As adults we realize utility power is easy to use. It seems equitable, and unlike coercive power, we don't have to scare anybody to get results. Here is a list of some of the most common reasons people give for using utility power:

It gets results.
It's logical.
It's fair.
It's often readily available.
We see it modeled by friends, peers, parents, church, the government, and the law.
We like the results we get.
It works.
It seems appropriate at the time.
It's easy.
It does not depend on conditions of trust.
It allows different responses.
It's nondisclosive.
It's low-risk.
It doesn't require confidence or competence.
It's a rational approach.
It's all we know how to do.
It's the only option.
It creates mutual back scratching (I owe you/you owe me).

DOES UTILITY POWER WORK?

Because utility power can be so easy and efficient, it has been noted by many in the business field as a useful managerial tool. Ken Blanchard emphasizes the importance of utility power as it relates to self-leadership. He recognizes that power in the workplace stems from many different social, intellectual, and emotional abilities. He suggests you can increase your power with co-workers by balancing areas in which you have great power, such as your knowledge of a specific job or task, with areas in which your power may not be as great, such as building relationships. His suggestion for handling a particular situation would be to ask a co-worker who has the ear of the department head to give you feedback on how she thinks the department head will react before making a presentation.[1] By cultivating relationships with people who have strengths in areas where you are deficient, you can increase what you bring to the table when dealing with others.

Blanchard is joined by Richard C. Huseman and John D. Hatfield in endorsing utility power as helpful in the workplace. Huseman and Hatfield have written a book dedicated entirely to the improvement of management through the use of utility power. *Managing the Equity Factor . . . or After All I've Done for You . . .* addresses the sense of fairness people come to expect from life, and more specifically from their employers. If they do not feel they have been dealt with fairly or received what they deserve, they will not perform as well or as willingly as they could. It is the job of the manager to reestablish a balance in the minds of her workers so they feel appreciated. If they feel they will be recognized for their efforts, they are more likely to raise the level of their performance and their dedication to the company's enterprise.[2]

Both on and off the job, financial transactions may seem to fit neatly into the utility power column, but sometimes this is not the case. Often we give up our independence when we "fall" for a particular item. It might be a stereo, a necklace, a kitchen appliance, or a car. Once we decide that we must have that particular thing, we have lost our freedom. We can no longer leave. If, for example, you fall in love with a car on a dealer lot and decide it is the only car for you, the salesman has you right where he wants you. The term used in the auto industry to describe such a person is a "laydown." The dealer can overcharge you, increase your financing rate, and take away any frills or benefits that normally accompany the purchase, and you will still buy. When this happens, you have left the world of utility power and entered the lose/win world of coercive power. If, however, you can get the same car somewhere else, or are willing to settle for a different car, you still have the freedom to negotiate because you can literally walk away.

Sometimes we find ourselves in situations where utility power is not an option. For example, the government might have a resource it can get from only one manufacturer because they are a sole-source provider. In this case the manufacturer can set the price at whatever it wants: the government needs the material and must purchase it. Normally the government would solicit bids for materials or products and award a contract accordingly, but with a sole-source provider, it is over a barrel.

INCREASING UTILITY POWER

Because utility power is both efficient and commonplace, you might want to increase your ability to use it. If you do, however, you should be aware that it also has significant drawbacks, which I will discuss later in the chapter. While utility power is a step above coercive power, it still pales in nature and substance to principle-centered power. There are a number of things you can do to increase your utility power, but as you do, realize that there will be limitations to your long-term results.

There are many resources available to you if you want to increase your potential to bargain, to make others feel comfortable in making deals with you. Many organizations and individuals offer public seminars to help you fine-tune your skills in negotiating, bargaining, purchasing, and dealing more successfully than the opposition. As I have studied successful negotiators, I have been impressed with the practical guidelines and suggestions described by William Ury and Roger Fisher, leaders of the Harvard Negotiation Project.[3] Any large bookstore will offer numerous collections of wit and wisdom, tactics and techniques for dealing successfully with others at the bargaining table.

I have observed that the following seven factors play a key role in determining how effectively you utilize utility power, whatever your approach: proximity, convenience, complexity, threshold, availability, cost, and awareness. As I illustrate each of these, you can ask yourself, Is there something I can do to increase my power so that I can be more efficient in influencing others to get the job done, get the task accomplished, or get the behavior changed? If you want to increase your utility power, pay close attention to these factors. If a particular relationship is based on coercive power, moving to utility power will create a huge improvement; but if your relationship is with someone you deeply care about, you may find that these factors, and utility power, will not take you far enough.

PROXIMITY

Are you close enough to your people that they know what you are going through? Do they feel they can approach you with problems and concerns? If not, you can work on increasing your proximity, or closeness, to them by decreasing the distance between you. There are many ways you can do this. You can seek to share the same experiences or try to understand their feelings by imagining yourself in their shoes. When dealing with others, get in their space, not in their face. You may think that you know their territory, their problems and opportunities because you once had that job or that experience. Trust me, things change. It is a vote of confidence and respect if you can say, "Yes, I was there once, but things have probably changed. What is it like now? What can I learn from you? When can we get together?"

At home, this might mean you take time nightly to sit at the end of your son's bed and discuss school, his friends, and anything else that's important to him. At the office, it might mean that you make sure you are sensitive to the concerns of your co-workers and involved in their activities. If the proximity between you and the people in your life is poor, you might grow too far from them to understand or even notice their concerns. The further apart you are, the less power and influence you will have with them. You may find it difficult to negotiate if you don't know what they want.

CONVENIENCE

In this age of convenience—Internet shopping, twenty-four-hour mini-marts, ATMs, and personal shoppers—people like to feel they can get what they need when they need it. They cultivate relationships in which it's easy to get what they want. If you can provide this for them, you have more power with them.

For example, the CEO of one of the most highly respected companies in the world has made it a practice to fly from the headquarters in the corporate helicopter on Friday afternoons to meet with the newly promoted senior managers. The managers are invited to attend week-long leadership development seminars, which involve many interesting exercises and activities, but the highlight of their week is when the CEO arrives for three hours of no-holds-barred, sleeves-rolled-up dialogue. No notes are taken, and no bosses are allowed in the room. No questions are taboo. The CEO reports that this is his way of cutting through the layers of his huge organization and getting the pulse of the rising leadership cadre. Although his time is in great demand, he feels this practice will have a long-term payoff in the growth and success of his company. As this executive recognizes, when you make it more convenient for people to get what you have, your power with them will increase.

You must be available to those you would like to influence.

COMPLEXITY

How much red tape do people have to go through to get something done with you? How many hoops do they have to jump through? If you make things difficult for them, they won't want to work with you and they certainly won't want to give you what you want. If you make things simple, they will be more inclined to come to you when they need something done, and what you have to offer will be more accessible to them.

A father who was accustomed to requiring background papers from his employees whenever they made a request used essentially the same approach with his own children. As a result, they usually went directly to their mother to avoid the interrogations they knew they would get from dad.

This is also true in a work setting. Red tape and unnecessary paperwork, complicated policies and procedures, archaic bureaucratic systems and structures—all will get in the way of your utility power being utilized efficiently.

THRESHOLD

Your threshold represents how big a step people need to take to get to you from where they are. If you lower your threshold, by diminishing the barriers between what people want and what you have, you can increase your power with them.

I have a client who took over a large manufacturing operation and found that a we/they adversarial attitude pervaded the ranks. He decided to change procedures, and informed his new assistant he would be implementing a genuine open-door policy so he could better develop his relationship with the plant employees.

The assistant, who was a fixture in the old regime, was appalled. He told his new boss that it had always been his job to make sure the factory workers, who were often stained with grease from the factory machinery, remained outside the expensively decorated executive suite. The mind-set that had been instilled in the assistant was to keep the executives and the factory workers separate, to prevent contact rather than facilitate it. The executive suite had become a barricade that, when coupled with the ever-vigilant assistant, effectively kept them apart.

Many of the old paradigms we cling to get in our way in just this fashion. We have notions of leadership or parenting that keep us from connecting with the people we are trying to influence. Through memos and policies, we keep them away. At home, we buy into the mistaken idea that we can influence our spouse or children at arm's length. I have been told by nurses that their hospital would be a great place to work, if it weren't for the patients. I have heard similar comments from school administrators and teachers, lamenting how the students were ruining their schools. And sometimes parents can be overheard to complain that their homes would be ideal places to live if it weren't for their kids that keep messing things up. Such ideas need reexamination. Sometimes they're not wrong, they're just skewed or incomplete. Maybe there's a reason, a time, and a place for division, but there's also a reason to come together. When we bridge the gap between ourselves and others our power will increase.

Ask members of your family or people you work with how accessible you are. They will tell you the barriers you throw up that keep them from interacting with you and being influenced by you.

AVAILABILITY

How often are you available to those who need you? If people feel you are there for them when they need you, you can expect that they will be more likely to do what you want when you need them.

I recently saw a public service message on television that humorously but poignantly highlighted the need to be available, to make time for each other. It depicted a businesswoman coming home after the typical hard day at the office. The mother greets her daughter, who is about seven years old, at the door. The young girl is filled with excitement and enthusiasm and can't wait to tell all about *her* day. The child is chattering nonstop as the mother moves into the kitchen, sits down at the table, gets out her organizer and her pen, and begins clearing up the last few details of the day, tying up loose ends. The young girl, impatient and energetic, keeps interrupting with fragments of conversation. The mother is preoccupied, making entries, checking off tasks completed, and reviewing commitments for the following workday. Her daughter, still chattering, interrupts again, "Mom . . . Mom?"

"Just a minute, I just have to finish this and I'll be right with you."

The mother retrieves a yellow note from the front of her organizer and continues writing. The child, impetuous, tugs at her mother's sleeve, "Mom, what are you writing in your book?"

Her reply is matter-of-fact. "These are my appointments—the people I need to remember, and the important things I need to do. I have to make notes so I won't forget." One more little tug. "Mom . . . ? (a long pause) Am I in your book?"

Think about the people you would like to influence. Are they in your book? I know a CEO who required all the senior people in his company to carry pagers so that he could reach them day or night, twenty-four hours a day. He expected them to be available to him at all times. I know another business leader who wears a beeper so wherever he goes, his people can reach him when *they* need to. What different messages these two executives communicated.

Are you available on your terms or theirs? If you increase your availability, you will increase your influence with them.

Cost

What does it cost to get what you have, in terms of time, money, effort, and sheer life energy?

I know a management negotiator who insisted on meeting with the union steward in a restaurant right across the street from the plant. He always arrived first and sat near the window, where everyone entering or leaving the plant could see that they were meeting. It always made the union representative nervous because the people he was supposed to represent could see him but did not know for sure if he was selling out or working on their behalf, and he made concessions quickly to get out of the fishbowl setting. Consequently, he was always reluctant to meet, and put off meetings as long as he could, which was a disadvantage to the management negotiator. Each raised the social costs to the other. If you can minimize the cost for others to deal with you, you maximize your power to negotiate with them.

Awareness

Finally, do people know what you have? They cannot access what you have if they do not know you have it. If they are aware of your abilities and needs and you are aware of theirs, you are more likely to be able to help them solve their problems.

To summarize, if you can increase your awareness, lower the cost of dealing with you, make yourself more available to others, lower the threshold between you, simplify procedures, make it more convenient, and get closer in many ways to the people you want to influence, your power will also increase. The more you can do for them, the more they will be likely to do for you.

THE DARK SIDE OF UTILITY POWER

Though utility power can often get us what we want, it also has a dark side, a side that might lead you to question just how pervasive you want it to be in your life. Although it feels better than the force and fear common in the world of coercive power, it is still temporary and conditional: if the situation changes in any way, your power could evaporate. In utility-centered relationships, everything is always up for grabs. You never have the assurance and peace that comes from a long-term, unconditional commitment. Since either partner can always walk away, you are always being compared against what else is available. This may seem to make sense in the continuous-improvement, delight-the-customer age in which we live. But it does not feel very good when the relationship you are focusing on centers around one of the few key people in your life, such as a co-worker with whom you work closely or a family member.

Business, by nature, seems to hinge on utility power. Though many great achievements emerge from contracts, agreements, and deals, when a utility arrangement goes bad, the results can be devastating. The leader of a large corporation once told me of such a case. We had spent the morning with a large group discussing utility power and its pitfalls in a company seminar. During lunch, he approached me with a problem. He explained that in a recent restructuring, the corporation had reduced the number of vice presidents from eight to four. Before the changes were implemented, they informed the four who were selected to stay to participate in restructuring the rest of the company. Shortly thereafter, they made an announcement to everybody else, including the four who were to be let go, regarding the changes. Within a year of the announcement, each of the four slated for outplacement was indicted for embezzlement. The charges were appalling—one took $100,000, another over $200,000.

The CEO was angry, saddened, and confused. His confusion stemmed from the fact that all four of the men had been with the company for years and were trusted. He couldn't understand why they would betray the corporation. As I listened to him recount the chronology, something clicked in my head.

I asked when he had discovered the embezzling. He explained it had been within the last two months. Then I asked if he had determined when it had started. All of a sudden his face turned white. He said, "I hadn't thought about it before. It apparently started right after we made the announcement that they would be out of a job. I didn't see the connection until now."

I replied, "It's not justified. But maybe we can all learn something from this. You made a statement to them when you pulled four in, and ignored the other four. You didn't give them any warning. They found out they were going to leave at the same time the rest of the company heard the news." "But we were just trying to protect them," he interrupted. "In a way it seems you made a different message very clear to them. Maybe the message they heard was, the company is looking out for itself—perhaps you had better do the same." This doesn't justify any kind of crime, certainly not even white-collar crime. But many otherwise honest people on a dark night sitting in an office staring at balance sheets that don't balance figure the organization is looking out for itself, so they had better do something to look out for themselves.

ADDITIONAL PROBLEMS WITH UTILITY POWER

With utility power we have created a transaction that can contain the good, the bad, and the ugly. For the most part we get what we want, but with every transaction, sooner or later the issue surfaces: What have you done for me lately? If the answer is "not enough," we lose power. The other party is free to walk away from us, leaving us in an undesirable position. If I'm a worker, this could mean that someone faster and cheaper comes along and takes away my business. If I haven't given my clients enough to win their loyalty, even temporarily, I could be replaced more quickly than I was hired. My power does not last. If I'm a parent, it may mean that if my neighbors pay my kids more to mow their lawn than I do, I may have to cut my own grass.

If marriage were treated as a transactional relationship and were based solely on the use of utility power, the results could be unnerving. Suppose you showed up at the breakfast table tomorrow morning and your partner had the classifieds open to the personal section. He/she is reviewing the listings of available partners. "This one is 'slim, trim, and wants to travel.' Oh, and here's one that's 'good-looking and independently wealthy.' Call on that one, honey. I want to check that one out." What if the next day followed the same scenario? How would you feel if every morning the relationship was up for grabs? Your spouse stays with you just until something better comes along.

Unfortunately, there does seem to be a growing trend toward the use of utility power in marriages. Prenuptial agreements, once exclusive to the rich and famous, have become commonplace. We sign contracts before the wedding, not because we lack love, but because we've seen the statistics. Maybe we've been married before, and it didn't work out. Or maybe we've seen our friends' marriages fall apart. To protect ourselves, to preserve our independence, we sign a document that provides for an equitable settlement when we tire of each other.

Currently, the average marriage in the United States lasts only 7.2 years. So we make a deal before we marry. We come to the altar offering 50 percent—50 percent of our loyalty, 50 percent of our fidelity, 50 percent of our possessions, our interest, and our time. When we add our 50 percent to our partner's 50 percent, we get 100 percent, a complete commitment. Right? No—that is bad mathematics and bad matchmaking.

When we enter into a relationship, whether personal or professional, on these terms, we may temporarily feel satisfied, but eventually we begin to worry. What if the other person finds someone who's better than I am? What if I get a better offer? If you're an employee you know that the boss might find someone more qualified, more skilled, or cheaper. If you're a spouse, you fear your partner might find someone younger, livelier, or more attractive. The result is an uneasiness that can detract from our happiness at home and our ability to perform at work. We decide we've got to put ourselves first because no one else will.

When we put ourselves first, we begin to use our power to manipulate others. A taxi driver told me he had life figured out. All he had to do was ask a few leading questions. "People love to talk. If you'll be their audience, you'll have them in the palm of your hand. But if they are drunk, just get through your shift." Under those circumstances, escaping with his life was a "fair" deal.

THE GODFATHER CONCEPT

Sometimes people do things for us, and then, out of a sense of balance, expect something in return. I refer to this as the Godfather concept, because, in essence, they are setting us up. They do something for you when you need it, and then you owe them. Later they come back to you and demand what you owe at an inconvenient time when you don't have any choice. In the case of the Godfather this could mean, "I've given you protection, now I want this money," or "I helped you out when your father died, so now you need to come through for me and bump off this guy." You may not want to do what they ask, but you are obligated. In this way, utility power, though efficient and useful when you got what you wanted, can be unpleasant or perhaps even dangerous when it comes time to pay up for what you got.

PERILS OF OUR LEGAL SYSTEM

Another downside to utility power is that once we make an agreement and it fails to meet our expectations, we seek recourse that perhaps ends in fairness, but rarely what's right or best. Our legal system exists to dispense fairness and balance the scales of what is owed between parties who are at odds. If I sign a contract with a painter to paint my house for a certain amount of money and after he is done I am dissatisfied, I might first try to negotiate a lower payment for his work. If we cannot reach a compromise, I might take my complaint and enter our complex legal system, which is adversarial by nature and is not necessarily designed to produce the truth. The system is set up to produce verdicts, and sometimes justice.[4]

The first place I might go is to a mediator, a disinterested third party. If she offers a solution that is not mutually acceptable, I move on to small claims court. If we can't reach a resolution there, we might move on to a jury of our peers who will then decide what's right. Or will they? Will they decide what is right and best or will they decide what is fair? Maybe the painter watered down the paint and I will need to pay another painter to repaint in a year, but the jury decides that I owe him for the time he put in on my house. Perhaps they order me to pay him a token sum for his shoddy work. Then I'm out some money and stuck with a house that needs to be repainted. Utility power got a result, what was ostensibly a fair result. Unfortunately, it was not the one I wanted and not the one the painter wanted. We both won, but didn't we also both lose?

This pattern is often repeated in the workplace. When you are hired by a company, someone from human resources lays out all the personnel policies, including scenarios that might lead to termination or reprimand. After leaving your briefing, you might conclude that the company has warned you it is looking out for itself. You are being paid to do a job, but only so long as it serves the needs and interests and policies of the company. You might then decide that you need to look out for yourself because no one else there will. I was teaching business leaders in Saudi Arabia about utility power once, and on a break a participant approached me and said, "We have an expression in our country that says the same thing simply—'Trust in Allah, but always tie up your camel.' " We may trust divine providence, but in the meantime (and in the short run) most of us are inclined or invited to look out for our own camels.

If, after you are hired, you feel the company is treating you fairly, everything might be fine. You might, however, feel you are being taken advantage of. If this is the case, you might fall prey to situational ethics, as did the corporate vice presidents I mentioned earlier. This is a term that describes the rationale involved when you make a decision based on what seems fair at the time and not based on what is right according to your deepest values and beliefs. I know of someone whose demanding boss coated his requests for extra hours without pay with promises of a future raise. When the raise did not come, the worker, who was otherwise an honest man, felt justified in compensating himself by unconventional means. He said nothing when a shipment to the warehouse was short one laptop computer. No one at the office knew that his son at college had mysteriously received a new computer of the same make and model. By looking out for himself and disregarding this worker's needs, the boss invited this kind of "fairness." I do not excuse this man's dishonest action, but I have been told too many stories rooted in just such cause-and-effect connections to ignore the lesson they teach us.

Though utility power may seem attractive in the beginning, it can easily deteriorate and create results far worse than we may ever have imagined. In these situations, each party is separated, brought together only by the transaction, and free to act independently, free to try to take what he feels he deserves.

THE CONSEQUENCES OF FAIRNESS

With utility power, this is what we *do:*

Deal
Bargain
Argue
Dicker
Exchange
Settle
Concede
Debate
Contend
Quarrel
Compromise

These are the results we *get* with utility power:

A deal
A transaction
A compromise
Low risk
Positive, external control
Situational ethics
Independent relationships
Temporary solutions
Performance agreements
Partial win/win relationships

GROWING BEYOND UTILITY POWER

Even though we spend much of our time in the world of utility power and it often provides results we want, there is another world available to us. It's a world we have all experienced at one time or another, and it's a world where we can develop a higher quality of relationship with those who are close and important to us. Bargaining and negotiating may suffice when dealing with those we do not know well, but do we really want to go for compromise with our spouse, our boss, or our friends? With some people we may want to pay the price to build a different kind of relationship.

UTILITY POWER SELF-ASSESSMENT

1. What types of utility power do you have that you can normally depend on?

2. How do you maintain your utility power?

3. How can you increase your utility power?

4. What relationships do you have in which the benefits of utility power are not enough?

CHAPTER 6

PRINCIPLE-CENTERED POWER—HONOR MAKES THE DIFFERENCE

> Power can be seen as power with rather than power over, and it can be used for competence and cooperation, rather than dominance and control.
>
> ANNE L. BARSTOW

THE POWER PRINCIPLE

The world created by principle-centered power is as different from the world of fairness as the world of fairness is different from the world of fear and force. It feels different. The results obtained are different. The quality of relationships is different. What is fostered is different. Motives are different. As fear is the source of coercive power, and fairness is the source of utility power, so respect, honor, and even love constitute the base of principle-centered power. We say that knowledge is power; that applied knowledge is power; that in the Information Age, information and information access is power. But those statements reflect primarily utility power. They represent something you may have that someone else wants.

There is another kind of power. Some call it referent power. Some call it legitimate power. It is based on respect and honor that go beyond some deal or exchange. It is not easily created. But it can outlast your lifetime. The power principle states simply: honor is power. In the relationships that are very important to you, such as with close family members, friends, and work associates, it is worth the investment to choose to operate from a base of principle-centered power.

Principle-centered power invites an open-ended question. The question is, "What can we do and be together?" It raises possibilities. It invites synergy, in which the contributions of all parties combine to create new options and new opportunities greater than—better than—anything you could do or be on your own. What is possible if we think and work together because we want to, because we trust and respect and honor each other? This type of power leads to sustained influence that stems from our deepest, most closely held values and aspirations. It can be profound. It can outlast our very lives.*

SOMEONE MADE A DIFFERENCE

I have selected a few typical descriptions from hundreds of similar statements I have collected over the years as I have taught. There are a wide variety of relationships represented here. People report having been significantly influenced by parents, spouses, grandparents, teachers, bosses, older brothers and sisters, fiancées, professors, clergy, neighbors, spouses, therapists, coaches, children, community leaders— the list is long. These descriptions were shared with intense feelings, feelings of respect, gratitude, confidence, and, sometimes, sadness. Notice the feelings and patterns in the statements. Why were these people so powerful? Why did this person do what he or she did? Why did their influence last for years, decades, and, in some cases, outlast their own lives? There is something important that can be learned by listening to thoughtful people describe in their own words someone who made a positive, significant difference in their life.

A MOTHER: She taught me that I win when I make others win. She taught me to "meet people where they are, not where you are." She taught me

*For a complimentary permanent reference card illustrating the power process, please call toll-free 1-888-7-POWER-9.

THE PRINCIPLE-CENTERED POWER PROCESS

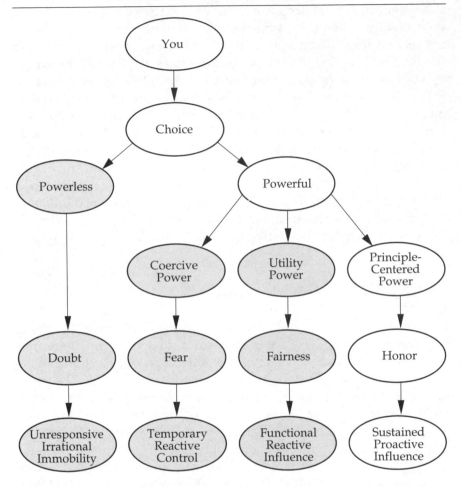

that leaders are "elected" because they serve the good of the group. She taught me that when the chips are down, I will come through because of what I know in my "central nervous system."

A GRANDMOTHER: Grandma empowered me. It was a very simple process. It did take time. It occurred over my lifetime, until she died. But it was so gentle and genuine and it gave me power. I didn't realize it until now. Grandma and I would spend hours listening to each other and she would never provide the answer; she provided the insight to come to my unique conclusion, which was right at the time.

A SERGEANT: When he did not know I was listening, he told another sergeant that "I would follow him anywhere." It was the highest compliment I had ever been paid, and it still is. He taught me to break rules but preserve principles.

A FATHER: With my father, I felt unique, special, talented, and also that I must honor a responsibility to give something back. He valued winning and achieving but also service to community. He made me feel good about myself if I accomplished both.

A BAND TEACHER: He wrote in my high school yearbook, "If I had a son I would want him to be just like you." With that this teacher affirmed me and gave me confidence in myself that I lacked. After that, I would have moved mountains for him. After he told me that, I always thought about what he would think before I did anything questionable.

A MAYOR: I was the city engineer reporting to him. He had a management style that drew the best out of me. He had a talent for delegating responsibility to me that said this is how I want it to look, but you are responsible. He would check in on my progress and even make suggestions, but I always knew it was my project and my responsibility.

AN EMPLOYEE: Although she worked for me, she was the one who taught me to see the best in others, to think of others before thinking of myself. She treated me like I was the best in my jobs and relationships. She made me a better person, and inspired me in doing things for others without recognition for my deeds.

A GRANDFATHER: I feel if he hadn't been in my life I would have been irreversibly dysfunctional due to the many traumas I had experienced. He provided me an inner sense of worth. I will always remember what he said to me as he lay dying of cancer. I related how much he had meant to me and how much fun I had with him. He said, "It was fun for me too." Those were his last words to me.

I am always humbled when people share such personal experiences with me. I want to be that kind of a person to the important people in my life. Most everyone does. I have had such people in my life and I will never forget them. No one has these wonderful experiences with everybody. But you may have had an experience or relationship with someone who was like the people described. Obviously, who the relationship was with is not as important as the quality of the relationship. Such relationships are invaluable partially because they are so rare.

But most of us have had someone in our life who really seemed to care about us and make an unusual investment in us. Have you had such a relationship?

Take a mental journey if you would for just a few moments. Mentally revisit this person. Go back to the relationship and experiences you have had with this person. They may not be alive today. That does not matter. Ask yourself the questions I have listed below. Briefly write out some answers. Take a few minutes right now and complete this exercise mentally, even if you do not write the answers. Allow yourself to feel the feelings that develop as you reflect on this person and their contribution to your life. What do you feel today because this person was, for a time at least, a part of your life? Reminisce and then answer these questions.

WHO MADE A POSITIVE, SIGNIFICANT DIFFERENCE FOR YOU?

1. Who was this person? What was their relationship to you?

2. How did this person treat you? What did they actually do?

3. How did this person make you feel? About yourself? About them?

4. Whether or not they are alive today, how do you feel about this person now?

5. Why did they do it?

WHAT DID THEY MAKE YOU FEEL?

What are you feeling right now, as the memories of this person and your experiences with them resurface? People tell me that as they think about such people they feel:

"Peaceful."

"I just feel good—like I did when I was with them."

"Immense gratitude and appreciation; thankful."

"Like I want to pass it on to somebody else."

"I miss them."

"I feel regret because they are gone."

"I'm sad because I never told them."

"Affection, fondness, warmth."

"I still feel accepted. I remember the acceptance I felt in the presence of this person. In fact, just recalling the person causes some of those feelings to come back and I feel accepted right now, and maybe acceptable."

"They are still there for me."

"I would like to be like that. I want to emulate that—that's something I want as a part of my life."

"It's important to me; I value that."

YOU ALREADY UNDERSTAND PRINCIPLE-CENTERED POWER

Suppose this person were alive today, but you'd had no contact or limited contact for a long time and then all of a sudden across the miles and the years they reach out. You receive a phone call or a letter and you discover that they are in some trouble, some kind of difficulty, and you could help. How would you respond? Would you be there for them? What if they needed cash, some kind of monetary help, and you were in a position to provide what they need. How would you respond? Any question in your mind or heart about what you would do? What if it was not money they needed. What if they just needed you? How would you respond? Would you do whatever it took? As soon as you could? You see, in a way I don't have anything to teach you about principle-centered power that you don't know because you

have experienced it already as a follower. You have been in a relationship in which someone has honored you. Because you allowed them
to influence you, you can become like them.

You might be thinking, "It was my mother I was thinking about. She
was not powerful in the larger community. She was not powerful like
world or national figures are. It wasn't a well-known official. It wasn't
a CEO, it wasn't a dignitary or high-level executive. It was my mom.
She was just mom and she loved and supported me no matter what."
Or perhaps it was a sister, brother, grandfather, or someone else who
wasn't known outside a small circle. Perhaps true leadership is not
about being well known. Perhaps we ought to reevaluate our ideas
about power and influence as we contemplate those who made a positive difference for us.

Now here's an exciting thought. We've talked about coercion and
force. We've talked about all the different kinds of deals we can make
with others and how those transactions are finite and when something
better comes along, it's over. Think about the people who are close to
you today—the people you live with, the people you work with every
day, the people who report to you and the person you report to. What
if they felt about you the way you've just recalled feeling about someone else? How would that change the nature of your work? How
would that change the nature of your life?*

THE POWER PRINCIPLE IN ACTION

I invite you to have a unique experience. Let your heart take the lead
more than your head as you read this section. Ask yourself does this
"feel right"? Does this "make sense" at the gut level? Does this "ring
true" for you?

We will be given power and opportunities through circumstance or
position to influence others toward good and worthy goals. Few of
our achievements, however, measure up to the great potential represented by those opportunities. Sometimes we do not even succeed in
sustaining power and influence with others. Why not? Two obstacles
can get in the way:

---

*If you would like to receive a complimentary worksheet to help you develop the char-
acter traits of those who have influenced you, please call toll-free 1-888-7-POWER-9 or
visit our Internet home page at www.covey.com.

1. What drives, motivates, inspires, and gives meaning to us may be the things we adorn our lives with, rather than the general good we can do in our relationships with other people.

2. We may seek the acclaim (praise, recognition, and status) others can give us. If we get our validation—our feelings of self-worth—from the way others treat us, we become controlled by others' opinions of us. In so doing, we lose sight of our original goals. We become externally controlled, and others—sensing our shift in focus—stop trusting our intentions, motives, and actions. We no longer strive to achieve such good and worthy goals. We no longer live what we teach. We become self-serving.

You may receive the opportunity to influence others. Indeed, you may even be invited or assigned to influence others. When you are given this power, you may be diverted from worthwhile goals by the temptation to use your power in ways that are ultimately counterproductive. If you attempt any of the following, the predictable consequence is that you lose power:

1. You attempt to hide, gloss over, or disguise something you are doing that is wrong; or avoid acknowledging any wrongdoing.
2. You feed, play into, or cater to the selfish, self-centered notion that you are better than others and deserve more than others, justifying yourself while condemning them. You become proud, thinking less of others who do not have the same power.
3. You focus on your own personal ambitions, and see others only as stepping-stones in your path. You use your opportunities to overpower others, seeing them as lower than you, and take advantage of others for your own progress, promotion, or self-aggrandizement.
4. You make decisions and take actions because of your superior knowledge or experience which deprive, exclude, or take advantage of others. By dominating or controlling them, you attempt to get them to do anything other than what is actually in their best interest in the long run.
5. You end up trying to force others to do what you want.

If you succumb to any of these temptations, your principle-centered power—a result of the honor given to you by those who choose to follow you because they trust and respect you, your values, and your goals—begins to diminish. Your capacity for long-term influence dissipates; your authority to act in behalf of others, influencing them for good, fades into impotence. Before you know it, you are left on your own, to struggle in vain, to attack those who are attempting to do what is right. Filled with fear and anger, you might even rebel against the common good.

There is a universal principle for being effective with others, maintaining power with others, and sustaining influence with others. This is the power principle. The power principle is simply stated: Honor is power. The more we are honored, respected, and genuinely regarded by others, the more power we will have with them. As Shakespeare wrote in *Richard II*, "Mine honor is my life; both grow in one; take honor from me and my life is done." Depending on how we deal with others, the honor they have for us will increase or decrease, and our power with them will increase or decrease. To be honorable is to have power.

HOW THE POWER PRINCIPLE IS UNDERMINED

Winston Churchill observed, "When one has reached the summit of power and surmounted so many obstacles, there is a danger of becoming convinced that one can do anything one likes, and that any strong personal view is necessarily acceptable to the nation and can be enforced upon one's subordinates."[1]

Under these circumstances, you might apply additional force, to coerce or drive others to do what you want. Or you might bargain or negotiate for a better set of options. But without realizing what is happening, you begin to lose power even faster as your actions become futile, irritating to others, and ineffective. Your efforts may then be weakened and even sabotaged by those you want to influence.

It is a natural inclination for most of us, when we get in a position where we feel or think we have power or authority over others, or have actually been authorized or granted power over others, to use our position to take advantage of them, to get from them what we want. It has become apparent, by watching human nature operate time and time again, that what most people do naturally, or are inclined to do, whether they feel they are in charge or have been asked to be in charge is to start attempting to coerce others right away.

That is the main reason we are prevented from claiming and taking advantage of the influence these opportunities present to us. That is why the promise of achievement and accomplishment rarely matches the reality. People do not get the chance to do worthwhile things when they are diverted by these many moral traps, behavioral pitfalls, and interpersonal snares. Our responses, driven by self-interest, cause those whom we attempt to influence to have less respect for us, to honor us less. And when we are honored less, our power dissipates. Eventually, our power can disappear completely.

THE POWER OF HONOR

If we want to increase our principle-centered power, we can develop and cultivate our honor rather than seek honors, status, recognition, and praise. Others will honor us when they know that not only do we have the capability to do what is necessary, but we have the inclination as well. Then we have both capability and worthiness, both competence and character.[2]

Principle-centered power has its roots in honor. When we live with honor, our principle-centered power grows.

What is honor? To honor is to have great respect. When we honor others, we respect them, we trust them, we believe in them. We tend to hold those who are honest and manifest integrity in their beliefs and actions in high esteem. A man or woman of honor has unquestionable integrity and dependability.

According to the dictionary, honor is uprightness; living with the highest moral principles; having an absence of deceit or fraud; adhering to truth. Honor connotes a fine sense of, and strict conformity to, what is considered right, especially in business dealings. Honor is uncompromising honesty and trustworthiness, a soundness of moral principle which no power or influence can impair. Honor suggests a combination of liking and respect, deference, homage, reverence, and veneration.

We live with honor when we are true to what we believe is right. We can honor our family, company, or country when we are true to the best that they represent. We are on our honor when we accept and acknowledge personal responsibility for our actions.

When we are honorable, we are worthy of being honored. We are honest, upright, and sincere. We are faithful to our cause, purpose, or belief. We are faithful to our duty and what is expected of us. We are genuine. We have high credibility. We are reliable. We are reputable, noble, pure, and scrupulous in our intent and in our actions. To be honorable is to live with honor.

Honor is both a noun and a verb. The verb is the way we treat those we respect. The noun is the result of how we live.

This approach feels different from the bargaining and negotiating we examined in utility power; and it is worlds away from the fear and force of coercive power. Before I summarize the effects and results of principle-centered power, one more distinction may be useful.

THE POTENTIAL PITFALL OF HONORS

Receiving honors is not the same as having honor. Honors are the various types of recognition that can come to us. Honors may include praise, status, notoriety, accolades, credit, fame, or glory. Some evidences of honors are medals, awards, badges, ranks, decorations, titles, commendations, and ratings. Honors can get in the way of principle-centered power. Utility power has its roots in honors. Honors are often the acknowledgment of our utility power.

The distinction between "honor" and "honors" is clear. Honor has to do with internal characteristics we possess, based on our deepest values, which may cause us to do certain things. Honors have to do with the recognition others give us because of what we have done. Honor has to do with our real and perceived intent or motive. Honors may come because of what we have done, regardless of our intent or motive.

We can have honor and be honorable without having honors bestowed upon us. Likewise, we can have honors bestowed upon us without being honorable. The honor that is a manifestation of your character and competence is not a list of characteristics or attributes. It is probably more accurate to acknowledge the ideals which are the sources of your actions than the actions or traits themselves as evidence of your being honorable.

THE POWER IN YOU

As you recalled an individual or a number of people who had made a positive, significant difference in your life, a couple of things may have happened. First, you have affirmed to yourself that you already know what I am talking about. You have experienced it. It is real. It is not Pollyanna or unrealistic, though it may be rare. Second, you were reminded that the source of great, durable influence with the people who are important to you is within you. Like the lieutenant telling the Air Force Academy cadets about his survival experience (see Introduction), it is what is within you, not the techniques and tools you acquire, that will make the difference, ultimately. Third, you have a source to turn to when you are confused, perplexed, or facing dilemmas in your own life. You can tie or anchor your understanding of principle-centered power to someone you already know. The magic here is not in my words—it's in the experiences that you have had with someone who cared deeply about you. You are going to carry the facts and feelings of those experiences with you. When you need to make critical decisions in the future you can be wise, avoiding short-term expedient actions by saying to yourself, "What is another way to respond to this situation? I don't have to act based on my fears. I can heed the biblical injunction to not attempt to influence with 'the spirit of fear; but of power, and of love.'[3] How would the person who influenced me so positively have handled this? How did they handle me when this sort of thing came up?" You carry this decision-making mechanism with you. What they were and what they stood for are embedded in your recollections of them.

THE RESULTS OF PRINCIPLE-CENTERED POWER

Principle-centered power is based on what you can do *with* others. Principle-centered power is the legitimate power created when individuals perceive that their leaders are honorable. Because they're honorable they trust them, they respect them, are inspired by them, believe in the goals communicated by them; therefore they desire to be willingly and wholeheartedly led.

Principle-centered power is based on honor. It's about honor that is extended to others from us and extended to us from others. Principle-centered power leads to self-control, ethical behavior, and proactive living. It's a phenomenon that leads to transformation, not transaction. We are changed by the relationships that have honor as their foundation. People are not loyal to a logo—they are loyal to other people. Principle-centered power creates more than a situational transac-

THE POWER PROCESS

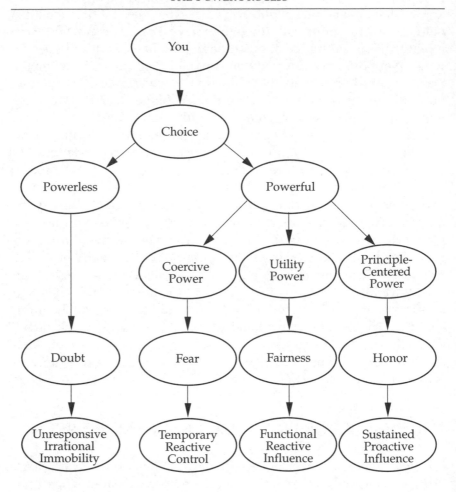

tion, limited by what else is available at the moment. Let us examine each of these results.

SUSTAINED POWER

First, it is sustained power. When you completed the exercise earlier in this chapter, did you recall someone who is deceased today? It is not unusual to have 20 to 35 percent of an audience indicate that the person who influenced them positively is no longer alive. I will ask them,

"You mean the influence didn't end when the person died? What's the source of that influence today?" People realize that they become a source of influence because the person who influenced them still lives with them, or in them. You are carrying the remembrance, the influence of that person with you. I would say that is sustained influence. How long does this influence last? What happens typically in a relationship? When it is based on coercive power, it lasts as long as the other person is afraid. When it is based on utility power, it comes and it goes, and it's fine while it's here. There is nothing "wrong" with it. It is just temporary. The question is, is that the kind of relationship you want with someone you would marry? Someone that you are working for? Someone that you're building an organization with? Someone you are dreaming with? Values can be passed intergenerationally. Has the influence stopped? No, it is living in you. It is likely that someone else will be affected because of how you live. When is it going to stop or are you passing it on to someone else? This influence does not stop because of some new management approach or self-renewal fad. It doesn't become outdated when the next self-help book is published. It doesn't lose potency if you relocate. You carry the influence with you; you become a carrier to pass it on to others.

PROACTIVE BEHAVIOR

Second, principle-centered power encourages proactive behavior. That means that we invite people to demonstrate truly ethical behavior. I demonstrated in Chapter 5 with utility power that often what we get is a kind of a situational ethic. It's the "What have you done for me lately?" mentality. It leads to constant evaluation, asking, "Can I get it better? Can I get it cheaper? Can I get it somewhere else? If I have an alternative, I'd rather do that than listen to you or deal with you. Is this still a fair deal?" With principle-centered power, we are talking about a relationship that goes deeper than that. A relationship that is not situational. A relationship that transcends situations. Proactivity means I make choices based on what matters most. What I value most. It is no longer a situational ethic. Now we're talking about true ethical behavior. Truly proactive behavior invites honorable behavior. You don't have to follow me around and see what I'm doing. You don't even have to check up with me. I'm holding myself to an internal standard that's higher than anything you would ever impose on me. I wouldn't think of doing anything else. Why? Because it doesn't fit with what I'm about. And if my behavior should slip below the level we both expect, I am self-correcting. I can do better. I can be better. I want to and I will, because it matters that much to me. We are inviting people to be true to their values, over the long haul, whether or not we are around to supervise and make certain that they are doing what we want.

It's more than initiative. Some people who study the Seven Habits of Highly Effective people get the mistaken idea that to be proactive means to jump up and do something. Take charge, take action. Action is a part of proactivity but it's more than just the action component. Between the stimulus and response there is an opportunity for choice. But what is the choice based on? Your deepest values or your temporary mood? What's happening right now or what you eventually want to have happen?

SELF-CONTROL

Third, this kind of power is no longer external. Principle-centered power focuses internally. Do you have control with principle-centered power? Yes you do. It's called self-control. It is no longer external. It is internal and it relies on the capacity that people have within themselves to be tougher on themselves, to push themselves harder when they are subsuming what they want in the cause of something that's greater. Ultimately that's what sacrifice is all about—giving up what I want now for what I want most. Giving up what doesn't matter as much, for what matters more. Sometimes the needs of the few are sacrificed for the needs of the many. Sometimes the sacrifice is just the reverse, and the needs of the many can accommodate the needs of the few. We find a community where a child is lost or has been abducted and a thousand people comb the hills for days looking for the child. Nobody is paying them. The needs of the few are worth the sacrifice and commitment of the many. Self-control, demonstrated in a group setting, is very powerful. Each person essentially says, "I give myself to it, because it is the right thing to do."

BUILDING INTERDEPENDENCE

Fourth, interdependence is cultivated. I described in Chapter 4 how coercive power tends to cultivate various kinds of dependence. Utility power, on the other hand, cultivates or encourages independence— both parties choose. We can choose to be together, we can choose to separate. What quality of relationship is encouraged by principle-centered power? Interdependence. There is high vulnerability when you're dependent. You have to have other people do things for you. It is a very high-risk situation. Dependence focuses on people outside yourself. You want others to take care of you. You want others to make you happy. You expect others to look out for you, making sure your needs are met. You can't do anything for yourself. As you move to utility power, you are less vulnerable; it's less risky. As you increase your capacity to provide for yourself, your confidence grows. "I can do it, I can take care of myself. This alternative isn't working, so I'll choose something else." Why would someone want to move from utility power to principle-centered power? If you're really close to someone and they really know your heart and they really know your weaknesses, can't they hurt you? Yes, and some of us have been hurt. I would say that with principle-centered power, you take a calculated risk. The potential gains—such as increased self-worth, honor, greater capacity to project genuine love, and more effective self-control—are worth the risks.

Interdependence asks, "What can we do and be together?" Interdependence asks the synergy question. Perhaps you remember in the first Rocky movie when Rocky decides to propose to Adrian. This is a simple but authentic love scene. Although it is a little rough, Rocky looks at her and at this stage she appears homely and shy. Rocky says, "Adrian—you have gaps." And she's crushed—this about destroys her. Is it her personality? Her education? Her figure? Her teeth? "But," he continues, "I have gaps too, but together we have no gaps . . . no gaps." Look what *we* can do. Principle-centered power is about what we can do and be together.

WHY WOULD OTHERS CHOOSE TO FOLLOW YOU?

Why would someone choose to work with you? If you are in a leadership role, why might someone choose to follow you? With principle-centered power, it is because they honor you. Why? Because you honor them. Honor is the foundation. What does that lead to? Sustained, proactive influence.

This approach has advocates in social arenas that might be surprising to some, including the Marine Corps and the Boy Scouts of America. At a recent week-long leadership development program I was conducting, a Marine colonel reported at the end of the week that his whole life had been built on the concept of honor, but until this week he never really understood what honor was. He left with that new understanding coupled with a new commitment and a desire to share his learnings with his troops.

The book *On My Honor, I Will* has the avowed purpose of sounding a "clarion call for a return to traditional values." Randy Pennington, president of the Pennington Performance Group, has written a fascinating and anecdotally rich volume with Marc Bockmon, in which they have taken the words of the oath of the Boy Scouts of America, and with an emphasis on honor, have described how this simple oath can lead to success in business. The authors document the perspective and attitudes of numerous successful business and organizational leaders on the difference that is made when honor, as taught in the Scout Oath, is either ignored or sustained as the foundation of their personal lives and the organizations they lead. Among those affirming their stance is former president Gerald Ford, who called their very practical book "A blueprint on how leaders became successful following the path of honor and integrity."

When we honor others and are honored, in turn, by them, our lives are transformed. The results are sustained, lasting for generations, easily outlasting our own few years on this planet. The influence invites proactive responses, encouraging people to make choices based on the values that are deepest in them. The results for all parties are positive. And there is control with principle-centered power—self-control. People will hold themselves to a higher standard than we could hold them to, if they feel ownership of the effort. Honorable behavior is inspired and interdependence is the result. Notice that in each case, when you choose power over powerlessness, you can predict the results. If you choose based on what you hope to avoid, you are choosing fear and coercive power. If you choose based on what you hope to obtain, your motive is fairness and utility power. But if you choose based on your deepest values, the most worthy principles you know, and the best that is in you, you are choosing based on honor and principle-centered power.

You not only already know a lot about principle-centered power, because you have experienced it, but you can be as powerful for good in the life of someone else as your honored person has been for you. Is it easy? No. It is a lifelong quest and pursuit. And there is a paradox that you will only have this kind of power when you stop wanting power at all. Which takes us to the next chapter. How do we learn to honor?

THE CONSEQUENCES OF LIVING WITH HONOR

With principle-centered power, this is what we *do:*

Persuade
Be patient
Be gentle
Teach
Accept
Be kind
Love
Learn
Discipline
Be consistent
Live with integrity

These are the results we *get* with principle-centered power:

Partners and partnerships
A mutual transformation
Synergy
Calculated risks
Increased capacity
Positive, internal control
Self-control
Ethical behavior

Interdependent relationships
Proactivity
Trust
Win/win solutions
Partnership agreements
Deeply satisfying long-term relationships

PRINCIPLE-CENTERED POWER SELF-ASSESSMENT

1. Have you felt inspired to do anything specific as you recalled the person who made a positive, significant difference in your life? What actions could you take to honor them? (Suggestions: communicate with them, express gratitude, pass on their influence to someone else. Dr. Norman Vincent Peale has challenged us all with his admonition "If you at any time feel a blast of appreciation or a sudden surge of gratitude, translate it into action.")

2. Think of a current situation in which you would like to increase your principle-centered power, to improve your influence with someone you deeply care about. How would your honored person deal with this situation?

3. What would it take for you to increase your power and influence with this person in this situation?

CHAPTER 7

HOW TO HONOR—TEN PRINCIPLES OF POWER

> Really great men have a curious feeling that the greatness is
> not in them, but through them. Therefore, they are humble.
>
> JOHN RUSKIN

IF YOU LIVE WITH FEAR, YOU WILL MAKE CHOICES BASED ON WHAT you want to avoid. Those who live in a world of fear do not even believe that the world of honor and trust exists. If you live with fairness, you will choose based on what you want to get. Those who live in a world of fairness may see that others live differently, but they either do not believe it can be better for them or they do not know how to get into that world. If you live with honor, your choices are based on what you value most. You know that you can do more with others than you can alone. You know that it is only through empowering others that you can achieve what is possible. You know that the best way to gain influence with them is to give up control of them. If others honor you, what is elicited in them is different. When you operate with principle-centered power, it invites others to feel, "I honor and respect what you are and what you're about. Because of that, I voluntarily commit my life, my efforts, my resources to partner with you in achieving worthwhile things."

Developing honor is a lifelong process. It is neither quick nor easy, but the value of the rewards it offers is immeasurable. If you want to have this kind of power with those around you, you must first win their trust, respect, and admiration. To do this, honorable people incorporate ten basic principles of power:

Persuasion
Patience
Gentleness
Teachability
Acceptance
Kindness
Knowledge
Discipline
Consistency
Integrity

In this chapter, I will illustrate each of these principles. My belief is that it is worthwhile to cultivate these principles in our lives. Even though force is easy, and deal making appears attractive, often it is better and always it is worth it to win with honor.

PERSUASION

We do not treat everyone the same. The people we respect feel differently when they are with us. We invest in them. We pay attention to them. We take time with them. We listen to them. And we usually tell them why we want to do something or want them to do something. It is an affirming thing to be told the "why" behind an action or decision. So one thing we can do when attempting to influence others is to share our reasons and the rationale behind our decisions and requests. While we make a strong case for our position or proposed action, we can still maintain a genuine respect for others' ideas and perspectives. Once they feel we understand where they are coming from, they are more likely to try to understand our opinions and desires. Ironically, it is our willingness to listen to them first that gives us the power to persuade others to agree with us and accept our decisions.

Persuasion starts as a mind-set. It assumes, from the beginning, that we are not going to have to "talk someone into" something. It assumes that we have to win them over. It assumes that we are willing to pay a price for their participation and involvement. It assumes that they are worth it.

General Dwight David Eisenhower, popularly honored for both his military expertise and political leadership, was someone who could get results with other people. He had such ability to build the people he led that he was wooed by both major political parties as a potential presidential candidate. He recognized the power of persuasion, and the difference between the effects of persuasion and coercion, when he said, "I would rather try to persuade a man to go along, because once I have persuaded him, he will stick. If I scare him, he will stay just as long as he is scared, and then he is gone." Though he could have relied on his position, rank, social standing, or military authority to demand compliance, he realized the merits of winning support rather than demanding it.

A well-known conductor once had trouble with his tuba players. Their performance was lackluster. They seemed disconnected from the other musicians. In frustration, the conductor called the lead player to the front of the orchestra pit while the assistant conductor continued the rehearsal. As the conductor began his plea for increased attention and professionalism, the tuba player held his finger to his lips, signaling the conductor to stop talking. As the tuba player listened to the rest of the orchestra, a smile crossed his face. "Got it!" he exclaimed. Without another word he returned to his seat and picked up his instrument. Turning to the other tuba players, he whispered, "You guys know what is going on while we oom pa pa, oom pa pa? Those violins over there are going duh da-da-da duh, duh da-da-da duh," and he hummed the beautiful Viennese waltz tune he had just heard for the first time. Having the big picture made the difference. From the tuba player's previous perspective, the conductor's requests had seemed meaningless. Sometimes we have to change our location before we change our perspective. Knowing the why is like having a mental change of location. When he understood *why* he was supposed to stay steady, as the foundation for a beautiful, lilting tune he had never even heard, he performed flawlessly.

When people are asked to do something, and not told why, they feel vulnerable. When changes occur, in pace or direction or focus, they become skeptical. In the absence of clarity from the leader, everyone brings their own sense of meaning and purpose to every situation. Without knowing the real why, people may supply meaning or reasons that are inaccurate at best or destructive at worst, and that may take them away from the direction in which you are trying to move. That is why one of the critical roles of a leader is to create, clarify, and communicate meaning.

Often, this issue of clarity and communication and sharing meaning comes down to a matter of timing. In the heat of a performance crisis or demanding deadline, it may be that the best you can do is to request, "Do what I ask now and I will get back as soon as I can to explain. Thank you." If the balance in this emotional bank account is high, you can make occasional withdrawals and the relationship will survive. In fact, it is a wonderful opportunity to make a deposit in that invisible but real account; how you function under stress and immediately thereafter signals to others how important they are to you.

Friedrich Nietzsche, the German philosopher, once observed, "I can endure almost any *what* if I understand the *why*." Explaining why is a difficult task for many of us. While we seek to persuade those above us, we often do not worry about persuading those below us. You wouldn't dream of asking your boss to do something or asking for something from her without explaining why you need it. How often do you do the same when you ask something of someone who reports to you or lives with you? A man convinced against his will is of the same opinion still. If they feel we respect them, they are more likely to respect us. Give others the benefit of the doubt. Give them the opportunity to voice their views before striving to win them over to your own. This is persuasion.

CONNECT YOUR MOTIVE WITH YOUR METHOD

Words are important. Words are powerful. Words between us can be weapons that hurt or tools that build and heal. A participant in one of my seminars, a teacher who specialized in dealing with at-risk students, shared these feelings about the power of words:

> One of the most powerful lessons I ever learned was from a person who taught and influenced me. What made a huge difference in her relationships with her students, parents, and fellow teachers were the words she used. Because she was a principle-centered person, her words came right from her heart, and deeply touched our hearts. She inspired us with her words and moved us to strive to be the very best we could be each day. Her words made us feel as if we were precious treasures.

Do your words hurt or help build relationships? Here is a practical suggestion. When you are in the middle of a power struggle, attempting to get someone to do what you want, ask yourself, "Do I really want to improve, right now, while I am with them, attempting to influence them?" Your true feelings will communicate eloquently through your words. Here are some statements that can help you connect your motive with your method, and perhaps both remind and inspire you in the moments of choice as you deal with others you would like to influence. Expressed with the right intent, these words can open possibilities. Not every phrase will feel comfortable to you. Select and implement those that elicit a positive, caring mind-set in you.

SELF-CHECK

1. Words to say to *myself* to check for persuasion:

Have I told them why?
Do they understand why?
Have I tried to help them understand why?
Would it help if they understood why?
Would I like them to understand why?

2. Words to say to *them* to demonstrate persuasion:

May I explain why?
May I share my reasons why?
Let me help you understand.
I would like to have the opportunity to explain why.
Do you know why we need to do this?
I would like you to understand where I am coming from.
Here is what I am feeling.
I would like to share my feelings.
This is why it is important to me, and to us.

PATIENCE

If we want to develop honor with those around us, we must be patient—both with the process and with the person. In spite of others' failings, shortcomings, and inconveniences, as well as our own impatience and anticipation for achieving our goals, we need to maintain a long-term perspective and stay committed to our values and to them in the face of short-term obstacles and resistance. This is not easy to do.

You probably became the person you are today because somebody had patience with you at some critical points in your life. Many people report to me that someone was patient with them, as they struggled along their life's journey. When you are patient with a person, you make a long-term investment in them. It's not an overnight fix. It takes a long time.

Emily Carr, a wise Canadian author, said, "I don't think you can explain growth. It is silent, it is subtle. You don't keep digging up a plant to see how it's growing."

To be truly patient, we are patient with the process as well as the person in process. We are not just humans doing. We are humans being. And, likely, humans becoming. We're all in various stages of development. I'm not where I was yesterday. A great gift you can give someone else, especially if there have been tough times between you, is to acknowledge the problems, authentically. "I know things have been difficult in the past but I am trying to change and I want to know, where are *you* now?" Free people by giving them an opportunity to change, to grow, to develop.

Lillian Hellman described a dynamic in all of our lives when she commented, "Sometimes, people change but they forget to tell each other." Allow others to change. Be helpful by giving people space to move on.

How do we learn patience? Plant a garden. What a lesson in patience! A very successful executive from a worldwide consulting company asked me in confidence how to fulfill his new assignment, in which he was supposed to mentor other executives in various countries around the world. He reported that he could tell others what to do, and make sure they did it, but he was uncertain how to "mentor." I suggested that he plant a small home garden. He didn't like the idea. He didn't have any time for it. He didn't have the know-how. He couldn't see the point. I persisted in my suggestion. Let me explain why.

I've got a home garden. I didn't grow up with any gardening background, but my wife, Shawny, convinced me that the enterprise would be worthwhile, and she has been right. Have you raised some vegetables successfully? It is an educational enterprise—and sometimes you get vegetables as well. We've got tomatoes; I *love* tomatoes. Do you know what it takes to successfully raise tomatoes? I mean to have a prize-winning, beefsteak, luscious, one-slice-fills-an-entire-sandwich tomato? Fertilizer. A little tender, loving care. Good soil. Water. You've got to weed the garden. Sunshine is essential. Can you have too much fertilizer, too much water, too much sunshine? Of course; there's a saying in Arabia, "All sunshine makes the desert." Can you have too little of these things? All of these ingredients demand wise balance. And there's more. Stakes or cages, to support the plants. Pay attention to timing. When you plant makes a difference. If I'm patient and plant at the right time, show a little love, water it, allow sunshine, have the stakes and everything in place, would you guarantee I'll get a good crop? No . . . What else do I need to do? I could hire a "consultant," someone who won the tomato contest at the county fair last year, to help me. I could construct some kind of protective cover, maybe a hot-house or a greenhouse to protect my tomato plant. Then I need to control the pests—find and exterminate or eliminate the flying and crawling and two-legged and four-legged pests. Remove the suckers at the right time. Prune the plant as it starts to grow. Harvest at the right time. With each additional step, I am improving the odds. The probability is getting better, as each of these factors is being added, that I will have a prize-winning tomato.

If I do everything I've described here, will *I* give life to the seed? No. *I* cannot. The life, or the potential for life, is in the seed. But can I kill it? Easily.

What is the point? I'm not really talking about tomatoes. What I'm talking about is influencing people. It is the art of management. Often we begin to think, well I'm in charge and I'm responsible, I'm ac-countable, I've got to meet these deadlines. Get the project in on time, under budget, get the chores done, finish the job. Perhaps my way of thinking about how I influence someone is a mechanical model and the internal dialogue is something like this: "I've got this person over here and she's just not quite working right. I've been watching her. Now when my videotape recorder wasn't working right, I took it to a repair shop. Do you know what they told me? They told me to get my head cleaned. I wonder if I could clean her head?" Can you "fix" peo-ple like you fix a piece of equipment? No, there is nothing we can do "to" people to fix them. Have you been successful in trying to fix peo-ple? I don't think you can do it. I haven't been successful in my at-tempts. When I try, it backfires. But what I *can* do, and what you can do, is what a gardener does. You can create the conditions that allow people to flourish.

Sometimes organizations flip-flop back and forth, between release and control, democracy and anarchy, centralization and decentralization, with programs du jour, trying the latest fad or technique, hopeful that with the next program or seminar they will finally get it right. We let people try. We dabble with participative management. We send our employees to a leadership course or an outdoor ropes course or down a river in inflatable rafts together. Then we wait to see what changes. Projects fall flat. People are friendlier but no more productive. So what do we do? We think, "I knew it wouldn't work. Centralize again. Take in the controls. More supervision. Check up on everybody, because the new fad didn't work."

With a garden, can you leave in the middle of the summer, take three or four weeks off, do nothing, come back and have a great garden? No! Is it a lot of work to have a successful garden? Yes! There are no guarantees, but there's a lot you can do to improve the results and the yield. The word for all of this activity is "empowerment." Empowerment has become kind of a buzz word, which is unfortunate because it's a wonderful concept and it means essentially you do what it takes, with no guarantees. I've had some marvelous planning sessions, shifting paradigms with senior executives, taking this one single metaphor and expanding it so that it applies to their current problems and challenges. What's the parallel for stakes and cages, what's the parallel for fertilizer, what's the parallel for getting good seed, or good plants to begin with? What's the parallel for good soil, for weeding, for sunshine? We can develop all of our people systems from that simple metaphor—ask yourself, What is it going to take to grow our people? You might respond, "This sounds like a lot of work and I'm not good at gardening." Well, if you don't like gardening, maybe you better get out of the garden. Your role, your assignment, your responsibility, your stewardship is to create the conditions that allow people to flourish and *if there is no gardener, there is no garden.*[1]

Principle-centered power, building with honor is an organic model, not a mechanical one. There are no guarantees, with people or with plants. The patience comes from our awareness that we are not really in charge—we are not really in control. The best we can do is work like crazy creating the best conditions. Because just as the life of the plant is in the seed, the life of the organization or family is the people.

So what do we do? There is a parallel for every single factor I have mentioned when we are creating conditions that build people. Harvesting, relocating, getting expert help, building a support structure, must all be considered. So must balance, the timing and harmonizing of all those factors. It is your privilege to work patiently at creating this balance.

Marie Curie spent much of her life in an effort to discover radium. After the 487th experiment had failed, which she and her husband, Pierre, had tried to isolate radium from pitchblende, Pierre threw up his hands in despair and said, "It will never be done. Maybe in a hundred years but never in our day." Marie Curie confronted him with a resolute face and said, "If it takes a hundred years it will be a pity, but I will not cease to work for it as long as I live."

We can afford to be patient when we are building another person, nurturing a relationship, or attempting to influence those we care about.

SELF-CHECK

1. Words to say to *myself* to check for patience:

   Are their efforts acceptable as a place to start?
   Must it really be done now? This way?
   Are the deadlines real?
   Where are the pressures coming from?
   Are the pressures real?
   Is this good enough for now?
   Are they good enough for now?
   Am I open to their opinions?

2. Words to say to *them* to demonstrate patience:

   You've made a lot of progress.
   We're in this together, for the long haul.
   We're together no matter how this turns out.
   I look forward to continuing working with you.
   I can see this is worth waiting for.
   Think about it; we'll get together again.
   I would like to talk again.
   It's coming, isn't it?

GENTLENESS

The best teacher is the one who suggests rather than dogmatizes, and inspires his listener with the wish to teach himself.[2]

EDWARD BULWER-LYTTON

We don't usually think of gentleness as a source of power. Yet there's nothing as powerful as true gentleness. Such sensitivity requires that we really tune in to others.

Gentleness means we are not harsh, hard, or forceful, especially when dealing in areas which are particularly sensitive or where the other person is vulnerable. Every one of us has areas of their lives that they are sensitive about, where hurts or wounds have left tender reminders or tough scars. If we are gentle, these are respected. We allow and ensure time and space for the healing of these wounds. Many of our wounds are self-inflicted; but they hurt nonetheless. It is a rare individual who can serve us, especially in these areas where we have hurt ourselves, and not judge us, not evaluate us, not condemn or criticize us for how we ended up in need in the first place.

Sometimes we are toxic to each other. Every one of us has been hurt in some way by other people. If we are not careful, we may "kill" the hidden, inner, tender parts of the people we live and work with. Our greatest joys and greatest sorrows have come in conjunction with our involvement in the lives of other people. Because of relationships that didn't work out, we have areas where we are vulnerable. People who really make a positive difference with us seem to sense that. They didn't come in and elephant-stomp all over those tender places that we've all got. They sensed it. They were gentle in those areas where we needed gentleness.

Many of us grew up in families that were not fully functional, or where there was a lot of pain. Perhaps some of this pain was inflicted on us, and we carry it as baggage into adulthood. A friend of mine who is a poet often talks about the ways we store our problems as we grow up rather than resolving them. He believes that when we encounter something that's difficult and we don't understand it, we just tuck it away. It's as if we have a little black bag on our belt in which we can hide our problems from view. If these problems stay in the bag, and are never dealt with, they build up over the years, and eventually they reemerge, sometimes uglier than they were before. He says as adults we've been stuffing so many things in this little bag that it's grown to be ten feet long. We come to work in the morning, and we're emotionally exhausted. Why? Because we've spent all morning dragging this tremendous burden around. We go into elevators and the doors won't shut, because our "bags" don't fit inside.

When you think about a person who made a difference in your life, do you remember them being gentle with you? Were they sensitive in the areas where you'd been hurt, where you needed some protection? Were they alert to your weaknesses?

One of my graduate advisers wisely counseled me, "Blaine, when you deal with the souls of men, take off your shoes. You walk on sacred ground." He had a real reverence for people and helped to inspire that in me. I liked his approach since I am vulnerable. Each one of us has some vulnerable places. We've been hurt, we've been wounded, we're unsure, we're fearful, even though it doesn't show. I spent two days teaching the producers and directors of a well-known television show. It was surprising that these people, who daily dealt with heads of state, political and business leaders, media moguls, bankers, and the movers and shakers of our society in the United States and internationally, were unsure of themselves. They needed affirmation, the reassurance that what they were doing was worthwhile. They wanted respect and acknowledgment. They wanted recognition. Underneath the apparent self-confidence and self-assurance, they were uncertain, vulnerable, and insecure. No matter what our position, we all have areas in which we feel vulnerable. People who powerfully influence us seem to sense these vulnerabilities and they tread lightly. They realize that we all wear masks of various kinds, and only gentleness can pry these masks from our tight, fearful grip.

This fear was poignantly described in a handwritten note that has been passed around from teacher to teacher, as long as I have been involved in education.[3] On my copy, it is entitled, "Don't Be Fooled . . . "

Don't be fooled by me. Don't be fooled by the mask I wear. For I wear a mask. I wear a thousand masks. Masks that I'm afraid to take off, and none of them are me. Pretending is an art that is second nature with me, but don't be fooled. I give the impression that I'm secure, that all is sunny and unruffled with me, that the waters are calm, and that I'm in command, and I need no one. But don't believe it. Please don't. My surface may seem smooth, but my surface is my mask. Beneath lays no smugness. Beneath dwells the real me, in confusion, in fear, in loneliness. But I hide this. I don't want anybody to know it.

I panic at the thought of my weakness being exposed. That's why I create a mask to hide behind, to help me pretend. To shield me from the glance that knows. I'm afraid your glance will not be followed by love and acceptance, I'm afraid that you'll think less of me, that you'll laugh, and that your laugh will kill me. I'm afraid that deep down inside I'm nothing. That I'm just no good, and that you'll see and reject me.

So I play my games, my desperate pretending games, with the facade of assurance on the outside, and a trembling child within. And so my life becomes a front. I idly chatter with you in the suave tones of surface talk, I tell you everything that's really nothing. Nothing of what's crying within me. So when I'm going through my routine, don't be fooled by what I'm saying. Please listen carefully, and try to hear what I am not saying, what I would like to be able to say. What for survival I need to say, but I can't say. I dislike the hiding. Honestly I do. I dislike the superficial phony games I'm playing. I'd really like to be genuine. I'd really like to be genuine, spontaneous, and me.

Can you help me? Help me by holding out your hand, even when that's the last thing I seem to want or need. Each time you're kind and gentle and encouraging, each time you try to understand because you really care, my heart begins to grow wings, very small wings, very feeble wings, but wings. With your sensitivity and sympathy, and your power of understanding, I can make it. You can breathe life into me. It will not be easy. A long conviction of worthlessness builds strong walls. But love is stronger than strong walls, and therein lies my hope.

Please try to take down those walls with firm hands, but with gentle hands. For a child is very sensitive, and I am a child. Who am I you may wonder? I am someone you know very well. I am every man, every woman, every child, every human you meet.

The fable Aesop taught about the wind and the sun, competing to determine who had the greatest power, makes a simple, memorable point. As the sun and wind argue about their relative strengths, they notice a lone man walking along a road, bundled in a greatcoat to gain protection from the elements. The wind boasts, "I can remove that coat. Watch . . . " and with great effort the wind attacks the man. The man only hugs his coat tighter. Gale-force winds surround him so that he can barely stand, but the coat remains intact. The greater the force, the greater the man's efforts to hang on to his coat. The sun then announces, "Watch *my* power." The sun rises as the winds die down. The air warms. The sun's rays gently fell upon the man. The man, beginning to perspire, unbuttons his top button. As the temperature increases, the man unbuttons the remaining buttons, slings the coat over his shoulder, and continues down the road. Which is more powerful, Aesop asks, the sun or the wind?

The capacity for gentleness is a reliable indicator of strength.

Nothing is as strong as gentleness; and nothing is so gentle as real strength. Are you gentle with those you want to influence? Could you be? Here are some questions you can ask yourself to remind yourself when you find yourself becoming like the wind and getting frustrated in the process.

SELF-CHECK

1. Words to say to *myself* to check for gentleness:

   Am I being gentle?
   Is this the way I would like to be treated?
   How would I respond if I was being treated this way?
   Do I know how they were treated before?
   Have they been hurt before?
   Am I inspiring hope?
   Am I being offensive?
   Am I being too direct?
   Am I being tactful and diplomatic enough?
   Am I considering their feelings?
   Is this the right time?
   Have they healed?
   Do they feel safe right now?

2. Words to say to *them* to demonstrate gentleness:

   Do you feel safe?
   Is this something you would like to consider?
   Are you hopeful that this might work?
   Do you believe you could do what I am asking you to do?
   Have you had an experience that causes you to be a little wary of what I want you to do?
   Is there anything else you would like me to know?

TEACHABILITY

Have you been taught by those who worked or lived with you? Are you willing to be taught? Many enjoy learning, but they do not always like being taught. It requires humility. It requires a recognition, first within and then to those who would teach you, that you do not know. If your ego, your sense of identity and source of security is the illusion that you "already know," you are vulnerable. You may be unwilling to let down the appearance. In fact, humility can be great strength. I have had many self-made millionaires as clients. I believe that every single one has shared with me the following thought, at some point in our professional work together: "I am successful, and I know why," they would say. "It is because I am very, very good at something, and I have built a (family, career, business, profession) around it. I know what I can do, and what I do well, I do better than anyone. But I also know that there are many things I am not good at. So I have surrounded my-self with people who have strengths in areas where I have weakness. And we have succeeded together."

If we operate with the assumption that we do not have all the an-swers or insights, we allow ourselves to value the different view-points, judgments, and experiences others may bring. When we approach others with open minds, and are willing to be taught, we learn that the key to influence is to allow ourselves to be influenced.

Listening enables us to come to the other person in terms that they understand, because we now approach them from their frame of refer-ence, their desires, wants, and needs. We all know this intuitively be-cause of our experiences with friends. Whatever your friend has to say is interesting. We connect with them. It is not a forced relationship. You want to learn from them. Few of us like to be taught; but from our friends, we will receive instruction.

While completing my doctoral coursework at the University of Texas in the 1970s, I worked on a comprehensive curriculum review and analysis of instructional design methodologies. The leader of our local church called me one day and asked if we could meet. He had some challenges in the Sunday school program administration, cou-pled with the implementation of a new curriculum. I graciously con-sented, confident that my recently acquired curriculum skills would enable me to donate a little professional time for a worthy cause. After all, my own children would be benefited if the program improved. As

I listened to his concerns I felt somewhat smug. The problems were simple ones. I could easily tell the Sunday school coordinator what to do. Toward the end of our interview, he paused and looked at me for a moment in silence. I don't know if it was my arrogance or my university status that had finally struck him. But he cut through my sense of self-importance with one question—a question he answered himself. "Do you know why we asked you to help?" My credentials passed through my mind, but I thought I would let him say it. "Because," he continued with a simple smile, "we know you love the children." I was truly humbled. It was not my expertise. My arrogance, born of postgraduate education, was possibly of value in dealing with their current problems; but that did not qualify me for the job. My capacity to listen, learn, and love was of far more interest to them. I took the job and thoroughly enjoyed learning from and being with their children. Some of the lessons learned as I supervised that informal Sunday school program were more valuable than my graduate studies.

As I have said before, if you want to have influence with someone, allow them to influence you. The key to influence is to allow yourself to be influenced. You will then earn the right to influence them. You cannot violate this basic principle and be successful, long term, with others. Are you teachable? Let me illustrate with an experience from a large manufacturing operation. The plant manager reported that when he took the position managing a twenty-four-hour-a-day, seven-day-a-week operation, there was such a negative atmosphere that he tried to help people shift their paradigms about themselves and their work. He decided to use a new slogan, "It's important; that's why you're here." He ordered a banner four feet high and fifty feet long with the new slogan in large letters printed on it, and hung the banner in front of the plant. He printed badges, T-shirts, hats, and posters, and got swept up in the new "important" campaign.

Three or four days into his new campaign he was out on the shop floor and asked a longtime supervisor what he thought of the new motto. "It's crap." "What did you say?" "Yeah," the supervisor continued, "it stinks. You've been here six months. Who do you think you are walking in here, looking over our shoulder and shaming us—'It's important; that's why you're here.' Spare us the preaching . . . " He turned to walk away, a smirk on his face as he glanced at the crowd of workers who had overheard the whole conversation.

Put yourself in the position of this new manager. You were trying to help. And what were the results? Arrogance. Ignorance. Rudeness. Your credibility is on the line. What should you do? Retaliate against this one outspoken informal leader?

This manager apologized to the supervisor. It was difficult. It took some emotional self-restraint. But by apologizing, he took the sting out of the dialogue. Then he asked the supervisor, "What do you think would work better?" "Well, how about this for a slogan, '*Because* it's important; that's why you're here.'"

Before the end of that shift, the plant manager had the banner taken down. Picture this scene, a week later. This same supervisor is approaching the building from the parking lot. As the supervisor and his friends get a little closer to the building, one of them notices the old banner up on the side of the building again. "Doesn't he get it? We don't need his signs." But as he neared the sign, he could see that the words had been slightly changed. He read it silently; it read, "Because it's important; that's why you're here." It was the same banner, but the word "because" had been written in. "'Because it's important,' isn't that what I said to the man the other day? Hey, that's my slogan!" How long do you think it took for the word to spread in that big organization, with thousands of employees, that somebody listens, somebody cares? Two years later, the banner still hung, and the slogan had become an explanation for why they worked together.

The plant manager who shared this experience with me mentioned with a smile that the maintenance supervisor became the champion of the new slogan. The supervisor had the opportunity to retire three different times after that, but he didn't until the plant manager left for a new assignment.

Are you influenceable? One of the keys to increasing your power with honor is to allow yourself to be influenced by those you wish to influence.

SELF-CHECK

1. Words to say to *myself* to check teachability:

    Do I think I know best?
    Am I really just trying to get them to do what I want?
    Is there another way to do it?
    Is there a better way to look at things?
    Is this the best way? How do I know?

What might I learn if I listen to them?
Am I willing to learn from them?
Do I believe I can learn from them?
What can they teach me?
Am I really listening?

2. Words to say to *them* to demonstrate teachability:

How do you see it?
Help me see what you see . . .
I would like to understand your perspective.
Help me see things the way you do.
How can I help?
Do I understand what you are saying?
What do you think?

ACCEPTANCE

The power of acceptance is great because there are no strings attached. That's what unconditional acceptance is. There are no strings attached to their approval of you. And in the presence of that acceptance a little flicker of hope is generated that gives us a positive belief about ourselves, a belief in our potential. Participant after participant has told me about someone who deeply accepted them, often when they did not feel acceptable, even to themselves; their postscript is usually, "I'll never forget it and I will never forget them."

Over a thousand years ago, an unknown poet wrote, "In every tribe, a man shall prosper by deeds of love."[4]

A BBC documentary called *Gandhi's India* included interviews with many people who knew him or took part in his work. Among those interviewed was a woman who gave this answer when asked to describe the dominant impression Gandhi made—"His great love."

Similarly, as I have reviewed hundreds of statements shared with me by participants who reflected on the person who had made a positive, significant difference in their lives, the overwhelming majority stated "acceptance," or as they more frequently named it, "love," as the dominant effect this person had on them.

I read with fascination the obituary of the CEO of Dain Bosworth, a large Midwest financial group. He died of cancer at age fifty-six. Apparently, this man was a remarkable human being. Two or three paragraphs in his obituary discussed the millions of dollars in assets, the returns on investment, and all the financial indicators of the growth in the company that were the results of this man's efforts. The remainder of the article talked about the man. Here are a few excerpts:

> He was an excellent leader, who cared about his company and the people that worked there. He listened to his employees; he listened to the people in the mail room with as much interest as he listened to the people in the executive suite, his colleagues said. He wanted to listen, not just to senior management, but to others throughout the company to try to get a broader view. His presence was very distinctive. He was a man of great passion. He believed in respect and dignity for individuals. He'd go to any length to help people. He had more sensitivity to people than anyone I've ever known. He had a tough life earlier. He was a recovering alcoholic and had been through some really difficult personal situations, so he reached out to others. People really cared about him. I guess it's because he really cared about them.[5]

If you've ever experienced unconditional acceptance, you know there is nothing like it in the world. You're never the same thereafter. When someone accepts you, they are telling you you're okay, even with your doubts and fears and inadequacies. There are no strings or conditions attached to their acceptance. You're loved whether you get good grades or lousy grades, whether you're underbudget and on time or overbudget and out of time. Unconditional acceptance is a marvelously liberating thing. It comes when you desire the best for the other person, withholding judgment, giving the benefit of the doubt, requiring no evidence or specific performance as a condition for sustaining high self-worth. This is different from performance reviews and appraisals. We're asking, What's the source of your regard for the other individual? Acceptance without conditions. If you have ever felt this, you know the tremendous power that comes with it. Do you mean I am okay? I am acceptable? Without any strings attached? Not because I am perfect or because I measure up but because I have inherent worth?

It may be that the need to love is more powerful and a greater, deeper need than the need to be loved.

Though it is invigorating to the soul to be accepted, it is often hard for us to learn how to *accept others* unconditionally. To do so means we have to desire the best for them, regardless of the effect of their success on us. We have to withhold judgment, give them the benefit of the doubt, and require no evidence or specific performance as a condition for maintaining our high estimation of them. We accept them not because of their accomplishments, or what they could do for us, but because of their inherent worth as human beings.

How often are your helping efforts an attempt to "do to" rather than to "be with?"

LEARNING ACCEPTANCE AT HOME

I had an experience one night at home which increased my understanding of acceptance. The youngest of my children awakened with a terrible cry and a wail. My wife was ill, so I dragged myself out of bed and tried to solve the problem myself. I fancy myself one of the new males who does diapers and windows, so I think I can do this. It's about two o'clock in the morning—the whole house was still except for the baby's crying in the nursery. Being somewhat groggy, I was anxious to stop the crying as soon as possible and get back into bed. My first thought was to *do* something. Pat him, get him a drink, or wrap him snugly in a blanket—whatever it took to get him quiet. Ten minutes later he was still crying, noticeably louder. Nothing I was doing was working. By this time I was thoroughly awake and determined more than ever to stop the noise and get back to bed. So I carried the baby downstairs, I walked outside with him, thinking the cool night air would distract him. Nothing worked. I turned on late night television and watched a few minutes of an infomercial. *They* certainly had some answers—with $49.95 charged to my Visa card, and somebody's cassette tapes, all of life's serious problems would be solved! I was beginning to feel that I was stuck in a gray land between reason and emotion where all of my training as an educator and all my good intentions as a father were futile before the irritating discomfort of an unhappy, crying child.

I started turning the house lights off (many of the house lights were on by now and I supposed some of the older children would be up soon asking why I couldn't get the baby quiet, what was I doing to him anyway, and why were all the lights on?) I walked slowly up the stairs to the nursery, resigned to my failure as a consoling, comforting father. I mean if an educational psychologist with a Ph.D. in learning couldn't stop a simple behavioral outburst like crying, who could?

As I closed the nursery door and turned off the light I found myself holding my baby wrapped in a soft blanket, gently swaying next to his crib. His cries were somewhat muffled as I held him close. I had exhausted all my alternatives—and he was exhausted. There was nothing left to try. Distractions hadn't worked. Threatening hadn't worked. Reasoning was fruitless. In fact, it finally occurred to me, nothing I had said had made any difference at all nor had anything I'd done made any difference. Feeling pretty foolish, I said out loud, "Guess I'll just stand here and hold you."

You can imagine my surprise and chagrin when within a few minutes the baby was asleep in my arms. What accomplished this miracle? Nothing I said, nothing I did, I just gave up and was with him. Nothing more. And somehow in his eighteen-month-old-brain and heart he sensed that, and that was enough. The thing that made the difference was the thing that for me was the very hardest to do. To stop trying to *do* at all. The lesson to me as I reflected on the entire episode the next day was a profound one. With an unhappy toddler I was stripped of all the tools I would normally use working with clients. Words, concepts, modeling, the use of metaphors and analogies, all were rendered impotent in dealing with another human being who had no knowledge of these interactive devices. When there was nothing left in my therapeutic arsenal I could only accept him without any conditions, without any strings attached, and that acceptance manifested by my willingness to just be with him was what was needed.

Try doing this with a teenage son or daughter, with an employee or a neighbor. It's hard. We're taught over the years to use Grandma's Law. "If you eat your peas, you can have some pie." You can have this, if you do that. Though this may be the way some relationships work, as we discovered in Chapter 5, there is another kind of relationship that is both higher and deeper. When we remove ourselves from the role of judge, we can accept others without limits or restrictions, and they may judge themselves more stringently than we ever could.

The beautiful thing is that acceptance is something we have control over. All those other things we want to control in other people's lives—spouse's habits, what our mother-in-law says, the way our customers or children don't respond when we want them to—are not under our control. But our acceptance is. So often we send the message, "I can accept you, but I can't accept your behavior. I am disgusted with your behavior." Then we project disgust. We say things such as, "I love you, it's just what you're doing that I can't stand." Well guess what? What do they feel from us? Not the love. They feel the disgust. They feel rejection, not acceptance. What acceptance we feel is so conditional that it is not felt at all. Unconditional acceptance is so rare and so wonderful that its impact is unmistakable.

Understanding is harder to give than advice, but it is usually more valuable.

A TEACHER'S LOVE

The power of unconditional acceptance was demonstrated to me in an unusual way with one of my children. Not too long ago, I was standing in a line along with other guests in front of a small group who had gathered to honor my son, when I was suddenly struck with an almost overwhelming wave of understanding and gratitude. Shawny and I were in the reception line because our fourteen-year-old boy, Benjamin, was receiving his Eagle Scout award. As I looked from my son, who was at the end of the line, out into the audience, I saw a woman seated at the back of the room. When I recognized her, tears filled my eyes. It was Suzanne Hess, the drama coach from my son's junior high school. I looked at her and then back at my son. He looked handsome in his uniform, but under his hair that was just a little bit too long, I could see his hearing aid. I looked back at the teacher, then back at my son, and a whole flood of memories entered my mind and heart.

I remembered when Shawny was pregnant with Benjamin. She contracted rubella, and because of possible complications, the doctors advised us to consider an abortion. They said our son could possibly have major problems as a result of the exposure that could lead to a lifetime of difficulty for him and for us. But for us, there was never a question about what to do. In fact, during the anxiety of those days, Shawny one day noticed the beauty of a rose growing on a bush and felt a strong spiritual prompting, "Don't worry—he will be as perfect as that." Our personal beliefs provided comfort and were the foundation for our decision. Although we were young parents, and unaware of all that could go wrong, we chose to continue the pregnancy and do our best to prepare to handle whatever happened.

When Benjamin was born, he seemed to be normal. The physicians told us we were lucky. We were ecstatic. Our prayers were prayers of gratitude and desire to be the finest parents a child could have, and we were soon consumed with the tasks of parenting the baby and his older brother. When Ben was about eighteen months, however, his babbling baby speech began to disappear and we weren't seeing normal speech develop—we sensed there was something wrong. When he was two, we discovered he was profoundly deaf. Rubella had struck after all, and left permanent nerve damage that prevented our son from hearing. Profoundly deaf! What should we do? The doctor told us that he would never be able to go to a normal school, because he didn't have enough hearing. He suggested that we get him in some kind of school right away, because he would need all the help he could get.

As we investigated options for teaching Ben, we found that some families had put their children in residential programs away from home. We couldn't think of that—he was so young. We visited various programs and could see that there were many different approaches to helping the deaf, with differing degrees of apparent success. In some of the educational settings, the children didn't even have hearing aids. We got a hearing aid for Ben right away. The aid was expensive and bulky. It was mounted in a harness, which Benjamin wore on his chest. For kids like Ben, the bulky body aid was the best we could do. We read everything we could find about how to help profoundly deaf children. We found a speech and hearing professional who worked with my wife, occasionally in our own home, teaching Shawny how to talk to him and how to sensitize him to sound. We heard about Doreen Pollock, a visionary clinician in Denver, Colorado, who was experimenting with an approach for capitalizing on the amplification of sound for deaf infants. She had very powerful hearing aids fitted for the children, who ranged in age from one to three years. When we visited her facility later, we saw preliminary results with children that showed they could be in a world of sound rather than a world of silence. Her idea was to utilize the residual hearing in these children. These children subsequently developed more normal speech and language than other deaf educators had believed possible. Looking back, we believe that we got help from many people along the way—people showed up to take us the next few steps in our journey with Ben.

I remember watching my wife kneeling down on the floor in our family room with Ben. She was equipped with a noisemaker and a bell, both of which she placed under a cardboard box. Our little baby, Ben, sat in front of her on the floor, with his hearing aid in the harness on his chest. Shawny reached under the box and rang the bell, and then lifted it up for him to see what it was that had made the noise. Then she placed the noisemaker under the box, rang it, and lifted up the box again. She repeated this process over and over again, each time asking him to indicate which device had made the sound—simple sound discrimination that any hearing person would take for granted. But he couldn't get it.

She repeated this exercise patiently, perhaps hundreds of times. After many attempts, he began to make the right connection. A tiny bit of sound was getting in and he was using it! Her whole focus was to help him use whatever little bit of hearing he had, to listen. An audiologist had told us, "Ben is profoundly deaf. That means a jet could fly through this room and he wouldn't hear it; he would only feel the vibrations." But with the help of his hearing aid, a little bit of sound started to mean everything to him, and in his mind, somehow, connections were being made. Without his hearing aid, he was totally deaf; but with his hearing aid on, to him, he could hear. Ben was inquisitive and a real watcher. We began a homemade book illustrating experiences Ben had. That "experience book" illustrates the first word he ever said, the second, and so on, until the words were coming too fast and we stopped keeping track. He could communicate. We took him to the elementary school, where a teacher said she would try him for six weeks. After two days she told us, "He'll be just fine." Ben ended up going to public school, and before long the school authorities agreed to have him attend regular school classes. He adapted well to school and with some loving and extra-mile teachers, he came to enjoy school very much.

Back in the present, I wiped my eyes. The drama teacher, Miss Hess, had caught my eye and smiled as she glanced at Ben, tall and straight, smiling as the Eagle badge was handed to him. He had not only been a fully involved Boy Scout, he had completed the independent work required for the Eagle with confidence. The drama teacher had played an important part in his developing that confidence.

The growing, learning school years had passed fairly smoothly for Ben until he entered junior high school. So many pressures; so many fears; so much adolescent insensitivity as children teased and pressured one another, trying desperately to find their own place and identity, often at the expense of others. Ben became very self-conscious of his hearing aids and of being "different." He struggled with the social scene and with acceptance. One day he came home from school and asked if I would rent the videocassette of the movie musical *Oklahoma!* We try to be responsive to our children's requests, so I agreed. Most of the movies today have closed captioning embedded on the videotape. With the closed caption feature on, Ben could follow the actual words of the dialogue as well as the songs. I located a copy of the video, checked it out, and we enjoyed it together as a family, but Ben stayed up that night and watched the movie alone, playing parts of it over and over late into the night.

I remember finding him downstairs at two o'clock in the morning staring at the television screen, watching the action as well as the words displayed across the bottom of the screen, like subtitles. I said, "Ben, are you crazy? Sure it's a good musical, but what's the intense fascination?" His reply was sheepish. The school had announced that the drama club was going to put on the play, and he wanted to be in it. Not as a part of the technical staff or stage crew—he wanted to be an actor in the play! I was astonished . . . puzzled . . . frustrated. A deaf student in a musical? I didn't want to discourage him, but I didn't want anyone to hurt my son or embarrass him either. I said, "Ben, you can't—that wouldn't work." My fears were speaking, not my faith. My fears of what might happen that would be hurtful were greater than my faith in his capacity.

Despite my protests, he would not give up. He watched the video again the next day. After a few days, he came to me and said that he wanted to be Will Parker. That's the tall, lanky cowboy who falls in love with the lighthearted and naive Annie after visiting and singing about Kansas City. It was a part that included extensive dancing, singing, and even a vocal solo. Ben said he knew who was going to get the part of Annie—it was a girl he really liked—and at the end of the play Will got to kiss Annie, and that was the part he wanted. I knew he was serious. But I wanted to protect him. If you were Ben's parent, what would you do?

Ben pleaded, "Dad, I really want this part. Will you help me?" I knew it would be difficult for Ben to sing—I had directed choirs and had witnessed Ben's "singing" firsthand. I recalled that Rex Harrison in the role of Professor Henry Higgins never sang in *My Fair Lady.* He sort of talked/sang, in rhythm, but without the lilting melodies. So I hesitantly agreed that maybe Ben could too. I also agreed to help. I play the piano, so we worked out an arrangement. I would play a chord each time he was to say a word; he would watch my fingers to know when to say the words, which he quickly memorized. He had natural rhythm, so he added a few gestures and hand actions. He had fun with it and we managed to laugh our way through. We practiced every night after school and finally it was time for the audition.

As is typical of most junior high school performers, the young people that showed up were not very polished or professional. But together Ben and I went through the audition—he read a few lines, sang his practiced solo, and then we went out for ice cream. "We'll be in touch for callbacks . . . " Miss Hess intoned as we left. I was proud of Ben. Few students in the school had the courage to try out for any of the productions. Young people are so self-conscious at that age. But Ben tried out. To me, he was a winner, and, gratefully, the whole *Oklahoma!* episode was now behind us. At least that was what I thought.

I got a call late that night from Miss Hess. She said, "Mr. Lee, I've got some bad news for you." I had anticipated the news and told her, "Hey, it's no problem. I was surprised but grateful that you would even let him audition. Don't worry about it. We didn't expect anything." Her response shocked me. "No, that's not the news. The news is . . . Ben got the part of Will Parker!" I was speechless. This *was* bad news. I tried to respond but could only stammer. All I could say was, "Are you sure you want to do this?" I envisioned him on the stage, faltering, perhaps humiliated by insensitive students. I imagined hundreds of hours of practice that could only end in defeat and embarrassment. Why? Why was she doing this? Then she said, "I couldn't deny him. He was the best prepared kid at the audition."

To Miss Hess, this was not really "bad news," although she knew it might seem like it at first. Work, yes. Risk, yes. Possibilities for growth for Ben as well as the other students, yes. This was a woman who accepted. She saw more in Ben than many other people saw. She saw past the hearing aids. She opened her eyes to him and caught a glimpse of his potential. Her acceptance of him was unconditional. And her patience was phenomenal as the weeks of early morning and after school rehearsals began. Miss Hess was a trouper, always encouraging, always believing in, and often getting after the kids in the play, pushing and fussing and inspiring them to learn their parts and work together.

The opening night of the play our entire family was seated in the front row, where chairs had been set up in the combination auditorium-cafeteria. The music started (piano and drums, as I recall), the curtains opened, and the musical began. The opening scene went well. The music moved along. Hey, these kids were pretty good! I started to relax. Miss Hess had taught them well. They had worked hard. It was a good production. The kids were doing a great job. Then it came time for Ben to sing his solo. He sauntered on stage with an exaggerated cowboy swagger, and leaned against the prop split-wood railing between "his" girl dressed in a big red and white checked skirt, and Aunt Eller, another teenage girl who played the part of a wise mother figure in the play, advising and guiding everyone. Then he started his talk/sing routine, right on cue, "I got to Kansas City on a Friday; by Saturday I'd learnt a thing or two . . . " His smile and enthusiasm and the sparkle in his eye captivated the audience. This was going to be okay. He performed the number beautifully. The audience even laughed when it was supposed to. When he finished his song, he started a dance with Annie, which led to a group hoedown and a big production number. I forgot my concerns and got lost in the plot, the action, the music, and the magic of a small-town school play put on by a bunch of kids who were trying their best to be as good as Miss Hess thought they could be. By the end of the play, he was a "hero" and even got to kiss Annie.

As the curtain closed and the music ended, the families who had come to watch their kids jumped to their feet with applause and enthusiasm. We pushed through the crowd as the curtains opened for the final curtain call, and friends and families pressed together for hugs and congratulations. I embraced Ben, who was grinning from ear to ear. He pulled me aside, into the wings offstage, and asked if I noticed anything during his big number. No, I hadn't, but it had gone very well, I assured him. He asked again. When he was sure I had not seen anything unusual or noticeable, he sighed. What, Ben? What was it? Was there a problem I had missed? No, he explained, it was just that he never could hear the piano while he was on stage during rehearsals, so the Aunt Eller actress and he had worked out a simple system. As they leaned together against the rail, she placed her hand just above his knee, then draped her skirt over her hand so that no one in the audience could see it. As the music started, she tapped his knee in time with the music, so he would know when to start. Once he got going, the piano player followed him. And it worked. This teenage girl did that for my boy!

As I stood in the line with Shawny and Ben that night, as he was about to receive his Eagle award, I felt all the emotion—the anxiety, the fear, the pride, and the gratitude—return from this experience, created because Suzanne Hess, the drama teacher, looking at my son, saw the boy, not the handicap. That teacher gave us all a gift. She inspired the teenage girl who helped him. As I stood there watching my boy and the teacher who had come to support and honor him, I thought,

"You should be up here, Suzanne. *You* are the one we should be honoring."* It made me want to live that way, to see the potential and the possibilities in other people and accept them, without conditions, without judging. What a powerful lesson she taught me that year. None of us had any way of knowing that within a year there would be a diagnosis of cancer, and this wonderful, optimistic, believing teacher would be gone. Although she died an untimely death, her influence, her legacy, lives on. Her funeral service was a tribute to the lives she touched; hundreds of teenagers, like Ben, and teenagers-turned-adults who had been blessed by Suzanne Hess over the years, turned out to honor her publicly and eulogize her among themselves.

As a side note, it is perhaps ironic that the play *Oklahoma!* barely made it to Broadway. The famous producer and impresario Michael Todd witnessed the New Haven tryout in 1943 and announced this evaluation: "No legs, no jokes, no chance." Nevertheless, *Oklahoma!* opened in New York on March 31, 1943, and was immediately acclaimed as one of the greatest musicals of all time, and ran for 2,248 performances. I wonder what the critics might have said about my son.

Because They Feel Your Love

When my son Adam decided to give volunteer service in South America, he spent time learning Portuguese before leaving home for two years.

Adam grew to love the Brazilian people he worked with in their communities and in their schools. Although he was only twenty at the time, he gained maturity and insight from these experiences far from home. In a letter to us he wrote:

> A love of all men . . . that is what I lacked in my early days here.
> The people here care much more about what they feel from you than what they hear you say. We influence them when *they feel our love.* I guess the key to serving or influencing anyone is to *love them.*

When I am not succeeding with someone, I ask the question Adam raised. How much do I love the people I want to influence? How much do I accept them? Am I being expedient with them, or do I really care about them? As person after person has told me, the individual who was the most significant, positive person in their life loved them. They felt accepted.

SELF-CHECK

1. Words to say to *myself* to check for acceptance:

   Can I separate their worth from their behavior?
   Do I love them? Can I?
   What "strings" have I attached?
   Do I accept them?
   Have I stopped judging them?
   Am I committed to them?
   Are they more important to me than the issue I am concerned with?
   Do I see their potential? Can I show it to them?
   Am I still judging them?

2. Words to say to *them* to demonstrate acceptance:

   You are not on trial here.
   Your feelings are important to me.
   We're together no matter how this turns out.
   Where are you now?
   What you feel is important to me.
   I want to understand.
   You are important to me.
   I love you.

KINDNESS

Kindness—it speaks for itself. We want to be treated that way. Do we treat others with kindness? Kindness means being sensitive, caring, and thoughtful. We act with consideration, politeness, civility, and genuine concern. Others feel our benevolence because it permeates our beings and becomes the foundation for all our interactions.

It is instructive that the Chinese symbols for kindness describe love and compassion in a friendly exchange between two human beings, mutually opening to the larger part of our joint human concerns and understanding.[6] Kindness is rare and yet more common than we might realize. Emerson invited us to look around, acknowledging what, in the turbulent jostling of day-to-day interactions, might otherwise be overlooked, when he said, "There is a great deal more kindness than is ever spoken. How many people we meet whom we scarcely speak to, whom yet we honor and who honor us?"

In their powerful and gentle book *Mentoring*, Chungliang A. Huang and Jerry Lynch share the following:

> The Shu Ching indicates that the length of a dynasty's governance is in exact proportion to the amount of love, compassion, and kindness showed by its rulers. The ancient story about the legendary kingdom of Shambhala serves as a model of peace and prosperity. The citizens were well taken care of by kind rulers, and in return they were kind, obedient, and giving to their rulers. They gave kindness and received the same in return. Confucius speaks of kindness as welcoming and protecting others; it commends what is good in them and forgives their ignorance. When people's dogs are lost, they go out and look for them, yet the people who have lost their hearts do not.[7]

Their suggestion is that the kind thing to do is help these people find their hearts. Only those who are motivated by kindness will move carefully enough to succeed in such a task.

They continue, "Loving kindness toward others will create a spirit of unparalleled reciprocity. Followers will become leaders, leaders will become willing followers, jointly overcoming hardship and honoring sacrifice toward mutual goals. With loving kindness, you will win hearts. Through compassion, you will gain loyalty and cooperation."[8]

Note the patterns of kindness, and the various ways kindness was expressed and felt in these excerpts from the descriptions of people who reported that someone made a positive, significant difference in their life:

> A SPOUSE: She lived her principles. Yet, she never attacked me for my failures. She was supportive and not judgmental. She is not passive, however. She vigorously defends the principles she espouses without seeming to denigrate others who do not live up to her own standards. I felt she was an anchor I could come home to. She was secure and so her judgment counted with me. When she believed in me I trusted her belief. She simply is what she believes.

> A HIGH SCHOOL COUNSELOR AND ENGLISH TEACHER: I couldn't talk plain and had no self-confidence, but she always encouraged me to speak. When I was a senior in high school I had no idea I would go to college. I talked to this woman and told her that I didn't think I could pass in college and she told me that she knew I would do okay. It may have been

her job, but she made her students feel like part of her family. I love her. Nobody else had that confidence in me. I did finish and taught Latin and English along with coaching.

Do you want this degree of influence with others? Then treat them kindly. Not in a patronizing, condescending, or naive way, but with a genuine regard for your common humanity, your common frailty, your common needs and desires. Kindness springs naturally from your own heart when you recognize in others what is also in you. What if there has been conflict, tension, offense in the relationship? Recall the words of Albert Schweitzer, the great humanitarian, who said, "Constant kindness can accomplish much. As the sun makes ice melt, kindness causes misunderstanding, mistrust and hostility to evaporate."[9]

A GRANDFATHER: He took me by the hand and made me know I was loved. He set examples of honesty, kindness, and charity. He gave to others when he didn't have to give. He was poor financially—but rich in important things. He made me feel that if you try hard and treat others with kindness—this is the best you can do in life. He just cared more for others than he did for himself. I hope my life can partially measure up to what he has meant to me. I feel deep love for him today.

A SON: He designates time to actually spend with only the two of us present to discuss, play, or just be together. He makes me feel that I am important to him, that he values me and my thoughts. Our relationship grows each time we see one another. I believe he recognizes the love a father can have and wants to develop his own insights into being a father and being my friend at the same time.

A HIGH SCHOOL MATH TEACHER: He treated me as if I were extremely capable. If I didn't understand what he was teaching, he acted as if it was his inability to get the point across, and he would try again with great energy until I understood. I felt very special, very loved, very capable. He changed my paradigm about myself. I worked harder than I had for any teacher in school. He holds a special memory for me, even though it was thirty-six years ago when I had a whole year of being with this wonderful person. I have never verbalized this before, but I guess he did it out of love and commitment to help students help themselves.

If we want someone to see our vision, following the path we have determined toward good and worthwhile goals, it is through the kindness that we show them that they first begin to see what we are really about. As the relationship deepens and we move along life's path ourselves, we can look back in quiet times and reflect on the power and pleasure of these mutual experiences. In "Lines Composed a Few Miles Above Tintern Abbey," William Wordsworth recalled the sweetness that can influence us:

> . . . *that best portion of a good man's life,*
> *His little, nameless, unremembered acts*
> *Of kindness and of love.*

In fact, the acts of kindness which spring from our own soul may be unremembered by us, but they are often remembered by those we are kind to.

Sir Walter Scott, Scottish poet, captured the power of gentle words, spoken deliberately:

> *Oh! Many a shaft, at random sent,*
> *Finds mark the archer never meant.*
> *And many a word, at random spoken,*
> *May soothe or wound a heart that's broken!*

Who was Sir Walter Scott? A gentleman's gentleman, loved by all who met him. It was reported that when little children came into a room where Scott was, they were instantly attracted to him and sat on the floor around him as he carried on a conversation. They felt his warmth. When a woman came into the room, whether homely or beautiful, she was attracted to him. Men of great renown or of little renown could approach Scott and feel totally at ease.

One of his friends once remarked to him, "You must have had a terribly impressive mother who taught you all of these things." Sir Walter replied, in effect, "No; I did have a wonderful mother, but actually that is not where I learned my lesson. When I was a boy of about eight or nine, I was out playing near the street. Seeing a dog, I picked up a big rock and, not knowing whether I would hit it or not, I threw it at the dog to scare it. It did hit the dog and broke its leg. The dog fell down on its front legs, crawled up to me, and licked at me."[10] This experience indelibly affected Scott. It, along with other experiences of his youth, helped form the values that were later reflected in his demeanor and in his interactions with others. He personally assumed liability for the entire bankruptcy of his brother's publishing partners and spent the majority of his adult years paying back those debts in a widely recognized act of nobility, responsibility, and uncommon kindness.

Have certain experiences of your life provided you with kind feelings? Maybe there is an appropriate time and place to respond with tenderness as we deal with other people. The manifestations of our own humanity may best be displayed as we act kindly toward those we wish to influence.

Ask yourself: do you have enough emotional reserve and control to treat others with kindness when they "deserve" it the least? That is, perhaps, when they need it the most. Such kindness may lead to our developing with them the kind of power and influence that will far outlast the moment, the incident, or the circumstance.

SELF-CHECK

1. Words to say to *myself* to check for kindness:

    Am I being respectful?
    Do I have their best interest in mind?
    Do they feel comfortable with me?
    Am I being considerate?
    Do I feel compassion and generosity toward them?
    Do I treat them the way they want to be treated?
    Have I shared my tender feelings?
    Am I holding back with my feelings?
    Have I asked their opinion?
    Are they important to me?

2. Words to say to *them* to demonstrate kindness:

    How are you feeling?
    Does this feel right to you?
    Does this work for you?
    Is this what you want?
    Do you feel respected?
    Is there anything else you would like to say?
    What is your opinion?

Do you feel you are important to me?

Do you feel my concern when we are working together?

KNOWLEDGE

Do you desire and acquire accurate information about the person you would like to influence? This is represented by knowledge of the person as they really are and as they may become—a fully functioning, actualized person of great worth, worthy of respect for what they are, regardless of what they own, control, or do at any given moment. Accurate, full knowledge about who someone is gives consideration to their intentions, desires, values, and dreams, rather than focusing on their actions alone. We can cultivate honor by desiring and acquiring this kind of information about the people in our lives. Do you make the time—do you *take* the time—to get to know someone you want to influence, beyond the simple intersection of your making requests and checking compliance? Or are we like Longfellow's "Ships that pass in the night"?[11]

Often, when Shawny and I are talking through the events of a day, I will mention a person I have interacted with that day. Sometimes, when I seem a little judgmental or evaluative, Shawny will urge me to get to know that person. "How well do you know them?" she will ask, and then gently remind me, "to know you is to love you." Not only is it true that we love most those we serve most, but we love most those we know the most. Everyone has a story. Everyone has a reason for their behavior. In their eyes, their behavior makes sense. From their perspective, their actions and beliefs are logical and reasonable. Everyone has a history. If we know how they got where they are, we are less likely to judge and more likely to understand and love. "If you judge people, you have no time to love them," Mother Teresa teaches. Our potential for influence with others is therefore a function of our knowledge of who they really are and who they can become.

A newspaper columnist recently asked his readers if they had had an experience in which they really got to know somebody, beyond the day-to-day, surface, casual conversation that sometimes passes for friendship. Unlike the ships only passing in the night, had they really connected with someone and in the process gained deep knowledge about them? Even in our own homes, the psychologists tell us we spend remarkably little time in actual, face-to-face interaction with our loved ones. When stopwatches are used to chart the time, the results are appalling; it appears that we spend but a few minutes in direct conversation that is more than direction giving. And so we can live in the same house or work in the same office month after month, year after year, and not really know each other. Our feeble attempts to influence each other then become jousting matches, with a word or an offer thrown at the other person, followed by a quick dodge by us as a counteroffer or volley of words comes back toward us. No wonder we sometimes feel impotent or powerless, incapable of getting "them" to listen to "us."

Reflect on your own social patterns. You see people you know and love every day. You park next to them in the parking lot, give them a brief greeting, engage in some superficial chat, but do you get beneath that level to see the whole person?

A number of readers replied to the columnist. One person wrote that "when a party has ended, when most of the crowd has gone home, and there are only a few people left, that is when men seem to get together and talk at a different level. It is a time when they seem to open up, when they want to share more than just polite conversation about the weather."

Someone else wrote, "I often have a sense of loss one feels when realizing something important didn't happen when it might have. This sense of loss very often hits me after I've spent time with one of my older brothers. We don't have enough real things to talk about, because the things that are real are too painful. So we talk about the scores of games or new cars or anything else that doesn't really matter." Do you identify with this feeling?

Another person shared, "I think it's possible to create a situation in which bonding is likely to take place. For example, I don't like to fish. But once I went on a fishing trip because I wanted to get to know this friend better. He was an avid fisherman and he invited me to go with him. I have marvelous memories of that trip. Not the fishing, but the talking, sharing by the campfire, walking through the forest in the crisp, morning air. Our friendship grew on that day. Today, this guy's my best friend."

One additional experience was described: "I want to tell you about a time of intense bonding between me and my son. It happened after he had broken his leg in a football game. I spent the night with him at the hospital sitting up and we talked for hours. Not about football, and not about the broken leg; but about what was really important in life and about how people needed to let other people know how they felt about them. It was the first time my son ever said the words to me, 'I love you, Dad.' It was truly a golden moment in my life."

I never met the people who shared these experiences, but I felt that in their descriptions they had identified something that I had experienced as well. Do you allow this kind of bonding to happen? Do you create opportunities for it to happen?

It is a challenge for most people to build their lives and their agendas to include the people we want to influence. But to know people we must make an investment in the relationship.

How do we do this? Sometimes, it can begin in simple ways by making time to be together *without* an agenda. I know a father who "dates" each of his children quarterly. The child (including the one in second grade) gets to plan the evening, and they have daddy for the evening. Some of the dates have included finger painting; some have been a movie and ice cream; some have included a Utah Jazz basketball game; one was an evening in the park, swinging and getting dizzy, then lying on the grass on a blanket watching the stars come out. I know a CEO of a very large consumer products company who arranges his schedule so that he is available to meet with the new managers as they complete a week of training after receiving their new assignments. During these sessions together, he says he listens more than he talks, and gets to know many of the rising stars in his organization. I know another CEO who has monthly breakfasts with a cross section of his organization, to just chat. I know a mother who arranges to be up when her teenagers arrive home from weekend dates, even though she has a full life and says her body and brain collapse each night about 11:00. Those quiet evening hours when defenses are down and emotions run high are wonderful bonding times that have paid off in sharing, risking, asking for and receiving guidance about issues that are never discussed in the harsh light of hectic daytime schedules. The ways are innumerable if the desire is strong enough.

Benjamin Disraeli, the British statesman, said, "The greatest good you can do for another is not just to share your riches, but to reveal to him his own."

One boss took an unusual interest in each new employee he hired. The company had thousands of employees, but this boss accepted the new employee, saw great potential in him, spent time with him, asked about his family, became acquainted with his children and spouse, always had time for him, gave him advice when he needed it, counseled him, praised him publicly, frequently, stood up for him, and always looked out for his best interests. He empowered this employee, making him feel good and creating confidence in him and his abilities. Does this sound like a boss you have had? Is this the kind of boss or spouse or friend you would like to have? Is this the kind of boss or spouse or friend you try to be? This employee reported later that he was still in contact with this boss, years after the boss had retired.

Another person shared with me the effects of his sixth-grade teacher getting to know him, not only as an insecure eleven-year-old, but as he might become as an adult. In his words,

> I was incredibly shy in the sixth grade, and came from a very poor family. This teacher gave me confidence. She said I was the smartest student she ever had—she said that to me and to the class. She told me how much potential I had. She took me to her home. She even took me to the junior high school I would go to the next year to introduce me to my teachers and to tell them what a good student I was. She said the only other student who showed my potential became the vice president of a well-known university.
>
> I still think about her and wrote her a letter a year ago. I am the first person in my family to go to college. I am very grateful for her care and concern. She made a big difference in my life. While I've never consciously thought about her comparing me to the student who became a vice president of a university, it is ironic that I serve today in that very capacity at a major university.

The people we influence are the people we serve. They are the people we remember and plan our lives around. They may be customers. They may be family. They may be friends. They may be the people we supervise and work with every day. How well do we know them? The better we know who they are, the better we can serve them and help them become what they are capable of becoming. We must pay a price to know them, but the potential rewards are immense. And when we love them, we can influence them in ways that may last their entire lives.

SELF-CHECK

1. Words to say to *myself* to check for knowledge:

   Do I understand what they want?

Do I know them? How well?

Can I see the whole person?

Do I know the person outside of this situation or task?

Have I "done my homework" on them as well as on what I want them to do?

How well do I really see them?

Am I willing to pay the price to know them?

2. Words to say to *them* to demonstrate my desire to know them:

Are you getting by?

Are you being treated well?

Are you happy?

Are you learning, growing, becoming?

What is your opinion?

What is important to you?

How well do I know you?

I would like to know you better.

I believe in you. How can I help?

Is there something about you I should know that would help us work together better?

DISCIPLINE

This chapter may be sounding soft, with descriptions of love, kindness, gentleness, tenderness, and acceptance. Let's look at the other side of the coin. There is a context for principle-centered power that makes love, kindness, gentleness, tenderness, and acceptance work. The word I like to use to describe this context is "discipline." Discipline is as important as any of the other power principles.

A disciple is a follower who is improving, learning, growing, becoming. Discipline means we acknowledge the errors others make, and we acknowledge the mistakes, but not in the old "boot camp" way of destroying someone, with a belief that they'll come rising like the phoenix out of the ashes, stronger and better than before. The discipline I am talking about is not about punishment. Effective discipline is done in a context of caring. Discipline can be negative and punitive, or it can be the foundation for understanding, growth, development, and positive change. Let us examine how discipline is a principle of power.

WHY DID THESE LIVES CHANGE?

A man told how his uncle always treated him as an individual. When he was having trouble in college, his uncle helped him through it in a way his parents could not. His uncle challenged him in a way that shocked him and made him really take stock of himself. He said, "It really made me mad at first, but years later I saw the wisdom of his words. He made me figure out what made me tick."

A man described a friend, who "taught me a way to choose not to smoke cigarettes. Nothing else had worked. It was not easy for me, but he saw me as I truly am, more powerful than my circumstances. I am committed to keeping his 'chain of empowerment' going by helping others who want to quit."

A man told how a professor helped. "I was at a shaky point in my life—a turning point. I was very much afraid and didn't feel very capable. I went from my parents' home to college to marriage and had supportive parents, but I was way out of my comfort zone. I panicked. These were first steps into the high-pressure world of graduate school. Everybody always seemed to be nice to me, but my professor challenged me and encouraged me to open new doors, to stretch. I truly respect, admire, and trust her."

TOUGH LOVE *Is* LOVE

One of the consistent themes across these inspiring examples is a willingness to love in tough ways. That may seem paradoxical, but it is real.

Perhaps you are familiar with the parent group named ToughLove. It is a support group for parents whose kids are out of control. They meet periodically to encourage one another to take back their homes and their lives, draw lines and stick to them, and find options for educating and helping their children. I used to be an owner of a school that attempted to deal with twelve- to eighteen-year-old kids from these families. It was a private residential school for adolescents who were acting out, manipulative, and leading lives that were destructive to themselves, their families, and their communities. In an earlier decade, most of them would have been called juvenile delinquents, too young to be in prison, but old enough to create massive problems for the social and legal institutions that tried to control them. We had nearly 225 students and over a hundred staff. These kids in this school had been given up on by almost everyone else. Tough love for these young people meant, "We're going to lock you up for the first six weeks when you arrive here because otherwise you would be on the street, steal a car, and be out of state."

You might be thinking, "Isn't that coercive, Blaine?" Yes, the people who operate primarily in a world of fear and force can usually see that there is a better way (for example, making utility deals), but they may not choose that better way. And they do not even believe that the world of love and trust exists. People who manipulate others, coerce others, force others, are quick to interpret *your* behavior as coercive and manipulative. Not until that paradigm shifts can they even begin to understand what you are trying to achieve. You can only deal with people where they are. We did not want to be punitive in our treatment. We could show them other students who were no longer in the locked area of the school and say, "See these students? They've got extra privileges. Do you want to be like them? Here are the rules. This is how you earn the right to move out of the high-security unit."

My first year at the school I learned an important principle from a counselor who helped start the school. One day he called me and said, "Blaine, we've got a problem down here. Could you come help me deal with it?"

A young man who had earned the privilege of moving out of the locked living unit, while working in the kitchen had bowed to peer pressure and had taken a glass half filled with water and added a half can of commercial nutmeg. I don't know how you snort a thing like that but he had tried it. It was an attempt to get high on something. Well, he was "busted," and put back into the locked unit.

What I had observed growing up was that if you catch somebody doing something wrong, you should make them feel bad so they won't do it again. That's the job of an authority figure. I thought he was going to attack this boy, but he didn't. The moment the teenager walked in, the counselor started talking about "next time." "The next time you work in the kitchen, how are you going to keep this from happening?" The teenager said, "I'm locked up, you know that." "Well," the counselor continued, "the next time you have the privilege, what can you do so that you won't give in to the peer pressure?" This is the way the dialogue went for twenty minutes.

Never once did he talk about punishment. The boy already knew what the consequences were. Never once did he threaten the boy verbally, psychologically, or physically. The whole discussion was about "next time."

I learned a very powerful though unexpected lesson that day. I asked the counselor about his approach after the boy left. He said, "Why make him feel worse? He already feels bad. You can't change what he has already done. Give him hope. You've got to deal with the next time or you have nowhere to go in the conversation."

The principle of "next time" is one of the most practical, liberating concepts that can help you change your orientation to influencing other people. If you focus on the past, all you can do is feel bad. What already happened cannot be changed. But a different future can be created. Next time I can be wiser. Next time I can try harder. Next time, if I see things differently, I can respond differently. There is hope in "next time." The positive approach to discipline focuses 20 percent on what went wrong, and 80 percent on what could be different next time.

Principle-centered people use discipline as a means of bringing out the best in those they influence. They acknowledge errors, mistakes, and the need for "course corrections" in others early on, while something can still be done. But they do so in a context of genuine acceptance, warmth, care, and concern, so that there is no misunderstanding their intentions and their real commitment to them.

The core of discipline is disciple. It means to follow, it means to learn, it means to shape, it means to grow. Discipline is the tough side of principle-centered power that makes such power complete.

The origins of discipline and disciple appear to produce three very distinctive connotations.

The negative usage includes the following:

- Controlled behavior resulting from disciplinary training
- Control obtained by enforcing compliance or order
- A systematic method to obtain obedience
- Order based on submission to authority or rules
- Punishment intended to correct

The neutral usage suggests:

- A set of rules or methods
- An active adherent, as of a movement or philosophy

- From the Old French *disciple*, from the Latin *discipulus*, pupil, and from *discrete*, to learn

The positive usage has an entirely different feeling associated with it:

- Training expected to produce a specific character
- Training that produces moral or mental improvement
- Self-control
- One of the original followers
- A branch of knowledge or teaching
- One who embraces and assists in spreading the teachings of another

Which form of discipline appeals to you if you are going to be the recipient? Which appeal to you if you are going to be the discipliner? Whatever you are feeling, discipline always has an element of confrontation or reproof. Reproof can also have both a negative and a positive emphasis. For example, the negative often is characterized as a condemning judgment:

- To voice or convey disapproval
- To rebuke
- To find fault with
- To reprimand
- To reproach
- Adverse criticism intended as a corrective or caution
- Sharp, angry criticism
- Formal or official censure
- Regretful or unhappy criticism arising from a sense of disappointment
- To check or repress
- To blame
- To bring shame upon or disgrace
- To disapprove

Do you get the picture? This kind of reproof is harsh and hurtful. Have you experienced it? How does it make you feel? What does it cause you to do?

But there is another possibility. And sometimes it is in the delivery that the difference is manifested. The positive emphasis is experienced as a warning given by someone who ultimately cares about your feelings and your results:

- To reprove gently but earnestly
- To admonish
- To counsel another against something to be avoided
- To caution or warn
- To remind of something forgotten or disregarded, as an obligation or a responsibility
- To give advice so that a fault can be rectified or a danger avoided
- To give gentle criticism with a constructive intent

The emphasis here comes from the overall purpose to which the reproof is being shaped. What is your real intent when you discipline? To tear them down? To build yourself up? To help them prepare for next time? Your long-term purpose will determine the tools you use and the possible outcomes that are available to you.

Often, the effect of positive discipline hinges on the timing and method of its delivery. The further you get from the event or behavior that was inappropriate or unacceptable that you are dealing with, the less effective the discipline. Ideally, discipline is not daily fare, but is provided as needed. Some child psychologists suggest that one correction for every ten positive reinforcements is a workable ratio. By that standard, what is your parenting pattern? How does your management style measure up? Not only should discipline be timely, but it should be done early, before patterns are ingrained, before it is too late, before so much time and so many events have passed and so much feeling has developed that it becomes almost impossible to take on the issue.

Further, discipline must be specific, clear, and penetrating.

To summarize, discipline, from a positive perspective, might suggest the following as you interact with children, employees, even spouses or others you care about and whom you want to influence:

Admonish and caution gently but earnestly with the intention of constructively warning, reminding, or counseling . . .
Quickly, as needed, but infrequently . . .
Specifically, precisely, clearly and with discernment.

Let me illustrate with a specific example. Consider what happens when you criticize someone—when you criticize them, have you noticed how their conscience will console them? "You're criticizing me? Yeah, did you see what I had to work with? If I had more time . . . " Do you see what's happening in the rationalizing, the "rational lies" that we tell ourselves when someone criticizes us? But when you love someone, their conscience will indict them. "Great job!" "Oh, I didn't put that much into it, " they protest. "No, really, it was terrific," you insist. They reply, "I'll do better for you next time." Look at the phenomenon: When you criticize someone, their conscience consoles them. When you love someone, their conscience will indict them.

THE POWER OF A LEADER WHO CARED

These sentiments are mirrored in a story a seminar participant once told me. When thinking of a person who had made a difference in his life, his high school principal had come to mind. He told me, "I remember vividly the day we had a school assembly. Three buddies and I went out behind the school auditorium. We all lit up. We knew we were safe: everyone else was in the assembly. And then, who should come around the corner but the principal. We were caught redhanded. My friends took off in three directions and left me just standing there. The principal collared me, and dragged me down the hall right in front of the auditorium right as the assembly was letting out. I thought I was going to die. Hundreds of kids saw me in this humiliating situation.

"He took me into his office, and chewed me out royally. It felt as if it lasted forever. Maybe it was only ten or fifteen minutes. I couldn't wait to get out of there. From that time on, I hated this guy. I waited for him to nail my buddies, but he never did. He knew who they were, but he did nothing. One day I saw him in the hall and I asked why he hadn't gone after them. It wasn't fair that I was singled out.

"Instead of giving me an answer there, he grabbed me by the collar, and dragged me back into his office. He sat me down, but the chewing out didn't even last a minute this time. I'll never forget what he said. 'I wish your friends the best. I don't know what's going to happen to them, but you could be somebody. *I expect more of you than this.* You're coasting through life. When are you going to do something with what you've got?' He turned around and walked out. I felt like I had been slapped across the face. He was right; I was coasting. And there is only one direction you can coast—down.

"I was a junior at the time. I started working a little bit in my classes and made a new group of friends. My senior year I had an A-average. I had been getting C's and D's before. I decided I wanted to go on to college, but when I applied, I couldn't get in. My grades were too bad in a previous term. My principal wrote a letter of recommendation on my behalf, and in response the university agreed to admit me on a probationary status. I chose the field I did because of this man. He became like a mentor, like a second father to me.

"Two years ago I gave the eulogy at his funeral. I'll never forget him. I will always be different because of him. He gave me something to live up to."

Do we care enough to communicate courageously when the situation warrants it? If you saw someone in a physical crisis, floundering in the water, or pinned beneath a vehicle, or about to slip from a precipice, you would likely respond quickly to do what you could; you might go for help, or jump in yourself, but you would do what you could. Discipline means you do whatever it takes, while you still have the time, to warn, to admonish, to instruct, to show and share a better way. Would the corollary be that when we do not help someone to improve, by confronting them and working with them on their behavior, that we do not care? Your communication might go like this: "I expect better of you than this. I believe that you can change and improve, to do better and be better next time. How can I help?" If you honor them, you will invest whatever is necessary to help them. Because of this genuine investment, they may come to honor you.

SELF-CHECK

1. Words to say to *myself* to evaluate my capacity and willingness to discipline:

   Am I demonstrating tough love?
   Do they have the tools to do what I ask?
   Have I prepared them?
   Do I have high expectations, commensurate with their abilities and
       potential?
   Have they been trained?
   Will our interactions elevate and refine them?
   Am I prepared to coach them?
   Have I demanded appropriate accountability?

Am I available to them?
Do I inspire them?
Are they ready to perform?
Do they understand what is expected of them?
Does their behavior or performance give me an opportunity to be in an "up" position?
Will this help them grow, develop, and become?

2. Words to say to *them* to demonstrate discipline:

I believe you have better in you . . .
Do you think this is your best?
What you are doing is not acceptable; I believe you could do better.
I may not trust you now, but I would like to.
Is this really your best?
I think you could do this.
Are you prepared to do this?
I believe you are ready for this.
If you really want this, I think you could do it.

CONSISTENCY

If we want to have the power that comes when others honor us, then we must strive for consistency in our living. The consistency to which I refer is not the consistency which is "the hobgoblin of small minds," as Emerson wrote, ever comparing and judging, looking for petty discrepancies and differences. It is the consistency of thought and action that comes from a set of beliefs and values that are at our core. Others will begin to honor us only if we treat them consistently, meaning that we operate from that very core which is our character. We are not capricious or transitory. We are not situational or variable in our acceptance, our patience, our love, and our discipline. When we are consistent, others do not view our actions as manipulative techniques brought into play when we don't get our way, or are faced with a challenge or confrontation, or are feeling trapped. Rather, our approach becomes a set of values that is our own creed, our personal code, a manifestation of our character, a function of who we are, and a reflection of who we are becoming.

The power of consistency is that our influence does not diminish from one situation to another. What we are in a certain setting, with a certain group, is what we are at other times and places. Someone has suggested that one manifestation of our character is the way we treat those who can do nothing for us in return. Sometimes our influence is greatest when we are not "trying to influence," we are just being. Something is noticed and felt by others, as has been reflected in many of the statements shared with me by those who think about the people who profoundly affected their lives for good.

These are recurring themes in those statements:

"He treated many other people the way he treated me."

"I think she was the kind of person who really believes in other people and is able to imagine or see them at their best."

"He was a good person who lived his entire life by the Golden Rule."

"I don't know why he treated me the way he did. It seemed like he treated everybody that way."

What we are communicates more eloquently, and more frequently, than anything we can say. To influence others, what we do not say may have greater impact than any few words, if we live our lives with consistency. A national educator taught this principle to a group of college students with these words:

> There is one responsibility which no man can evade; that responsibility is his personal influence. Man's unconscious influence is the effect of his words and his actions on others. Every moment of life man is changing, to a degree, the life of the whole world.
>
> Man can cultivate sweetness, calmness, trust, generosity, truth, justice, loyalty, nobility, and make them vitally active in his character.
>
> This comes from what a person really is, not from what he pretends to be.[12]

If we live with consistency, what we radiate has the capacity to influence others greatly. Our power does not vary. It does not fluctuate. It is not diluted. Others do not have to wait us out or make apologies for us. In computer jargon, "what you see is what you get," regardless of the circumstance, the issue, the challenge, or the setting. This is what Roger Dawson refers to as "Reverent Power," having a consistent set of standards and not deviating from them. Dawson suggests that this type of power is the most powerful influencing factor of all. "The longer you project that you have a consistent set of standards from which you'll never deviate, the more people learn to trust you. From that trust grows a tremendous ability to influence people."[13] Of course, the main point here is that the reason for the consistency is not a desire to have greater negotiating strength. The consistency comes from the commitment to principle; the power and influence that derives from that is a by-product.

Consistency does not mean you *do* the same thing to every person in every setting all the time. It does mean that you look to the same core principles each time you act.

A biographer of Gandhi and compiler of his writings described the humble leader in this way:

> The amazing thing about him was that he adhered in all its fullness to his ideals, his conception of truth and yet he did succeed in molding and moving enormous masses of human beings. He was not inflexible. He was very much alive to the necessities of the moment. And he adapted himself to changing circumstances. But all these adaptations were about secondary matters; in regard to the basic things he was inflexible, he was firm as a rock. There was no compromise in him with what he considered evil. He molded a whole generation and more and raised them above themselves for the time being at least. What a remarkable achievement.[14]

Gandhi himself described his striving, writing, and living in an insightful context which explains how he lived with consistency:

> At the time of writing I never think of what I have said before. My aim is not to be consistent with my previous statements on a given question, but to be consistent with truth as it may present itself to me at a given moment. The result has been that I have grown from truth to truth; I have saved my memory an undue strain; and what is more, whenever I have been obliged to compare my writing even of fifty years ago with the latest, I have discovered no inconsistency between the two.[15]

There is an apparent contradiction or paradox here. Consistency results when we are not trying to be consistent. As Oliver Wendell Holmes said, "Those who honestly mean to be true contradict themselves much more rarely than those who try to be consistent." If we live with a consistent effort to be true, there is a greater likelihood that others will honor us. They can afford to. They may disagree with us, but they know where we stand, and perhaps more importantly, what we stand for. We have demonstrated that our greatest allegiance will be to the standard we try to live by, no matter what. Such commitment invites and inspires a similar commitment in them.

SELF-CHECK

1. Words to say to *myself* to remind me to be consistent:

Is this a gimmick or technique? Or is it really me?
Is this coming from the best, highest, and deepest in me?
Are my commitments unchanging?
Am I reliable?
Am I looking for someone to blame?
Am I trying to be consistent?
Can I be counted on?
Have I checked my own motive and heart?

2. Words to say to *them* to demonstrate consistency:

Is this what you expected?
Is this how I treat others?
Were you surprised?
Do you feel I am being inconsistent?
Are we in agreement?
Is my leadership predictable?
Do you feel blindsided?
Can you count on me?

INTEGRITY

Integrity means we are committed to matching words, feelings, thoughts, and actions so that we live with congruence and without duplicity. We are authentic. We then have no desires other than what we appear to have. We have no desire to deceive. We are without malice. We are without guile. We do not feign appearances or affectations in an attempt or with a desire to deceive, take advantage of, manipulate, or control. The greater our integrity, the greater our power. We demonstrate the trustworthiness that stems from both *character*—what we are—and *competence*—what we can do and are likely to do.

Do the Rules Apply to You?

In Randy Pennington's book on honor as a foundation for ethics in the business world, he observes, "Strangely there are some in business today who want the benefits of Scout-like ethics without having to actually adhere to those standards themselves."[16]

Some years ago I was invited to teach a group of very senior executives for a worldwide company headquartered in the South. A few moments before I was to begin my presentation, my host invited me out into the hall with a worried look on his face. "I've just been beeped," he explained. That meant the CEO had paged him; each of the senior vice presidents was required to carry a pager twenty-four hours a day so that they could be reached whenever the CEO needed them. "The CEO is not coming to your seminar. He just told me that he read some of your material over the weekend, and resented the waste of time. Nobody who worked for him was going to lead a balanced life! Word has spread and our leaders have formed two groups, one aligning itself with the CEO, and my group, who want to improve and challenge the mediocre status quo." Needless to say, we had an interesting day together. The CEO did not attend our session, and about half of the leaders who spent the day with me did so with body language and countenances that announced, "I don't want to be here; the boss doesn't believe in this principle-based stuff; and you can't teach me anything!"

It was a painful day for all of us, as I attempted to walk the fine line between encouraging those who wanted to improve while defending the need to improve to those who wished they were somewhere else. The influence and example of the CEO was unmistakable and powerful. The capstone occurred at the end of the day. My host, apologetic and still committed to helping his own group become more principle-centered, escorted me down from the executive suites to the ground floor of their corporate headquarters, where we lingered and discussed the events of the day. I noticed outside the glass doors at the entrance that about two dozen well-dressed business executives were standing in the cold breeze outside the building, smoking. "Is that a club?" I inquired. "No," was the reply. "We just adopted a smoke-free policy here at the headquarters and it is a little awkward for some of the employees." I recalled having smelled tobacco smoke when I was in the conference room on the fifteenth floor of their beautiful facility—I am alert to such things because my voice and my throat, as a professional speaker, are my instruments, and I am careful to protect them. I mentioned the smoke I had smelled. "Oh that—that was coming from the CEO's office. The no smoking policy applies to everyone but him." Now whether you smoke or not is between you and your physician. But I couldn't help wondering how much more powerful this particular CEO might have been if those who worked for him saw him supporting, rather than working around, the policies, practices, and principles that applied to everyone else. There is a direct connection between the power of a leader and his individual quest for integrity.[17]

The goal here is to eliminate the difference between our diction and our action, between our creeds and our deeds. Corporate headhunters often cite lack of integrity as *the* obstacle too big to get around when a prospective executive is being considered for a new assignment. "A lack of integrity is often the knockout punch for candidates who are otherwise very strong," reported Hal Johnson, managing vice president of Korn-Ferry, a nationally ranked executive search and placement company.[18]

MATCHING WORDS, FEELINGS, THOUGHTS, AND ACTIONS

When you match your words, feelings, thoughts, and actions, with congruence and without duplicity, you are exercising integrity. To paraphrase Robert Louis Stevenson, a man or woman of integrity cannot be perplexed or frightened; they go on in fortune or misfortune at their own private pace, like a clock during a thunderstorm.

Gandhi was one of the greatest examples of integrity this century has witnessed. I have been inspired by what I have learned about his life, and I have been specifically taught about integrity by reports of how he lived. In an attempt to stop Gandhi and his crusade for freedom, the British government imprisoned the Indian leader. Their move backfired, however, as Gandhi was perceived as a martyr and his cause continued to grow. They cracked down in India, implementing and enforcing stricter laws against the native people, yet support for Gandhi's mission remained unhindered. Finally the British government invited him to come to England to attend the Round Table Conference, and perhaps to speak before the House of Commons, the lower house of Parliament.

When Gandhi arrived at the great hall where the historic meeting was to take place, a swarm of curious reporters, eager to catch a glimpse of the famous leader, gathered, poised to encounter the man. What they saw surprised them. They assumed he would be charismatic, striking, and powerful, but instead he appeared small and weak. He was dressed in the simple robes of his people. The press wondered aloud as to the source of this power. He held no political office, had no great wealth. Perhaps he was a magician with words. They waited to hear what he had to say.

Gandhi came up to the front of the hall and approached a bare podium. He stood behind it and began his remarks to the members of Parliament. He spoke out of the abundance of his great heart, describing the plight of the Indian people. He explained the evils of British rule and the need for home rule in India. It was to this cause he had dedicated his life. He made a soft-spoken yet bold call for England to leave India.

Some in the audience were legitimately moved. At a human level, they started to relate. What would it be like to have no freedom? Gandhi did not dwell on the pain and ugliness of his countrymen's bondage, however, because he had a vision that drove him beyond it. He began to paint a picture of the possibilities, a panorama of possibilities for the Indian people. He spoke twenty minutes, thirty minutes, forty minutes, an hour. At one point in the presentation someone began to applaud, then nervously stopped. Gandhi was unfazed—he was not speaking for their applause.

Gandhi went on to speak for nearly two hours. By the time he concluded, a transformation had taken place within the room. These were the people who imprisoned him. These were the people who passed new laws to subdue and suppress his people. Yet as a unified body, the entire room rose to its feet and gave this man a standing ovation. It lasted for minutes. Some of the British statesmen even jumped up on their chairs and started stamping their feet.

Meanwhile the press looked on in disbelief. They wondered how it could be possible that their officials were embracing their supposed adversary. Many in the audience rushed near the front of the hall to be near this man from whom they had felt so much. The reporters were irritated because they could not get through the crowd to interview Gandhi.

Then they noticed Gandhi's secretary, Mahadev Desai, at the front of the hall and quickly moved toward him. They asked if he would answer their questions until Gandhi was accessible. He agreed, and they proceeded to bombard him with questions such as, "What's Gandhi like when he's not up in the front? Has he always been like this? How long have you known him?" Then someone said, "I couldn't help noticing that he stood behind this podium for nearly two hours mesmerizing these politicians and he had no notes. The whole time he spoke, not a note. How does he do that?" Expecting the secretary to reveal a secret oratory technique or gimmick, they were surprised when he said, "You don't understand. You don't understand Gandhi. You see, what he thinks is what he feels. What he feels is what he says. And what he says is what he does. What Gandhi thinks, what he feels, what he says, and what he does are all the same. He does not need notes. You and I think things, which sometimes may be different than what we feel. What we say depends on who's listening. What we do depends on who's watching. It is not so with him. *He needs no notes.*"[19]

When I first read the secretary's account, it occurred to me: these words provide an operational definition of integrity. What he thinks, what he feels, what he says, what he does—they all match. There is congruence in his living. There is power in his life. Integrity means more than "walking the talk." It includes doing what we say, but it also means the walk and the talk match the values that represent the best way we know to live and to be.

I'm Not Gandhi

I use many notes when I teach or speak. In fact, as a child my mother once caught me in a lie and admonished me, "If you would always tell the truth, you would not have to remember what you said." Wise counsel for us all. I am not Gandhi. But I am seeking the truth, as he did, and striving every day to live it a little better.

Gandhi's mother, like mine, instructed him. For example, she taught him that eating meat was wrong, inasmuch as it necessitated the destruction of other life. And so young Gandhi took a pledge to his mother to remain a strict vegetarian throughout his life. Many years after his mother had died, Gandhi himself was very ill and not expected to live. His physicians tried to persuade him to drink a little beef broth to save his life, but Gandhi remained resolute. He told them, "Even for life itself we may not do certain things. There is only one course open to me, to die but never to break my pledge."

A third anecdote about Gandhi may be instructive. A mother once brought her child to him, asking him to tell the young boy not to eat sugar, because it was not good for his diet or his developing teeth.

Gandhi replied, "I cannot tell him that. But you may bring him back in a month." The mother was frustrated as Gandhi brushed her aside. She had traveled some distance, and had expected the great leader to support her parenting. She had little recourse, so left him. Four weeks later she returned, not sure what to expect. The great Gandhi took the small child's hands into his own, knelt before him, and tenderly cautioned, "Do not eat sugar, my child. It is not good for you." Then he embraced him and returned the boy to his mother. The mother, grateful but perplexed, queried, "Why didn't you say that a month ago?" "Well," said Gandhi, "a month ago, I was still eating sugar." What power in example!

This kind of integrity is rare. It is powerful. Pierre Corneille, in his play *Horace*, left us this challenging thought: "We hold in our hands the power to end our sorrows; he who is willing to die can brave any calamity." It is an odd thing to some that a person would have such congruence that they would give their life for something they believe in, rather than deny it or betray their deepest beliefs. "Greater love hath no man than this, that a man lay down his life for his friends."[20]

"Imagine what it would mean in the world if all of the present-day leaders of nations had that kind of integrity. What if we could depend on their word in any situation? What if trust and confidence were the foundation of every relationship? In trustworthiness, Gandhi excelled. Everyone understood he was absolutely honest, that he could be trusted, that his motives were right. When Gandhi said something, everyone knew it was exactly what he meant. Millions trusted Gandhi; millions learned from him; multitudes counted themselves as his followers. Strangely enough, only a few ever attempted to do as he did. Gandhi's greatness lay in doing what everybody could but does not do."[21]

SELF-CHECK

1. Words to say to *myself* to check for integrity:

   Are what I think, feel, say, and do integrated?
   Does what I say match what I do?
   Are my words and deeds, feelings and thoughts in harmony right
      now?
   Are my intentions and actions united?
   Do I have a sense of completeness and wholeness?

What motivates my feelings at this moment?
Am I feeling centered or cornered?

2. Words to say to *them* to demonstrate integrity:

Do you believe me?
Do you trust me?
Do you believe you can trust what I say?
Do you feel my words and deeds match?
Have you been able to count on me?

IMPACT—IS IT WORTH IT?

I have repeatedly referred to Gandhi in this chapter. It is not that there are no other examples. Neither is it that I am a devotee of Gandhi. I simply attempt to seek what he sought. I am on the same journey. Someone approached Gandhi late in his life and openly lamented that it would be wonderful if they could be like Gandhi and do what he did, but . . . they were not like Gandhi, they were not great, they were not some mystic or spiritual or religious leader. Gandhi's response is instructive. Gandhi did not want to be labeled or judged. Here are his words with my commentary added in italics.

"I claim to be no more than an average man. I believe I have less than average ability. I'm not a visionary. *I struggle like the rest of you.* I claim to be a practical idealist. *What does that mean? That means I've got one foot solid on the ground but I'm reaching for something better. As Robert Browning said, a man's reach should exceed his grasp, or what's a heaven for?* Nor can I claim any special merit for what I've been able to achieve with laborious research. *If you know anything about the man's life he didn't just one day say, "I think I'll skip a few meals and change the world." He practiced, he disciplined himself for years, and when he walked into that fiery furnace of civil disobedience in the cause of Indian home rule, he knew what he could do. He knew what he was capable of. A wise man observed, "I can't say to you I'll be your servant unless I can say I am my own master." And he, as much as any man, was his own master. Independence precedes interdependence. Independence is an achievement, Interdependence is a choice that can only be made by independent people. Then, he gives this challenge to us:* I have not the shadow of doubt any man or woman can achieve what I have if, *if—what is the if?* if he or she would make the same effort and cultivate the same hope and the same faith."[22]

So what's the challenge for you and for me? Are we willing to pay that price? Are we willing to cultivate the same hope? The same faith? In what relationships is it worth paying that kind of a price?

You can expect to realize remarkable, disquieting results as you begin to live the power principles:

1. You will be more careful what you ask of others.
2. You will be more confident when you ask anything of others.
3. You will grow in your ability to influence others.
4. You will come to understand the relationship between principle-centered power, influence, and leadership.
5. You will have continuing influence with others without forcing them.
6. You will have increasing peace of mind.
7. You will become wiser and more effective as a parent, salesperson, friend, teacher, and leader.

In the next chapter we will explore how we can multiply principle-centered power in our lives and the lives of those we really care about—those we would like to influence.

CHAPTER 8

HOW TO INCREASE PRINCIPLE-CENTERED POWER

> Reason enables us to know, in part, about the truth, but it can never provide us with the truth. We cannot know any principle we do not live.
>
> RODNEY TURNER, *educator*

WE CREATE LEGITIMATE, PRINCIPLE-CENTERED POWER WHEN PEOPLE believe we are honorable. When others honor us, they will trust and respect us. They will be inspired by us. They will believe deeply in the goals we communicate and will want to follow us willingly and wholeheartedly. Have you experienced this kind of power as a leader? As a follower? Have you listened to or been influenced by someone primarily because you honored and respected them? The principles of power discussed in Chapter 7 are the source of principle-centered power. To the extent that these principles are a part of our lives, to that extent we will have enduring power and influence with the people we care most deeply about.

SOMEONE CAPABLE AND WORTHY

Many years ago, I heard a story of a man who learned an elementary lesson in principle-centered power from his father. The boy lived on a small family farm where he and his father seasonally hauled sugar beets to a nearby factory in a wagon drawn by four horses. The boy's job was to hold the reins as the wagon was being loaded. But as the load began to get heavy, his father would take over, because the horses could pull more when he held the reins. These horses had learned to have confidence when someone capable and worthy of their trust held the reins. They seemed to know that the father would not ask them to do anything impossible or unreasonable. It was as if they knew that he understood their potential. When the father held the reins, the horses were at their best. They were united. Their efforts were coordinated. They worked together. Their spirit peaked. They had learned, over time, that the father acted in their best interest when he held the reins.

Whether horses or people are involved, the ease with which any load is moved is largely determined by who holds the reins, and how they are held. A skillful leader knows how to communicate to the team through his style, his voice, and his manner. In addition, he communicates nonverbally what he believes and how he lives. Both competence and character are evident. As a result, he makes accomplishment easy for others. Under his guidance, the members of the team can coordinate and unite their efforts.

ALL OF US IS BETTER THAN ANY OF US

This principle-centered power is manifested in the same way whether the setting is at work or at home. The members of a group are inspired by the ability, fairness, and purpose of the principle-centered leader. The organization, the team, the family, or the neighborhood becomes stronger than it was before; and the total strength is greater than the combined strength of its individual members.

Remarkable achievements result as people work together under the guidance of this kind of leader. As Ray Kroc, the visionary and legendary founder of McDonald's, frequently noted, "All of us is better than any of us." But the difference between one group working synergistically, creatively, and with increased capacity and another group of individuals who are merely looking out for their own interest is dramatic. With principle-centered power, the likelihood or probability that magic will occur multiplies many times.

In the sugar beet story, the son learned, in time, to do what his father had done. As the boy's experience increased and his judgment improved, the horses came to sense and rely on his skill. Eventually they were able to improve their performance so they worked for the son as though the father himself held the reins. Through modeling, the power of example, careful teaching, practice, and some deliberate risk taking, the son gradually gained his father's power.

FACTORS THAT AFFECT THE POWER PRINCIPLE

We cultivate and increase our principle-centered power in the same way. I have identified five critical factors which consistently aid those who grow in their ability to influence others in principle-centered ways. In this chapter I will discuss these five factors which can predictably affect your power. Each factor addresses a question which may be significant in the mind of the person you are attempting to influence. Visualize those you would like to influence, and listen to their voices as you ask yourself these questions:

> Where are you going? *Vision*
> Are you coming with me? *Risk*
> Can you be honorable? *Capacity*
> Have you been honorable with me? *History*
> Why should I listen to you? *Credibility*

WHERE ARE YOU GOING? VISION

LESSONS FROM A FARMER

I learned a personal lesson about vision one summer years ago. When I was about twenty years old, I spent some time in Kansas. I'd grown up in Southern California as a city boy, so the farm life I observed in Kansas was fascinating. One day a companion and I were sitting in a car by the side of the road. We noticed a farmer plowing his field, moving steadily back and forth, as he slowly sculpted the entire field with straight furrows of freshly turned up soil. As I watched him navigate his tractor across the field, I thought to myself how easy farming had become. I commented to my companion, "Gee, he's got it rough. All he has to do is sit up there in that big cab, which is probably air-conditioned, listen to a little country-western music, and steer."

The farmer stopped a short distance from where we were parked. We introduced ourselves and talked about the differences between Kansas and California. I decided I would share my observation with him. Remember, I was twenty. I'd been to college for two years, and thought I knew what life was all about.

I said, "It sure is easy being a farmer today, isn't it?" I watched as the farmer turned red with anger. A pair of gnarled hands came reaching through the window, and I was sure he was going to throttle me. But it was his words, not his hands, that got my attention as he released me from his grip and started grinning.

"Do you have any idea what it's like today with federal subsidies? Do you know what it's like with all the big farmers we have to compete with, and the financing we've got to arrange?" I knew nothing of these things. He continued with fervor, illustrating with a dozen reasons why I didn't know what I was talking about.

Genuinely sorry I had offended him, I interrupted his speech. "Really, sir, I didn't mean to be rude, but we've been sitting here for a while and all we've seen you do is drive back and forth."

The farmer shook his head and gazed at me oddly. "Okay, sonny, have *you* ever driven a tractor?" I had not, but at this challenge I responded with more bravado than wisdom. "No, but what's difficult about that? I've been on the freeways in California. I guess I can drive a tractor."

Realizing the trap I had just set for myself, the farmer grinned and said, "Come here, sonny." I climbed out of the car. I was about a foot and a half taller than the farmer.

As I stared at the tractor and the imposing plow behind it, I asked, "Should I climb up?" He responded, "Be my guest." I climbed up into the cab; it was filled with controls and switches and blaring country music.

The farmer showed me how to start the engine, how to shift, and then he got down. He said, "Okay, now I want you to cross this field. When you get to the other side, you'll see a fence. Turn around there and come on back. Your buddy and I will wait here for you."

"This can't be too hard," I thought. I started the engine, and turned to look over my shoulder. The farmer and my friend had backed off. I glanced down and noticed the rear tire on my right side was almost into the furrow the farmer had just finished plowing. I thought, "Okay, that's the key. I've got to keep that tire right next to the furrow and I'll plow straight like he did." I then put the tractor into gear.

As soon as I did, the tractor lurched forward, throwing me. He hadn't warned me about that! I looked down at the tire and noticed it was starting to squirm right into the furrow. I pulled hard on the wheel to correct, but, forgetting how small the front wheels were, I overcorrected and veered nearly 90 degrees from my target. I quickly pulled the wheel the other way and gasped as I plowed straight through the neatly aligned furrows the farmer had just plowed.

No matter what direction the tractor took, I kept my eye on the right back wheel. I supposed that if I could just match that wheel with his furrow all would be well. I quickly lost confidence, however, as I looked behind the tractor and saw the effects of my weaving on the field. It looked as if a huge snake had zigzagged its way across the freshly tilled earth. I turned around and was startled.

No more than ten feet in front of me was the fence at the edge of his property. I knew there was no way I was going to turn the machine around without causing damage to the tractor or myself. Panicking, I squinted through the perspiration dripping off my brow, reached up, and in a single, glorious moment of cowardice, turned off the engine.

As the engine died down, a surge of relief raced through my body—I had survived. My exuberance was short-lived, however, as I heard the farmer howling with laughter in the distance. I couldn't move. I was frozen in place. The farmer made his way across the field, thumbs in overalls, delighted with my poor performance. "Got a problem, sonny?" he chortled. "Okay, I deserve it," I conceded. Not yet ready to relent, he opened the door of the cab and triumphantly informed me, "My nine-year-old drives this tractor."

Humbled, I apologized as best I could. "I really made a mess of things. I feel bad, I'm sorry. I guess I kind of blew it back there." With a voice hinting of patient forgiveness he replied, "Yeah, you did. You made a big mistake." "I think I made a lot of mistakes," I muttered.

What he said next surprised me. "No, you made *one* mistake." "Yeah, getting in the tractor," I thought.

He paused until our eyes met. "Your mistake was, *you looked down.* Any farmboy knows you can't look down and plow straight."

"But I thought I could line up the tire with the furrow," I finally offered, weakly. His reply was stern, yet gentle. "You can't do that.

You've got to pick a spot in the distance and keep your eye on it the whole time. It'll pull you straight in the direction you want to go."

It was a pearl of wisdom. I didn't fully appreciate it at the time, but what he was telling me applied to far more than farming. What he defined was the essence of having a vision.

THE DIRECTION YOU WANT TO GO

Do you have something out there that's worth pursuing, that's pulling you in the direction you want to go? I told this story recently and someone came up to me during the break and said, "I had to laugh at your story. I grew up on a farm and that's sure the way it is. You've got to look out to plow straight. You can't look down. Growing up, I did pretty well most of the time, but my problems always came in the fall. I'd be plowing the field, and I'd be doing just fine until some geese would fly by. I loved to watch them fly in formation and I found that I always tended to lean in the direction I looked, so I would end up with crooked furrows, just like you."

I thought—how true that is of us all. Don't we all tend to lean in the direction we look? And so we find what we are seeking, because that is what we see. The difficult part is choosing our direction, deciding where to look and where to go—what is worth going for. If we pinpoint our direction from the beginning—establish our vision clearly— and keep our eyes fixed on it, we have a much better chance of ending up where we want to go and becoming what we want to be.

What vision drives your behavior? How clear is that vision? The clarity of our vision may determine the influence we have with others and their willingness to follow us. This is true in the family, where children look to parents for definition of life goals and values. It also holds true in the workplace, where employees look to their leaders for definition of company standards and expectations. Max DePree suggests that the first job of a leader is to define reality. This includes not only where we are going, but also why it is worth it to go there.

VISIONS AND MISSIONS

The popularity of creating visions in the form of mission statements grew in the 1980s and then, like most management fads, the practice diminished. Too often the effort was an off-site, special-assignment experience in wordsmithing. But the process is vital. Effective people and successful organizations in all ages have had a passion for something that mobilized and channeled and gave meaning to their lives. What is your vision? What is the grand why of *your* life? Before others choose to follow you, they will want to know where you are going.

Our vision not only drives us and pulls us; it can drive and pull others. We can set goals that are too big for us and throughout our lives grow to stretch and fill them.

It is vision that gives energy and passion to our reason for living. Most of us are very specific and deliberate as we select vacation spots, new homes, majors, careers, business associates, and spouses. But what is the overall focus of our lives? Charles Garfield, Olympic champion and peak performance coach, suggests that peak performers are always driven by a sense of mission. It is the ultimate mission that kindles the imagination and motivates people to higher levels of achievement over long spans of time. Anybody can get excited about something momentarily, but what happens when the tent folds and the circus moves on? The vision must be there to ensure that commitment remains.

If people are willing to commit, and to follow you because of the dedication of your life and the vision you paint, how good a painter are you? How real is that panorama for you? How real can you make your picture, so your followers have a sense that it's worth fighting for or sacrificing for or living for? How clear is your vision?

WHAT ARE YOU LOOKING FOR?

We tend to find what we look for. We see what we look at. We have to create new ways of seeing, by releasing old ways of seeing. What we focus on is critical. Experienced mountain bikers know that when you are on a narrow trail, if you look at the loose rocks, you will likely hit them. If you focus on the spaces between the rocks, you won't hit the rocks. The rocks in our lives may be the obstacles we run into. In fact, as Jack Paar observed, "All of life is like an obstacle course with myself the chief obstacle."

Obstacles are the things we see when we take our eyes off the goal. So we watch, look, and see carefully. We focus. We keep a worthy end in mind. The Palo Alto Research Center operated by Xerox, and largely responsible for the vision behind modern personal computers, has for years operated with the slogan "The best way to predict the future is to invent it." The spiritual reality, the vision, comes first and de-termines the physical reality.

What Are You Willing To Die For?

Throughout time people have been willing to give their lives for their vision. While the fires were being lighted around the stake at which the nineteen-year-old French peasant maid Joan of Arc was to be burned alive, she was given a chance to gain her freedom by denying what she believed in. In telling of her courage in the play *Joan of Lorraine*, Maxwell Anderson describes how she chose the fire rather than her freedom with these words: "I know this now. Every man gives his life for what he believes. Every woman gives her life for what she believes. Sometimes people believe in little or nothing, nevertheless they give up their lives to that little or nothing. One life is all we have and we live it as we believe in living it and then it's gone. But to surrender what you are, and live without belief—that's more terrible than dying—more terrible than dying young."[1]

What Are You Willing To Live For?

A few years ago I was invited to attend a gathering of professional speakers where Art Linkletter, the author, businessman, and legendary host and live television pioneer was being honored for a life-time of achievement. As we shared across the table at dinner, I was impressed as he related the story about his daughter's drug-related death, and his subsequent personal involvement in the anti-drug movement of the late 1960s. Although he was impressive as a speaker, and quickly became part of a small cadre of first-person, I-have-a-story-to-tell orators who were in high demand on the huge rally circuit, he felt that his energy was quickly waning. His enthusiasm dissipated. He had trouble sleeping. He felt terrible. His drive was gone. What was wrong, he wondered, after a health checkup showed that medically he was fine?

Then one day, as he crossed the stage to address an audience of thousands of hopeful parents and nervous teenagers, to tell for the umpteenth time the heartbreaking story of his daughter, it hit him. His life had lost its power because all of his efforts had gone into something he was *against*. It was negative energy. It had become destructive in his own life. And the biggest question, in his mind, became: I know what you are against—but what are you *for?* In that glaring confrontation, his own soul cried out for life, for living. He changed his speech that night and never gave the other speech again. He was going to be *for* something. For goodness, for families, for trust and communication and understanding and service and compassion and, yes, for healthy living.

What beliefs do you live with? What vision do you live for? What cause or purpose or goal is worth your best? Invariably we give our lives for something, we invest or spend our hours and days for something. What is it for you? Your power with others will increase as your commitment to something outside yourself increases, gets clearer, and intensifies.

I have been impressed with the mission of the Points of Light Foundation, a nonpartisan, nonprofit coordinating organization started in 1990. Begun as a result of the inspiration and challenge of then President George Bush, the foundation has served in catalytic ways to inspire, inform, and instruct hundreds of other organizations, to help them link efforts in an attempt to "ConnectAmerica," to bring people together, to encourage and support volunteers at the local level to solve the serious social problems of our day. As the volunteers in hundreds of cities have grown in numbers, so the vision of this organization has grown, from recognizing worthy service at the grassroots level, to building in interdependent ways to enable more people to do more good.

Good people are attracted to good ideas, whether they emanate from a foundation or an individual. The result? In Los Angeles, a Day of Dialogue brought together hundreds of people to talk about race relations. In Michigan, a school and a company helped young people find a way to learn and work. In Washington, D.C., a recovered crack addict went back to school and got a job through an organization that links suburban and inner-city communities. In New Jersey, a company started a program for employee volunteers to teach co-workers to read and write. In Maine, a community turned out to build a home for a family whose house trailer had been repossessed. The list grows daily. These situations occur because someone was committed to something, saw it before it was real, and through the power of their vision enlisted the support from others who chose to follow them because what they saw was worth following.

What Do You See When You Open Your Eyes?

In *Jacob the Baker*, Rabbi Noah ben Shea shares this timely parable:

"As Jacob told his stories he would from time to time shut his eyes. It was as if he were remembering what to say, not by searching through his mind, but by remembering what he saw. Somewhere, he had a perfect picture, and the words he spoke were a description of this vision.

"'What do you see when you shut your eyes, Jacob?' asked a little girl.

"'Well,' Jacob said, 'once upon a time there was a man who had a vision and began pursuing it. Two others saw that the first man had a vision and began following him. In time, the children of those who followed asked their parents to describe what they saw. But what their parents described appeared to be the coattails of the man in front of them.

"'When the children heard this, they turned aside from their parents' vision, saying it was not worthy of pursuit.'

"Jacob leaned toward the little girl who had asked the question.

"'What do we discover from this story?'

"The children were quiet.

"'I'll tell you,' said Jacob.

"'We discover children who deny what they have never experienced.

"'We discover parents who believe in what they have never experienced.

"'And, from this, we discover the question is not, "What do I see when I shut my eyes" but "What do you see when you open yours?"'"[2]

What do you see when you open your eyes?

The great Italian sculptor, painter, and architect Michelangelo considered himself primarily a sculptor. How did he make men out of marble? He learned to see the finished product in the raw material.

> In every block of marble I see a statue;
> See it as plainly as though it stood before me,
> Shaped and perfect in attitude and action.
> I have only to hew away the rough walls
> Which imprison the lovely apparition
> To reveal it to other eyes, as mine already see it.[3]

Helen Keller observed, "I would rather be blind, than have no vision." Those who can "see" in a visionary way can greatly influence others.

REAL VISIONS FROM REAL PEOPLE

Good people are attracted to great ideas; capital too finds a home where enthusiasm and possibility link arms. What paths would you like to go down? Adventures in living are not limited to faraway places.

I would like to ask you two very big questions which may be key to helping you unlock your vision. First, *if you did not have to work for a living, what would you devote your life to?* Second, *if you knew you couldn't fail, what would you do with your life?* If you're uncertain of your vision, your answers to these questions might help you to begin to define it. They represent your greatest hope and most sincere desire. Possessing time and resources and lacking fear, what would you do? What could you do?

> *You've got to have a dream, if you don't have a dream—how you gonna make a dream come true?*
>
> BLOODY MARY, *South Pacific,* CHORUS OF "HAPPY TALK"

THE SOURCE OF CAPTIVATING VISIONS

A biblical proverb advises, "Where there is no vision, the people perish."[4] What leads us to discover or uncover a vision that compels us, that gets us up in the morning? What is it that pushes us in the face of obstacles? Is there something that would cause you to sacrifice, to give up something you want because you want something better? Is there something worth that in your life?

Where does a vision come from? I do not have a complete answer, but the vision-making process seems often to have at least four components: crisis, information, serendipity, and intuition. If, in the middle of a genuine challenge or trial you can get totally involved in the problem, be open to previously unforeseen possibilities, and learn to listen on the inside, direction, purpose, and vision may come. Let me introduce each of these elements and illustrate how they work together.

Crisis Mobilizes and Clarifies

Financial hardship can knock us out of our comfort zone and give us the motivation to seek a solution. For some the impetus is loss of a job, for others it is loss of a loved one. Whatever the crisis, it serves as a wake-up call. It compels us to examine what we are doing, why we are doing it, and how we are going to go on. We are forced to open our eyes and, unblinking, stare in the face of our current, situational reality. The crisis creates the energy we need to question the status quo, and to propel us forward.

With external factors in turmoil in the world today, with organizations downsizing and merging and outsourcing and transforming, with technology exploding and job skill sets appearing and disappearing overnight, many people are experiencing crises. Some are financial, some are emotional, some are professional, and some are primarily personal. Recent data suggest that most people who are outplaced, downsized, or displaced from their jobs are actually happier afterward, although not initially. Even when they are making less money, ultimately they report being happier.[5]

The crises in our lives can be new beginnings. But we have to be willing to step outside of our comfort zones, or be shoved out of our comfort zones before we usually look around for new solutions. Sometimes our responses are like those in the tale about the little child who had never talked. The boy was seen by the best doctors, but no medical problems were discovered. The parents lived with the problem until one morning, while his family was eating breakfast, the boy looked at his parents and calmly announced, "The eggs are cold." His parents looked up in amazement. "What did you say?" He repeated, "The eggs are cold." They both leaped up. "You can talk—it's a miracle! When did you start talking?" "Oh, I've always been able to talk," the boy replied. "But until now everything has been just fine!"

The problems and difficulties we face can be enormously useful if they serve to shift our paradigms, to wake us up, and to cause us to mobilize our resources and move in the direction of our dreams.

Information Immersion Illuminates

A second element contributing to the discovery of a vision is what we learn as a result of being thrown out of our comfort zone. The energy driving our fear can be channeled to curiosity as we dig to discover all we can about the problem or crisis we face. What do others know? What has been tried? What has failed? What is wrong with the situation as it is now? What is right with the situation? What resources are available? Who else is working on the problem? What could be done if resources were available? What is possible?

We continue this process of examination by immersing ourselves in data. What similar experiences have others had and how have they been resolved? The search may capitalize on the technical capacities of the Internet, databases, libraries, or the social dialogues possible through modern computer networks and bulletin boards. We are not just looking for *an* answer at this stage, or even *the* answer; we are tooling up to deal with the problem, in perhaps new ways.

Serendipity Provides Happy Surprises

A third element I have observed that often contributes to the uncovering of a vision is serendipity. We want to learn what our options are before we choose a path, but in the process we may end up creating new options. It is easier to identify new options if we believe new alternatives are possible, *even if, at the time, we don't know what they are.* As we consider new possibilities, we must be open to the unexpected. The solutions we find might not be ones we had ever dreamed possible. Those who act with this orientation are said to experience serendipity.

The word "serendipity" has Arabic origins but comes from a reference the English author Horace Walpole made to a Persian fairy tale about three princes. In the story, the three Princes of Serendip were always making discoveries, by chance or accident, as they traveled about in search of something else. These happy accidents are the essence of serendipity. The modern application of this idea is that this ability to make fortunate discoveries is observed usually in those who are out adventuring, whether their adventures are geographical or mental. If we are doing, trying, looking, with a mind-set and readiness to discard what we have when we find something better, we are more likely to detect or uncover our vision. If we do not maintain an openness along the way, we may miss something that is worth more, or is better than, what we were initially looking for. If we are pursuing something that does not exist yet, at least for us, we must not quit too soon.

Psychologist Joanna Field explained her awareness of this process in herself as follows. "In my journey, I began to have an idea. Not as the slow shaping of achievement to fit the preconceived idea of my life, but as the gradual discovery and growth of a purpose that I did not previously know." If we are willing to drop the known and embrace the new, or see what is old in new ways, we are more likely to see what others may not see or have not yet seen. And what we see with new eyes, when they are fully open, may be our own defined purpose for being—our vision.

Inspiration or Intuition Ignites

Finally, choices must be made. Closure must be reached if your activities and actions are to have focus, if your passion is to be bridled and channeled toward worthy outcomes. How is this done? One CEO told me, "When we face a crisis, I get all the data I can get; I get all the information I can collect that bears on the problem. Then I pay the price, by doing my homework, by researching everything I can that relates to the issue. At the same time I keep the door open to new, unforeseen options. Finally, I sit in my office, all alone, and push all of the documents away. Then . . . I don't know how to describe this other than I just *listen* on the inside. And if I get a tingly feeling on the back of my neck, I move ahead. And if I don't get that tingly feeling on the back of my neck I don't do it. This process has seldom failed me."

This fuzzy, imprecise, intuitive sensing is different from logic, and only seems to work after the other components—crisis, information, serendipity—have occurred. If you just sit around waiting for warm, enlightening feelings, you may be fired or locked up. But when those inner impressions come after research, thought, introspection, and the commitment to openness, it can be a powerful, passionate, confirming experience. Many people have described an experience with intuition as something that was "given" to them from some outside, higher source, a source that lifts and stretches them.

Whether they define it as spirituality or common sense, they believe the source of the intuition resides beyond their own sensibilities and sensory perceptions. Most have described this experience as intensely personal, as coming from a place outside themselves, perhaps coming from God. Some indicate that this feeling or awareness has been with them since they were children. Oprah Winfrey described to me how she felt, even as a child, that she would do something significant someday, although she had no idea what that might be. That early feeling guided her, encouraged her, inspired her, and gave her confidence to move forward into areas which were not only unknown to her, but for which there were no roadmaps, no models, and few guideposts.

Have you had such an experience? Have you had a feeling or impression in quiet moments about your purpose, your passion, your life's work? It might not occur in full-blown fashion. It may go through cycles of gestation and fruition, but it becomes increasingly clear and compelling as you move forward. Sometimes this inspiration comes in a dream, or after weeks and months of thoughtful reflection and mental incubation, with thoughts that won't go away, but keep interrupting and displacing other, more mundane or routine thoughts. Sometimes the inspiration that provides focus and power in our lives comes through the facilitation of another person. Coaches and mentors, teachers and respected friends, parents and bosses—all can play a role in helping us have a clearer view of our possibilities.

> *In the last analysis, your future is not going to depend on economic conditions or outside influences or circumstances over which you have no control. Your future is going to depend on your purpose in life.*
>
> ALBERT E. N. GRAY, *The Common Denominator of Success*

Your overarching purpose in life is your guiding vision. It is perhaps not necessary to create or look for crises in pursuit of a vision—crises seem to find us, if we are in the thick of life's challenges—but as they occur, collect all the information you can, be open to previously unexpected possibilities, and be receptive to inspiration and intuition in their many forms. If you want to increase your capacity to influence others with honor, clarify and cultivate your own vision.

ARE YOU COMING WITH ME? RISK

To have a vision is to begin with a belief about what is possible and what is worth striving for. But many who can believe in possibilities do not have the courage to move toward them. Ayn Rand has noted that, "Throughout history, brave men and women have gone down new paths armed with nothing more than their own vision." Are you willing to go down new paths, and not just dream about them? As someone once said, "Many have the ability to look at events and trends and describe a future state. However, few are willing to take the risks of acting on that vision unless the current state is bad. To reform or change tactics when things are working, based on your vision of the future, requires courage."[6]

To have courage means that you are willing to take risks. Walter B. Wriston, former Citibank chairman and one of the most admired businessmen of our time, wrote about risk in the context of governance and economics.[7] His observations form a worldly-wise place from which to develop an understanding of the necessity and power of taking appropriate risks. Ponder his beliefs developed over a lifetime of successful business- and people-building:

"Play it safe; if there was ever a prescription for producing a dismal future, that has to be it."

"Uncertainty is the opportunity to make the world a better place."

"If we observe the world around us, Americans as individuals seek out risk."

"The model for perpetual motion is the marriage of management with entrepreneurship. This requires the willingness to take risks."

"If wages come from work, rent from real estate, and interest from savings—where do profits come from? Profits come from risk."

"The only way to avoid risk is to leap into the arms of an all-knowing government . . . The society that promises no risks . . . may be able to protect life, but there will be no liberty, and very little pursuit of happiness."

How far are you willing to go in your pursuit of happiness, while maintaining liberty? This pursuit may require that we get outside of comfort zones, move away from the tedium of mediocrity, let go of safety and security and move in the direction of our dreams. As someone has quipped, even the turtle makes progress only when it sticks its neck out. We must be willing to take risks—calculated, deliberate, faith-filled risks. For most of us, that is a scary proposition. We feel safer if we stay in the pack, stay in the mainstream, not making waves, not attracting attention, not challenging or questioning or pushing the limits. It feels safer if we don't get close to the edges of our knowledge, our experience, or our faith.

WHAT WOULD *You* DO . . . FOR THEM?

I was coaching a professional speaker at one time who was nationally prominent. He had a best-selling book, he had more money than he could spend, he had a network of followers and clients all over the country—most people felt like he had it all. There were articles about him in the major newspapers and magazines. His area of specialty was financial security. What he did for a living was to persuade large groups of people to change the way they spent their money, the way they invested their money, and the way they looked at financial security. People respected and trusted him, but it was hard for many of them to imagine that they could do what he had done. In other words, he reeked of credibility (he had done it) but he did not always inspire possibility (you can do it too). And as I worked with him, it became clear that he had developed a lifestyle in which he was getting further and further from his own humble beginnings. He was also becoming insulated and barricaded emotionally from the lives and lifestyles of the people who came to hear him talk.

As we visited together before he was about to make a major presentation, I challenged, "Do you know how scary it is for some people who are sitting out there in that audience? You're up there on the platform looking distinguished, with confidence and know-how and power, surrounded by all the trappings of success. You tell them what you have done with the resources you have created, but the people out there don't have those things to work with. You're saying so glibly, just go out and do this and this and this and you can become like me—do you feel what they're feeling?" He reminded me about his beginnings and told me that, of course, he remembered what it was like in the old days, the lean years, the tough times. So I asked him, "Are you willing to try an experiment? You are planning to give a speech tonight that you have given over and over; you could give it without thinking. Why don't you give a different presentation?"

He was visibly startled. His presentation began in an hour. He replied, a little nervously, "Okay, I can try that for my next speech in Atlanta." I said, "No. I mean tonight. In an hour . . . " He recoiled. "Do you know what goes into a presentation? The planning, the preparation, the practicing, the polishing, the timing?" His body language and words revealed pain, anxiety, fear, and nervousness. "I'd make a fool of myself out there, I couldn't do that." He began pacing in front of me.

I asked, " How badly do you want them to feel that you are being congruent and that you can empathize with what you are asking them to do? You've been working in this field for years—you can talk easily about what it takes to achieve financial security. I challenge you to give a different presentation tonight than you have ever given before. Leave your prepared speech here and go down to the ballroom right now and talk to some of those people, individually, that you're going to be talking to as a group later." There were going to be nearly a thousand people in the audience for his speech.

I continued, "Go down and talk to them individually, find out what's in their hearts. Get some sense about what's going on in their lives right now. Then get up there on that stage and relate to them." "I couldn't do that," he said. The words of a poem came to mind, a poem I had heard him share with audiences before.

> *"Come to the edge," he said.*
> *The people answered, "We are afraid."*
> *"Come to the edge," he said.*
> *They came.*
> *He pushed them.*
> *And they flew.*[8]

He smiled. "All right; *for them,* I will do it." And that night, he went to "the edge." I believe it was the finest, most powerful, most informative, and most inspiring speech he had ever given. There was an authenticity and potency in his words and manner that came from his willingness to risk. The whole evening became a significant learning experience for this man, who was humble enough to take the advice (an invitation to "come to the edge") that he routinely gave to others. I believe this experience was a turning point for him and for his career. I know from feedback we subsequently received that his example and teaching influenced thousands of people beyond the attendees in the ballroom that night.

ARE *YOU* WILLING TO COME TO THE EDGE?

This kind of risk taking is not the typical extreme, life-and-limb-threatening jeopardy which is foolhardy and unnecessary grandstanding. Nor is it the tight-fisted, white-knuckled living-on-the-edge state of emotional frenzy or panic of the amateur daredevil. This kind of risk is not about drawing attention to yourself. It is not about self-aggrandizement or braggadocio. It is much harder than that. It requires what Susan Jeffers has called "feeling the fear and doing it anyway."[9] Dr. Jeffers offers practical suggestions for taking healthy risks with the insight that as long as we are growing, we will continually be in unfamiliar territory, so we will always be taking risks, moving from the awkwardness and pain of newness to the power of competence.

Willingness to risk means giving up something that is easier for something better; it means a willingness to go without certainty for an uncertain, but likely, prospect. It means to consider the loss if you do *not* take the risk. It means counting the cost of risking and counting the cost of not risking. Peter Drucker has suggested that people who don't take risks make, on average, two big mistakes a year. People who *do* take risks make, on average, two big mistakes a year. What do you have to lose? Risking means taking your choice and accepting the natural consequences of those choices. It means to visualize and assess the worst thing that could happen if you do not risk. It may mean giving up the confidence of a known present, for humble, patient faith in a better future. It is not to know, but to trust and believe when you cannot possibly know the full outcome ahead of time. And it means to be willing to do this all for someone else.

GROWING FROM DEPENDENCE TO INTERDEPENDENCE

Stephen R. Covey teaches about a maturity continuum, in which we grow from dependence through independence to an ultimate interdependence in the quality, key relationships of our lives.[10] In Chapter 5 I showed how when we are dependent (or co-dependent or counterdependent) we are highly vulnerable. I want to expand on that idea. When we are dependent, we are literally at risk. Our safety, our happiness, our well-being, our very lives may be in someone else's hands. Dependence means high risk. Think about the wailing infant, lying in a crib, waiting for someone to hold, feed, change, and comfort him. This is high risk. Some people never leave this state. All their lives they are in danger because they are at risk.

As we move toward independence in thought and action, in feeling and competence, we lessen the risks. We are increasingly self-reliant.

The risks are reduced. Others cannot hurt us so easily. We can take care of ourselves. We have options. We have means. We are not so vulnerable. We can protect ourselves as we prepare for the unknown. We can adapt to changing requirements and needs and opportunities. To the extent that we are independent, we cannot easily be attacked, overwhelmed, or taken advantage of. We may not have unlimited resources; we may not even be wealthy; but we can do pretty well with what we do have. Some people become relatively independent and stay at that level most of their lives. We certainly want our children to become more independent as they age and mature. We enjoy them more as their own ability to do for themselves expands. Independence is a predictable, worthy, reasonable goal for those whose relationships have been primarily dependent.

There is a third way. There is a third quality of relationship that is possible. As we begin to value the differences in other people, as we expand our thinking to include rather than exclude others, as we think in terms of "we" and "us" instead of just "I," new synergistic alternatives are created. We can move from the stable, predictable, and reassuring comfort of competent separateness to a new state—interdependence. Interdependence suggests that we count the cost, we have our eyes open, we know the possibilities for failure as well as success, and with a leap of faith we take calculated risks by connecting with other people.

Can we be hurt by someone who is our partner in an activity, whether it be business, marriage, or friendship? Absolutely. There is always the possibility that someone will let us down, not show up, leave us behind, go their own way, not measure up, not keep their promises or commitments, or in some disappointing way not be there when we expected them to be. Our expectations can not only be violated but destroyed. Why then might we be willing to risk under these circumstances? Because the potential payoff is worth it. Because the other person is worth it. What we gain from a partnership, an alliance, or a marriage can be worth so much more than the potential losses. That means we will likely be hurt along the way.

It is a fine line to walk between the potential greatness and possible weakness inherent in us all as we build with others. Perhaps this is the thinking behind the biblical counsel for us to be "wise as serpents, and harmless as doves."[11] Our eyes must be open. It is clear that some options are only made possible in interdependent, risky, intense relationships.

194   THE POWER PRINCIPLE

LEARNING TO TRUST—THEM AND US

Willingness to risk means not only that you are trustworthy, but also that you come to trust others. In fact, it is impossible to be interdependent if you cannot trust. Principle-centered power requires that you trust. You cannot honor someone fully you do not trust. To choose a path when the outcome is not known, when the path includes the involvement and participation of others, is this kind of risk.

For some, willingness to risk means choosing to trust again a mate who has been unfaithful. For others, it is the experience of believing that you can love again when your love has been abused, mocked, played with, or betrayed. Still others find the greatest risk in believing in their own possibilities. *Parade* editor Walter Anderson points out that there are "no tidy formulas to face risks." Yet, he writes, "the risks worth taking are those that lead to the most fulfilling life. Vulnerability can make you stronger. By revealing ourselves, we gain the true confidence that comes only from being accepted as we really are. Before all else, each of us must take a fundamental risk—to be true to ourselves."[12]

What keeps us from being true to ourselves? Sometimes it is fear, fear of the worst or fear of the best that is, potentially, within us. Sometimes it is a lack of enlightenment or awareness. We just don't know what is possible. Here is a challenging perspective:

> Our deepest fear is not that we are inadequate. Our deepest fear is that we are powerful beyond measure. It is our light, not our darkness, that most frightens us. We ask ourselves, Who am I to be brilliant, gorgeous, talented, fabulous? Actually, who are you *not* to be? You are a child of God. Your playing small doesn't serve the world. There's nothing enlightened about shrinking so that other people won't feel insecure around you. We are all meant to shine, as children do. We were born to make manifest the glory of God that is within us. It's not just in some of us; it's in everyone. And as we let our own light shine, we unconsciously give other people permission to do the same. As we're liberated from our own fear, our presence automatically liberates others.[13]

IT MIGHT HAVE BEEN

John Greenleaf Whittier captured the pathos of unfulfilled longing and unrealized potential in a simple, romantic poem about a peasant maid who had a chance meeting with the town judge. There was an unmistakable attraction; both were eligible; and each thought of a possible life together. But theirs was to be the classic tale of impossible love, of risks not taken. He would have to swim the tide of tradition and custom; she would have to cross the invisible but real walls of prejudice. Neither could bring themselves to take the risk, and so their lives went on, separately. They each married another, leading to a high-society but hollow life for the judge and service with squalor for the maid, and neither felt the quiet joy that could have been created by their union. The poet ends his tale with these haunting words:

> She took her burden of life again,
> Saying only, "it might have been."
>
> Alas for maiden, alas for judge,
> For rich repiner and household drudge!
>
> God pity them both, and pity us all
> Who vainly the dreams of youth recall.
>
> For all sad words of tongue or pen,
> The saddest are these: "It might have been!"

If we are willing to take the risk, to come to the edge with others, they may respect our courage, develop their own beliefs and confidence, and choose to follow us. We can then influence them with power because we will have more power with them.

CAN YOU BE HONORABLE? CAPACITY

Robert Mager, the father of behavioral objectives and instructional design, makes an interesting distinction in his best-seller *Analyzing Performance Problems.* He suggests you diagnose people problems by asking, Could the person perform the way you desire if their life depended on it? In other words, if it was important enough, do they have the ability to do what is needed?

This same idea applies to living with honor. In interpersonal interactions, ask yourself, What could I do and be if my life depended on it? That is, could you develop and communicate a vision or a goal if it was important enough to you? Could you risk for others if it mattered enough? Your capacity is what you could do if it was important enough to you.

Reflect on your ability and capacity to act in the ways described in Chapter 7. Could you? Is it possible for you to persuade the person you would like to influence? To be patient and gentle? To teach and accept with kindness and love? To learn about them, to discipline, to be consistent, to live with integrity? You cultivate principle-centered power as you increase your ability to live this way, with these behaviors and attributes as the hallmarks of your interactions with others. Perhaps the best way to increase your ability to live with honor is to increase your ability to live the power principles.

HAVE YOU BEEN HONORABLE WITH ME? HISTORY

As Thomas Carlyle wrote, "Conviction is worthless unless it is converted into conduct." What's your history with the people you would like to influence? Why should they trust you now? What happened the last time you interacted, and the time before that? What happened since you've been with this company or in this town? What happened yesterday? At the local level the questions are asked over and over again: "What have you done *to* me lately? What have you done *for* me lately? How much of a deposit have you made *with* me recently?"

THE EXECUTIVE COMPLAINT

Let me illustrate with a personal example. I was invited to present a seminar in a five-star hotel in Naples, Florida, giving a presentation to the CEOs of the major children's hospitals in the United States, Canada, and Australia. It was a powerful group of leaders—people whose lives were committed to helping kids. I listened to their complaints and their problems for what seemed quite a long time.

During a break, the president of one of the largest hospitals came up and said, "You know, we're complaining a lot here, but when we started the organization five years ago, we met at a picnic table in my basement. Then at our first annual meeting, we met at the Holiday Inn. Now look where we are—the Ritz Carlton." He reviewed with me their history with their clients, who were doctors, university professors, parents, benefactors, and their respective boards of trustees. The challenges for these CEOs came when each of the groups demanded to know, "What have you done for *me* lately?" The issue was not capability, it was history. "What have you done with what you had, and how has that benefited me?" everyone wanted to know.

My Wife Sacrificed Her Trip

As I left the hotel room where I had been speaking, I thought about the challenges and opportunities of these CEOs. But I had a hard time not personalizing the issue. When I had originally made plans for this speaking engagement, my wife was going to accompany me. But recently our eight-year-old son had been having some personal challenges and my attempts to influence him had not been satisfactory. Shawny said, "I'll stay home those three days. Why don't you take him with you to Florida?" We thought about it and decided that that was the most important thing I could do with my son at the time. I didn't need to lecture him or explain things to him; I needed to spend time with him, working from his agenda, doing something together, building a positive memory. Acting in honorable ways, investing in him and in us, giving him a gift of time and my genuine interest might give him a stronger foundation to think through his situation and make his own wise decisions. Showing him that he was of worth, and that he was worth investing in, gave him the capacity to self-correct. So often we want to, and then attempt to, "fix" other people, when they actually have the capacity to correct themselves. They can make the needed course corrections, developmentally and over time, if we supply the raw materials, the patience, and the space.

So, we didn't stay at the grand, beautiful hotel; we stayed at a motel where he'd be more comfortable, where his splashing in the pool would not be an annoyance to anyone. We didn't go to the museums in Miami; instead we went out to the Everglades and took a ride in an airboat. We stopped at the roadside alligator farm. We had fast food. We watched cartoons together in our motel room. We did not spend a lot of money, but we spent some pretty focused time together. Because I made that investment with my son, my emotional account balance with him grew. And Shawny, who chose to forgo that trip, had made a significant deposit with both of us, because of her selfless spirit of service and sacrifice.

Do you want to influence someone? Ask yourself how honorable you have been with that person. Would they report that the power principles had been demonstrated in your relationship and interactions? Ask yourself not what your capacity is, or what you *could* or *might* do, but what you actually have done.

WHY SHOULD I LISTEN TO YOU? CREDIBILITY

For some years I directed and taught the National Speakers School, where professional speakers who were already excellent came to get coaching on how to be even better. I'd tell them, "When you get on the platform, the first thing anyone wants to know is why they should listen to you. What have you done? What have you accomplished? What are you accomplishing now? What do you radiate that confirms or negates your words? How much congruence is there between your behavior and your words?" That's what credibility is all about. It is the example of your life that is the foundation for trust. Trust comes when others perceive the match between your words and your actions. Have you actually done what you are inviting others to do? Have you been there, in the trenches, where they live and breathe and struggle? Are you doing so now, under the same circumstances and in the same situations in which they must act? Have you earned the right to be listened to? Why should they believe you?

Credibility has received attention by those who would inspire and inform potential leaders. Entire volumes have been dedicated to understanding the importance of credibility if you want to effectively influence others.[14] What is credibility? It is the capability or power we have to elicit the belief in others that we can be trusted. It is a direct function of our trustworthiness. Can we be believed? Our capacity to be believed is determined or perceived by individuals; we may communicate or interact in carefully crafted ways with groups and masses of people, but individuals make their own conscious or unconscious decisions whether to believe us. It is always the life of the leader that gives credibility to the vision.

CREATING HOPE, CREATING TRUST

When we make commitments to others, when we communicate intent, when we make promises and create expectations, the direct result is hope. Hope is a belief about the future, about something that can or might or could happen. If the expectations we create are realized, and others learn about this, then we move beyond hope to trust. Are you believable in the eyes of those you would like to influence? You may extend trust on a conditional basis to those you interact with, not knowing for certain if they will be loyal, competent, reliable, and responsible. You cannot control the actions and thoughts of others, so your offer is genuine but conditional. It is conditioned upon the realization of your expectations.

But, you can be unconditionally trustworthy. As you strive for such trustworthiness, your perceived credibility will increase. Others want to know if you are reliable. If you say you will do something, can they have confidence that you have the competence as well as the inclination to do what you have said? Have you done it before? Are you doing it now, under current circumstances and in the face of current realities? Is it realistic to expect similar performance in the future? Can you be believed? A lesson many have not learned yet is that we spend too much of our time on appearances, the sound of things, the way we are quoted, the spin we can put on events, and our ability to manage the images rather than focus on the realities. Credibility is not about looking good, it is about being good.

Sometimes we miss the obvious—that trust, or the lack of it, is the core problem. In surveys we have done of executives throughout the country, the number one factor inhibiting improved quality is lack of trust, meaning, "We don't trust senior management." It is often experienced but it's not often talked about. I had a senior executive in one of my leadership seminars who had worked most of his life in a major airline company. He said some of the executives had recently tried to bring the trust problem to the surface, using data from a culture audit that an outside consulting company had completed. Every organization has discussables and undiscussables, and the trust issue was an undiscussable for this company. This group had tried to bring the issue up indirectly with the CEO but they were brushed aside. After a while they bluntly stated in a senior staff meeting that they thought there were significant problems in the company with trust. The CEO just exploded, "We don't have problems of trust! I don't want to hear about this anymore. I *trust* that you people will do exactly what I say! Don't bring it up again." At last report, this CEO still has not dealt with the issue, and continues to shoot the messengers who dare to bring bad news from the front lines.

The trust that results from creating credible expectations has certain important characteristics. Such trust is:

- The result of interactions between two or more individuals or groups.
- A belief and hope that apparent trustworthiness will be extended in the future.
- Ongoing, real-time, and as fresh as the last interaction.
- Influenced by each individual's history.
- A social and cultural reality.
- Represented by the current level and relative stability or precariousness of the emotional bank account balance.
- A relative, dynamic factor that is not just in one person or group but is a function of the overall pattern of behavior manifested by related groups, and is highly influenced by what has happened most recently.

Trust is not:

- Blind faith.
- Lemming-like followership.
- A suspension of the desire or ability to make independent assessments, with courageously but respectfully expressed differences.
- Giving up deeply held values, dreams, or desires for the "good of the organization."

How Long Does It Take to Create Trust?

Credibility has cultural and national derivatives. In the United States, for example, credibility is easily created, easily destroyed, and easily re-created, especially if the individual takes responsibility. People are quick to forgive if full ownership is taken. For example, when Chrysler was challenged in what became a highly publicized scandal alleging the practice of adjusting odometer miles on executive cars, then-president Lee Iacocca immediately took full responsibility, informing the press, and condemning the practice. The scandal fizzled to a footnote.

Every group, every association, every company, even families and interest groups have bonding and ritual experiences that allow outsiders or newcomers to cross the threshold, establishing credibility. "Walking the talk" is so obvious, it is common sense. But what is common sense is seldom common practice. The perceived credibility that derives from being observed to do what you say, listed last here, is probably square one. Your example speaks so loudly. You may have observers when you least expect them. In critical situations, when you should speak up to stand for something, the words you don't speak may outweigh all the words you have ever deliberately spoken when you knew the spotlight was on you.

WHERE ARE YOU NOW? YOUR OWN POWER INDEX

How do you measure up in these five areas—vision, risk, capacity, history, and credibility? As you continue to develop your capacity to win with love, these five factors and the questions they represent constitute both a to-do and a to-be checklist for those who desire sustained, principle-centered power with others.

The power you have with others varies with different people and also varies with the same person in different circumstances. You may find it useful to assess yourself in a relationship with someone you would like to influence. This might be someone you work with or someone you live with. After you have completed the following exercise, invite the other person to answer the questions. Comparing responses could lead to an interesting and eye-opening discussion as you share perceptions.

Each self-assessment has two scores. The first is your estimate of your capacity or skill level in the area indicated. The second is your estimate of history, of how frequently you have demonstrated or are demonstrating this attribute with a particular person. There are no right or wrong answers—these are indicators of areas of strength and areas you might want to improve. Identify the target individual you want to influence (spouse, peer, salesperson, child, neighbor, boss) and keep that person clearly in mind as you answer each question below.

SCORING KEY:

Capacity	History
9—master	9—always
7—high	7—usually
5—average	5—often
3—low	3—occasionally
1—no skill	1—never

Capacity	History	Your Self-Assessment

1a. Ability to persuade this person?
1b. How frequently or how recently have you been persuasive with this person?

2a. Ability to be patient with this person?
2b. How frequently are you patient with this person when you are trying to influence him? Has this always been true?

3a. Capacity to be gentle and teachable with this person?
3b. Are you typically gentle and teachable with this person?

4a. Ability to be accepting and nonjudgmental with this person?
4b. How frequently do you demonstrate acceptance of this person?

5a. Ability to be kind and sensitive to this person?
5b. How frequently are you kind and sensitive with this person?

6a. Ability to really know and understand this person and their potential?
6b. How frequently do you really focus on knowing and understanding this person and her or his potential?

7a. Ability to confront this person's mistakes with compassion?
7b. How frequently do you confront this person's mistakes with compassion and positive discipline?

8a. Ability to be consistent, treating this person similarly, regardless of the situation, your goals, or your moods?
8b. How consistent are you in manifesting these characteristics as you interact with this person?

9a. Ability to have integrity with this person, matching your words, deeds, feelings, and thoughts in your interactions with them?
9b. How frequently do your words, deeds, feelings, and thoughts match as you interact with this person? How often is this true for you?

Power Index Scoring

High	70+	Medium 55–69	Low 54 or less

Pattern		Interpretation/Comments
Capacity	*History*	
High	High	Good match. Be patient, results will come.
High	Medium	Good capacity. Analyze obstacles.
High	Low	Good capacity. Motivation is an issue. Does it matter enough for you to make the investment in the relationship?
Medium	High	Rare. Working hard with somewhat limited resources.
Medium	Medium	Good match. Doing what you can. Consider improving capacity through application of *The Seven Habits of Highly Effective People*.
Medium	Low	Mismatch. Evaluate your desire and interest. How badly do you want to improve this relationship?
Low	High	Rare. Possibly overdoing it. Improve skills to make it less difficult.

| Low | Medium | Rare. Working hard on the relationship. Capacity will probably increase over time. |
| Low | Low | Urgent candidate for personal and professional development. You are doing what you are capable of, but there is lots of room to grow. It can only get better. |

INCREASING YOUR PRINCIPLE-CENTERED POWER

1. Which capacities are your strengths? Which need improvement? Can you be more honorable with this person?

2. Which history areas are your strengths? Which need improvement? What is your pattern of behavior with them? Have you been honorable with the person you would like to influence?

3. What does the difference between your history and capacity scores reveal about you? About the person you want to influence?

4. Put yourself in the shoes of the person you would like to influence. Try to understand them by getting inside their world. Listen to their heart. Look back at yourself through their eyes. From their perspective, how would you answer these questions?
   A. Where are you going? *Vision*

B. Are you coming with me? *Risk*

C. Can you be honorable? *Capacity*

D. Have you been honorable with me? *History*

E. Why should I listen to you? *Credibility*

CHAPTER 9

PARENT POWER—HOW TO HONOR YOUR CHILDREN

The trouble with being a parent is that by the time you're experienced, you may be unemployable.

AUTHOR UNKNOWN

INFLUENCING WITH HONOR IS NOT EASY, BUT IT IS WORTH IT. IT takes courage, awareness, and wisdom. It requires that you add commitment and knowledge to provide a foundation for your good intentions. It also helps if you have models and mentors. In this and the next three chapters, I will illustrate how influencing with honor takes place in four significant roles—parent, teacher, salesperson, and leader—in which your primary goal is to influence others. These four roles are complementary, and often overlap and support each other in specific ways. If you want to have more power in these roles and relationships, you must learn to influence with honor.

The most important place for you to begin any worthwhile change might be in your home, starting with you and spreading to the people who know and love you. You begin as a parent. Many of the attendees in the public seminars conducted by the Covey Leadership Center tell us that their immediate application of what they learn is usually at home first. Success in application of principles of effectiveness at home inspires efforts to build stronger, more effective relationships at work. So start with your own family. Whether your children are young and at home or raised and are having families of their own, you can increase your ability to influence them with honor. It is our family relationships that matter most. Even though it may not be our primary goal, if we can be comfortably and increasingly powerful at home, we can use the positive experience we gain there as a pathway for building power through honor outside our homes.

THE DEMANDS OF PARENTHOOD

What is a parent? The role of parent might include birth parent, adoptive parent, stepparent, grandparent, foster parent, or any relationship in which you feel a biological, legal, or spiritual kinship in your stewardship for another person. I will focus primarily on the traditional biological relationship, but these principles apply to any of the other relationships as well. Parenting is about taking care of your family. If you have children, you will never stop being a parent. One of our marketing brochures at the Covey Leadership Center has these words on the cover: "The Seven Habits really hit home—so that's where I am taking them." Some believe that there is nothing which can compensate for failure at home. If that is true, then perhaps the greatest, most important work you will ever do will be within the walls of your own home.

What happens at home is important; it is challenging to have a family. It can be financially, emotionally, and physically draining in a way unlike almost any other work. As I have watched leaders in multibillion-dollar operations carry out their work, then seen these same leaders struggle to deal effectively with their own spouses and children, I have been amazed at how difficult it is to be a happy, successful, honorable parent. Victor Brown, Jr., who directs a worldwide private social services program, commented on this challenge and the strength it requires: "The fact is that an emotionally healthy and emotionally well-nourished person is as much able to undertake strenuous emotional activity as the physically healthy person can undertake physical activity. . . . Family living is not for emotional weaklings."[1]

We are most vulnerable and potentially most powerful when we are home, with the people we love and care about the most. We are vulnerable because these important people see us without makeup, without carefully weighed words, and without caution but with fatigue, impatience, fear, and irreverence; in our casual clothes and sometimes in our underwear. At home, it all "hangs out." We are potentially most powerful because at home we are living without pretense; we are giving our time and attention and energy to the things we care about. Seeing us "as we really are" can inspire others; without the need of appearances, image grooming, and event orchestrating, we are free to be. The power of our example, coupled with the lack of any ulterior motive, is immeasurably potent.

The privileges and powers of parenthood dramatically outweigh the problems. The possible joys are worth the necessary risks. When you decide to have children, you must do so with your eyes open, expecting and preparing for the significant changes that will inevitably take place. Elizabeth Stone expressed this sentiment: "Making the decision to have a child is momentous. It is to decide forever to have your heart go walking around outside your body." But that is a risk Shawny and I have taken, and I am continually learning in the laboratory of life called the family.

In my work I have observed families in which a particular path to power was predominant. In the following sections I will illustrate what happens in families as parents build relationships based on powerlessness and the three paths to power—fear, fairness, and honor.

PARENTS WHO FEEL HOPELESS/HELPLESS

It *is* a struggle to be an effective parent. The beliefs you have create a self-fulfilling prophecy to which your children are remarkably sensitive. Your children need you; your increased proactivity can become a foundation that ultimately empowers them. They will take heart when they see you taking action, however small or indirect that action may be.

Carlfred Broderick, a practicing therapist who also trains therapists to work with intergenerational family systems, believes that most kids who are out of control, acting out, not doing well, and not becoming responsible are usually the result of one of two things—too little structure, involvement, and influence from the parents, or too much. Too much control is discussed in the next section. Too little appropriate involvement can be the result of parental lack of awareness, modeling, energy, self-esteem, interest, knowledge, or too much stress and over-load.[2]

Barbara Bush, concerned with the many difficult challenges facing the modern family, gave this insightful challenge at a college gradua-tion while she was first lady. She used the metaphor of the home, with a focus on the importance of creating power within the home. The message is an invitation for all of us to continually challenge ourselves to shift from being powerless to being powerful, starting wherever we are. She said:

> Whatever the era, whatever the times, one thing will never change: Fa-thers and mothers, if you have children, they must come first. You must read to your children and you must hug your children and you must love your children. Your success as a family, our success as a society, de-pends not on what happens in the White House, but on what happens inside your house.[3]

You can make a difference, with your own children. Get help. Talk to someone you respect. Join a self-help organization. Visit with a pastor or police officer or school psychologist. Alternate roles with your spouse. Take a parenting class. Visit the bookstore, select and read a good book on parenting. Try a new approach. Don't give up. Much is at stake. You can make the difference your children need. It may be the most important thing you do in life.

PARENTS WHO FORCE THEIR CHILDREN— COERCIVE POWER AT HOME

Do you find yourself making your kids do what you want, but not lik-ing the result? Do you intimidate your children, whatever their age, and find yourself not liking what you become while you are doing it? Has anyone ever approached you after they have observed you with "helpful" suggestions on another way to raise or discipline your child? It is possible that you are getting the results you want with your kids, but only on the surface, and only temporarily. Coercive power al-ways creates the illusion of order and obedience, but seldom does compliance lead to internal, self-directed behavior in children. There are terrific challenges in getting children to do what we want them to do. But the most immediate, most readily used method may not get you what you actually want.

It is not surprising that most parents use coercive power with their children under certain circumstances. For some it is an isolated occurrence. For some it is a lifestyle, perhaps mirroring what they experienced in their own homes as they grew up. Not knowing any other alternative, they act out of ignorance, fatigue, or fear. Too much structure and control is often the result of fear in the parents, but it usually is justified under a banner of "what's best for you," in the name of religion or democracy or some other social authority. Sometimes we abuse our children when we think we are accomplishing some great good. It is a tricky business that requires common sense, enlightened awareness, self-control, and the ability to tune in to your deepest sensitivities as well as your children's.

There is a particularly disturbing public service announcement on television which portrays a young girl, bandaged, saying to the camera, "She burned me for playing with matches." The thirty-second spot is designed to sensitize us to the horrors of child abuse. Whenever I see that portrayal I recall an incident that occurred when I was education director for a large private residential school for difficult children. While reviewing the intake folder for a new student one day, I found a statement from the examining physician about scars on the boy's arms. The boy was quite self-conscious about the scars and always wore long-sleeve shirts, even in the summer, to hide them. The patient history described the cause of the scars—the boy's father had caught him smoking when he was eleven, and as punishment, took a lighter and set his clothes on fire. Indignation evolved quickly to anger as I thought about a parent doing this to his own son. I began to make mental notes about what I would say to the father when he arrived later with his son. There are many forms of abuse, from neglect to verbal, sexual, physical, and emotional invasions and attacks; but this was as heinous a thing as I could imagine. How the boy must hate his father, I thought. How could someone become so hateful and hurtful to their own child?

Two weeks later I had an appointment with the father, who had traveled from out of state to bring his son to our school. My pulse raced as I anticipated the encounter. It would be difficult to be professional under the circumstances. The father entered by office, acting sheepish and making no eye contact. My first impression was that he was not the bully or brute I had imagined. He was slight, and wore baggy, almost sloppy clothes, although I remembered from the intake folder that he made a reasonable living. I invited him to sit and began the preliminary discussions, the small talk, the obligatory review of rules and regulations and policies of the school. His eyes darted about the room. He was obviously uncomfortable with me and with himself. He nervously scratched at his left arm. I couldn't help noticing that he, like his son, wore a long-sleeve shirt.

The father noticed my eyes following his movements and the color immediately left his face. "Oh," he interrupted. "I see you noticed my scars . . . " I had not until then, but yes, there were old, wide discolorations and smooth patches on the back of his hand. "Most people do," he continued, without looking directly at me. "There was an accident . . . when I was young . . . my father . . . " His voice faded. "Yes . . . " I encouraged. "Well, I was burned. Dad caught me trying to smoke, and he . . . " He stopped talking altogether and his head dropped.

I could not believe what I was hearing. Could it possibly be? This man, hurt and disfigured as a child by a father who was too angry or drunk or ignorant to be rational, had done the same thing, under the same circumstances, to his own son? It was true. The inhuman crime had been passed on, and now, in a second generation, a new child had learned to deal with his own hurtful and dysfunctional parents by becoming a problem that they could not ignore.

I was glad I had not said anything to the father at first. I pitied them both. And I determined to do everything in my power to give this man and his son, these two hurting and damaged people, another view of what they could have and be together as we worked together during the next twelve months.

CAN WE BREAK THE PATTERN?

Where did we get the idea that we could make people improve by making them afraid? Or that we could help people do better by making them feel bad?

It is normal to fear, on behalf of our children. There is much to fear in the world today. But you must balance realistic fears with a hope for the possibilities that are also in your children. Perhaps you fear you will do the wrong thing. Perhaps you fear what might happen if you don't control or coerce your child. In any case, the fears you have as a parent are usually manifested in your attempts to control your children. What are you afraid of? I have observed closely the phenomenon of fear in myself as a parent and in other parents.

Sometimes fear is disguised as concern. A father attending our leadership program was having a great week, learning, growing, and trying out new ideas. He approached me late in the week for help with his son, a college student. Simply put, the son refused to do what the dad wanted, so the dad in a direct but mechanical way forced compliance. The boy was not allowed to make his own choices and live with any degree of freedom. The father insisted on telling me how much he loved his son, how he attempted to do things with him, and how he wanted his son to "have so much." In the father's words, "I just love him and want so much for him, but he is not doing anything with his life—he should be in an engineering program, he is so smart. Yet he is wasting this opportunity that I am paying for!"

I started to talk to the father about career choices and the many shifts in the selection of a major that are common among college students, drawing on numerous experiences I had had counseling students while I was teaching at the university. Then, I gradually sensed something in the father that seemed incongruent, and felt prompted to ask him, "What are *you* afraid of?" No response. Then, angry and visibly frustrated, "I am not afraid of anything! My son needs the help, not me—what do I need to do to help *him*?" But I felt he was afraid of something. I asked him to think about our conversation and told him that I would think about his situation and visit with him again later. He came back the next morning and confessed, with tears streaming down his face, "You were right. It is *not* my son; it is me. I *am* afraid." "What are you afraid of?" I asked gently. "I am afraid that he will become just like me."

WHAT DO YOU FEAR?

This father wanted to be helpful to his son, but his fear controlled his interactions with the boy. His son, feeling the control, resisted somewhat weakly, but with enough determination that the father's fears were coming to life before his very eyes. The harder he pushed his son, the less he got what he wanted. He was filled with fear, but his fear was hidden under his anger. The son interpreted the anger and control as disapproval and disappointment and took steps to prove, if only to himself, that he could make choices, that he could direct his life, and that he, and not his father, was in charge. Neither the father nor the son was getting what they really wanted. They both felt awkward about their relationship and they felt bad about each other.

Our children are not bad, and you are not bad. Your methods may not be getting you the results you want, but that can be changed. Inappropriate or unacceptable behavior in your children must be dealt with, but if you do it out of anger or control, you are likely to end up with a relationship that is painfully alive or regretfully nonexistent.

Educator Kathryn J. Kvols suggests you examine your beliefs to determine if you are likely to be coercive. Your methods are likely to continue, perhaps in altered, less obvious, but equally damaging forms until your beliefs change. Are some of these a part of your privately held beliefs?

- A child must suffer in order to learn.
- You must control your child.
- Your child must be afraid of you in order for you to be able to make them behave.
- The child must know that you are the adult, and they are only the child.

Kvols's book will help you identify the extent to which you tend to be a coercive parent and offers practical suggestions for changing to more effective approaches.[4]

The consequences for parents who are at odds, in adversarial relationships, who have a disorganized life can be severe. For adolescents, depression often accompanies suicidal thoughts, as an ultimate expression of helplessness. But common risk factors often involve family dynamics: physical or emotional abuse, constant parental arguing, or loss of a parent through death or divorce.[5]

ANOTHER WAY

Sometimes you may be at your wit's end and are doing the best you can, yet still falling far short of what you had intended to accomplish. Sometimes, when you are emotionally spent, discouraged, and worn out, you could use a good suggestion. I recommend *Discipline: 101 Alternatives to Nagging, Yelling, and Spanking: Ways to Stop Hurting Your*

Kids and Start Helping Them by Dr. Alvin Price and Jay Parry.[6] Price and Parry have compiled a healthy, fun, workable, and positive collection of alternatives that lead to creative and ingenious solutions rather than anger and hurtful parental acting out when children misbehave. They deal directly with the frustration parents often feel and provide answers when you are stuck in ineffective ways of responding. If you feel that you are controlling your children excessively, I recommend you study *Control Freaks: Who They Are and How to Stop Them from Running Your Life,* by Gerald Piaget, and *Imperative People: Those Who Must Be in Control,* by Dr. Les Carter.[7] All change begins with an awareness of where we are, what we are doing, or what effects we are having that we don't want.

As we all learn sooner or later, the impact we have on those we love and live with can be indelible and long lasting. But that awareness alone does not simplify or smooth the process of influence. It is tough to communicate in the ways you want; it is also tough, when you are living with others, to *not* communicate. It is inevitable that you will be an example, for good or ill. At your worst, someone has joked, you can serve as a clear warning to others; at your best, your children become better just because you are there. It will feel better when you leave coercion behind and invite an arrangement that will work for both you and the child. It will be worth your while to consider a shift to a different type of power.

MAKING DEALS—THE POSSIBILITIES AND THE DANGERS OF UTILITY POWER AT HOME

Everything I would like to say about the problems with deals has already been said and supported well in another book, *Punished by Rewards: The Trouble with Gold Stars, Incentive Plans, A's, Praise and Other Bribes,* by Alfie Kohn.[8] I strongly recommend that you read this book. It changed how I think and deal with my children. It will change how you think about influencing your children, and will enlighten you about a huge assortment of problems we create for ourselves in relationships outside of our homes when we negotiate deals with others. We tend to do as parents what was done to us when we were children, without counting the cost or thinking through if it is getting us what we really want. The difficulties associated with building awareness and developing new skills have been noted. When you see the process of parenting as more than a set of deals to get the work done or eliminate the annoyances of disappointing or disapproved behavior in your children, you can be liberated to a different kind of relationship with your own children. In the process, you will come to see negotiation for what it is, an approach that seldom offers what it promises.

In essence, Kohn's masterful, carefully documented book teaches a new answer to the question, Do rewards motivate people? The answer is they absolutely do—they motivate people to get rewards. Kohn profusely documents and makes a compelling case for the problems with the carrot as incentive. Six reasons are illustrated: rewards actually punish, rewards rupture relationships, rewards ignore reasons, rewards discourage risk taking, rewards reduce intrinsic motivation, and rewards in the form of praise are controlling and ultimately ineffective.

It is not effective and, Kohn contends, it is not right to treat children (or anyone else, for that matter) like pets in some big experiment where we decide what is going on and who gets what. Practice does not make perfect, as many parents have noticed. But practice, especially the repetition of a way of dealing with our children in our attempt to get them to do what we want, does make permanent. Children do learn, when we make deals with them. They learn to make deals. And they learn, unwittingly perhaps, that many things are not worth doing unless one is rewarded for them. The long-term effect of making deals leads to a mind-set that says I won't do anything unless I have a deal. It is difficult to transition away from contrived consequences. We all learn what we live, as parents and as children. We can stop controlling, in the seductive, deliberate way characteristic of utility power, and shift to another, better way. Don't disagree with me out of hand; read the book soon. In the meantime, read the next section and see if the alternative to deal making is not practically attractive.

PARENTS WHO INFLUENCE WITH HONOR— PRINCIPLE-CENTERED POWER AT HOME

Some parents seem to make a positive, significant difference in the lives of their children without demeaning them or making deals with them. They live with honor. They still experience the highs and lows that are a part of life, but they are not overwhelmed by either success or failure in the short term. They recognize that things will not always go the way they want, but they believe fundamentally in the capacity their children have to self-correct, given time, good examples, and an atmosphere of loving acceptance. Happy families are different in how they apply the principles of power. They are not scripted. Living with honor is not a matter of technique, nor is it a series of steps or formulas. Living with honor requires a healthy view of yourself and your children; and with that perspective you adapt as needed, with the changing needs of both parents and children. Your goal is understanding more than compliance; growth more than regimentation. And you recognize that living honorably in a family is a somewhat messy, unpredictable process that never ends. You will learn from your children as they are learning from you.

Parents who influence with honor see the various roles they play as different lenses through which they can view, understand, and help their children. For instance, parents have significant roles as leaders and teachers. Dr. Benjamin Spock, who as an active ninety-three-year old spent his days revising his book on baby and child care, which had already sold nearly fifty million copies, concluded that with all the changes in demographics of modern society, what was most needed today is parents who can give their children firm but loving leadership. I agree. Parents *must* be leaders, leaders who show the way, then inspire, teach, and live with courage.

Some parents extend their teaching role into the place of the school. There is a growing group of committed parents who have removed their children from public or private schools and have created home schools. In cooperation with the school districts, they teach classes, develop curricula, evaluate performance, and coordinate learning for their own children. Groups of parents sometimes organize for large group activities, such as drama, chorus, and athletics. Studies suggest that children who are home-schooled enter college with skill and achievement levels on a par with their age-mates who participated in traditional schooling. Home schooling is time-consuming and an enterprise not to be entered into lightly. But most of those who choose to teach their own children report benefits that make the extra effort more than worth it.

WHAT WORRIES THE CHILD?

Many children are hurting and worried. They may be fearful and unsure. A recent poll sought to determine the biggest concerns, problems, and challenges facing teenagers today. Here are the top five, as reported by the teens themselves:

1. Loneliness
2. Disappointment with self
3. Conflict with parents
4. Negative peer pressure
5. Pain—death and problems in the world

Whatever we do, we can help our children with these issues if we create the safe, trusting conditions that enable them to feel safe with us, because they know we not only have their best interests at heart, but we honor them in the communication process. Because we honor them, they come to respect themselves. One study of teens pregnant without the benefit of marriage concluded that the problem was not ignorance of contraception methods and the conception process, but low self-esteem, feelings of inadequacy, and uncertainty about their own acceptability. Perhaps if they felt an increased sense of honor for themselves, they would choose healthier, alternative ways to feel accepted. Their needs are now and the time is now to make a difference in their lives. The Chinese say that "the dawn does not come twice to awaken a man." Teaching and leading and loving our children must be a priority. You cannot skip a month or a year or a season and reenter the relationship where you left it. You must act early, when their interests are transparent and the issues are small; then they may less reluctantly approach you later when their interests are disguised and the issues are huge.

CHANGE YOUR PERSPECTIVE, CHANGE YOUR APPROACH

A thoughtful friend gave us an embroidered, beautifully framed quotation as we started our family. Today, Shawny has hung it above the washing machine in our home, as a reminder and an invitation. I have been unable to identify the author, but I wish I could personally thank him or her for the inspiration and wisdom formed in a few lines, which has often caused us to choose to spend time with our children when other voices called for our attention elsewhere. It is entitled "Children Won't Keep."

> *Cleaning and scrubbing can wait 'til tomorrow*
> *For babies grow up, we've learned to our sorrow.*
> *So quiet down cobwebs; dust go to sleep;*
> *I'm rocking my baby and babies don't keep.*

With children, you are constantly choosing—do you get after them or do you support them? Do you care for them? Be careful to not invest more time in taking care of things than in taking care of these important people. Do you do too much *for* them and thereby diminish your opportunities and energy to do things *with* them? This is always a matter of wisdom and judgment, and you don't have to "get it right" every time to honorably influence your children. I remember an experience with our teenage son who wanted a bicycle. He didn't want just any bicycle, he wanted a high-tech mountain bike with full suspension and custom parts and a high price. I didn't know that such bicycles were even available. And from a parent's perspective, this boy was unreasonable; he had not been pursuing mountain biking. He was not a member of a bicycle club, his old bike was rusting in the carport, and he didn't have enough money.

It seemed like an open-and-shut case to us, but he persisted. He read bicycle magazines. He spent hours at the bike shops, looking over the new, expensive specialty bikes. He tried to convince my wife and me, alone and together, that it was not only a good decision, but that life as he knew it might end if the purchase was not only approved but financially supported by us, with a loan he would eventually pay back. We tried to listen objectively, but his desires seemed so outrageous that we quickly grew impatient and started drawing lines. The kitchen became a no-communication zone. Certain subjects became taboo at mealtime. Tension mounted. I pushed him to see my way. After all, I was objective and *knew* what was best, and I *was* the father.

The arguments lasted all summer. A critical moment finally arrived when a group of his friends decided to take an overnight bicycle trip. Our boy needed a bike for the trip. We had to make a decision. We wanted him to learn something from the experience, but we had also been worn down by the endless arguing that by now seemed to deteriorate quickly into a shouting match with hurt feelings and little communication as the only outcome. I finally gave in. We had not been able to convince him to forgo the expensive bicycle and purchase something reasonable. But the harder I pushed, the harder he pushed back. It seemed that the issue changed—it was not about a bicycle but about trust and the freedom to make independent choices. The day before the big trip, I told my son he could purchase the bike he so desperately wanted, and that I would loan him the money to make the purchase. I still remember the grin on his face as he headed out the door with my check, his money, and an eager friend, finally "free" to get the bicycle of his dreams.

That evening, when I arrived home, I greeted my son and asked to see the bike. He said I couldn't see the bike because he hadn't bought it. I was astounded. What was going on? What about the big trip? What had happened? A slight smile crossed his face as he looked at me directly and said, "Dad, I couldn't buy the bike. As long as you wouldn't let me get it, I had to have it. But when I actually had the money in my hand, and was standing in the bike shop in front of the bike, I couldn't do it. I couldn't spend that much money on a bike I would seldom ride."

I was speechless. I had thought all along that I had to talk him out of the purchase, that I had to prevail against his friends' influence, that I had to do whatever it took to make sure he did not make this big financial blunder. As long as I took responsibility for the purchase, he felt free to let me, and to badger us with his wants and demands. When he finally felt responsible, he made the decision we wanted him to make, but he made it for personal, private reasons, as his values came up against his wants and desires. I gained new respect for my son that day. What about the big bike trip? He borrowed his brother's bicycle, went on the trip, and had a great experience. He decided it was a better deal to rent a bicycle from his brother than to go into debt to me and spend his entire summer earnings for something *he* knew he was not really interested in.

A happy ending for our son and for us. And the lessons learned lasted for many months, until school started and he decided that what he really wanted was to become a professional golfer, so he would need a set of rather expensive golf clubs, and a bag, and . . . And so the need for parents to parent goes on. But with each successive communication, each session of give-and-take, each apology and each reaffirmation of love, we grow. We are learning to honor each other. After the bicycle incident, my son approached me and thanked me for supporting him, listening to him, and staying with him while he worked through the issues. And he hugged me as he slipped my original check—the bicycle loan—back into my pocket.

As parents, we do not "arrive" and the process does not end. You, like us, will never finish the process. We pause and see what we have learned and what they have become, and we go on. The never-ending nature of parenting reminds me of the couplet expressed by the comedian Phyllis Diller:

> *Cleaning your house while your kids are still growing*
> *Is like shoveling the walk before it stops snowing.*

DO YOU WANT TO BE RIGHT OR HAPPY?

The other day, my wife, Shawny, and I were having a rather heated "discussion." I was having a little fun with the issue, but she was taking it pretty seriously. At one point she turned to me in exasperation and said, "All right, Blaine—do you want to be right . . . or do you want to be happy?" That really got me thinking. What do you want in your intimate relationships? When arguments and conflicts arise with your spouse, check your motive. Do you want to be right? Or do you want to be happy? Will you allow pride to get in the way of peace? Enzio Busche has suggested that pride asks *"Who* is right?" while humility asks, *"What* is right?" If we are truly humble, we will open our hearts and then we can learn the principles that are most useful, that will enable us to influence with honor because we have truly honored our children. Sometimes we will learn the most valuable lessons from our children, if we will listen.

LEARNING FROM OUR CHILDREN

Not only do we influence: we are influenced. In fact, we have little influence with our children unless we allow them to influence us. This does not mean to let them run over you, nor does it mean to completely let them have their way with you. (Although I heard a comic suggest that if your children want to learn to drive, don't stand in their way!) But it does mean that you give them choices and allow them to exercise those choices according to their age and maturity whenever possible. It means you require respect from them and you model respect by giving it to them. This approach avoids the permissive versus rigid dichotomy because when you truly honor someone, you not only expect much of them, but you are willing to help them achieve it. You do not abandon them. You do not smother them. You honor them. And you affirm that you honor them by listening to them, deeply and without judgment. A client illustrated his growing capacity to listen empathically with this incident:

> One day my son was telling me that he didn't want to go to his class roller skating party. Normally, I would have cut loose with a barrage of reasons (my reasons) why he needed to go. For example, he would be seen as antisocial, he should support the activity, maybe he would enjoy it, what would others think, etc. Instead, this time I tried to just listen. I reflected back to him what he was saying. I rephrased his words. I listened for his feelings as well as the "facts." I had never spent that much time listening to him, as I always knew the answer to his problems. Right? Eventually, he reminded me that he had asked for new roller skates last year, and I had told him he was getting too old for roller skating. He took it to heart and decided I was right; he was too old. But, in the first thirty minutes, he had ten other reasons why he didn't want to go. He ended up not going, but what mattered to me was that we both finally understood each other by the end of our discussion.

You can develop your listening skills. You can even learn to listen under pressure, or when the subject is you. The best book I know that helps develop the practical side of listening with empathy is *I Don't Have to Make Everything All Better* by parent and family therapist Dr. Gary Lundberg and writer Joy Saunders Lundberg.[9] With numerous encouraging and helpful examples, the Lundbergs demonstrate how to validate our children, our spouse, and others without robbing them of the responsibility for their own behavior.

EXAMPLE TEACHES MORE POWERFULLY THAN WORDS

The subtle power of example was underscored in a simple way recently in my home. We have built a tradition of family prayer, all of us kneeling in a circle in our home at the beginning and ending of each day, to express gratitude, to acknowledge blessings, to ask for heavenly help with specific challenges and opportunities, to pray for friends and family members. Each of us, including the youngest, takes a turn offering this family prayer. It is sometimes humorous and always awareness building to listen to our children pray, in innocence and with simple faith. Because of an accident that led to reconstruction of my left knee, I kneel on my right knee only. One morning in the middle of our prayer, I opened one eye to see if our youngest was still in the circle with us. I nearly laughed out loud when I looked around the circle and observed that each of my children was kneeling on their right knee, just as I was!

A colleague at the Covey Leadership Center tells of an incident in the life of his great-grandfather that has become a part of their family folklore, establishing a kind of intergenerational wisdom of what effective parenting is about. The great-grandfather had instituted the habit of eating breakfast with his family daily, and after breakfast going around the table kissing each child on the forehead. It was a time of regular physical contact and a moment of reassurance that each was loved. One Valentine's Day the routine changed. His eight-year-old son, Wesley, had sent a mean-spirited, anonymous valentine to the neighborhood bully, and was giggling and bragging about it in whispered tones to his older brother during breakfast.

Apparently overhearing enough to understand what had happened, the grandfather made no mention of it, but when the meal was finished, he kissed each child on the forehead, except Wesley. Then turning from the table, he indicated that he would like to see Wesley alone; that translated into "Come into my study; we need to talk."

What Wesley must have thought and felt as he followed his father out of the kitchen was not recorded. All the others knew about what followed was what they learned from Wesley sometime later. He entered his father's study, noticing that he had pulled the big family Bible down from the shelf. The father pulled his son close and read a passage from scripture, then excused the boy. Just as the boy was leaving the room, the father called out, "Remember that I love you." My colleague said he heard Wesley, as a man of eighty-four, recount this tender experience with his father, tears streaming down his cheeks.

One moral of this story is that perhaps the answers to our problems are found in scripture. Perhaps another moral is that the key to memorable teaching and enduring discipline is respect, intensity, and privacy. And maybe a critical learning from this family incident is that if we have cultivated an atmosphere of trust and love, with expectations of standards to be pursued, the course corrections we make with our children can be made with a lighter touch than we think. I asked my colleague if this incident provided a pattern he followed with his children. He indicated two things: first, he struggled because some of his children responded to a word or a look, but others required louder, more intense attention; and second, that he always wanted to be more like his great-grandfather. This good father continued to learn from and be inspired by an intergenerational example that is too rare today.

Without the blessing of intergenerational wisdom, we may get most of our cues about parenting and success and values from the media messages bombarding us and our children daily. It appears that something "out there" will finally make us happy, if we can just get it before they are "nearly gone," because they are "going fast." We sometimes are off the mark when we think we know what will make our children happy. Too often, our children's dreams are reduced to shopping lists. And as parents, you may get sidetracked or derailed into thinking that there is something you can buy that will fill the growing vacuum in their lives. There is not. As this father learned so many years ago, you may provide part of the answers your children are seeking if you give them part of yourself. The best reinforcer you can provide your children is often the most personal—a gift of time and energy and genuine interest from you. The best offering you can make to your child is yourself.

ENCOURAGEMENT FOR HUSBANDS AND WIVES

If you are a single parent, with major emotional or financial responsibilities for your children, you may feel isolated, alone, and solitary. You may feel that the system, your former spouse, or the world is unfair. You may be filled with anger and resentment. Or you may have sized up your situation, acknowledged the new realities you are facing, and chosen to move on, making the best of a difficult situation. The fact is, children don't just need two parents; they need two parents who love and care for each other and them. One parent who cares for them is preferable to two who don't really care for each other. Therapist and educator John Rosemond has made it his business to debunk what he calls the myth of single parenthood. Yes, he says, it can be more difficult to be on the front lines alone, all the time; it is also less complicated than having to coordinate your entire life with another person:

> Raising a child on your own is surely different from raising a child within an intact family, but it is only as difficult as the single parent thinks it is. One single parent curses his isolation, saying that he has to make all the decisions. Another rejoices at her independence, saying that she gets to make all the decisions. If you believe that raising a child on your own will be an insurmountable hardship, it will be just that. If, on the other hand, you convince yourself that raising your children independently is one of the greatest opportunities for creative living you've ever had, then you will use that positive force to create opportunity after opportunity for yourself and your children. . . . No, you can't be a mother and a father too, but you can be a whole, fulfilled person, with more than enough vitality to share with your children. Do you want to believe it?[10]

For those of you who are married, yet who struggle with spouses who are not everything you dreamed they would be, I have a specific suggestion: hang in there. When you get to the end of your rope, tie a knot and hang on. As both Benjamin Franklin and Jesse James have been quoted as saying, "If we don't hang together, we will hang separately." Let me provide two reasons for my encouragement. The first reason comes from a professional observation. I was visiting with a friend of mine, a therapist in private practice who specializes in the problems of adolescents and families. I shared a concern about a twelve-year-old boy I knew who was acting out and was being rejected by his family.

My friend's first question was not about the boy, but about the family. The animosity and family fighting were escalating to the point of threats to place the boy in a foster home. She asked if both of his parents were still in the home. Yes, I answered, but they have many problems of their own. She considered the presence of both parents a major variable in the prediction of serious antisocial behavior among children, and a major source of influence on what would happen later to the child. Essentially, her professional opinion was that if both parents were still at home, that is, if the family unit was still intact, *even if there were strained relations between the mother and the father,* the boy had twice the chance of eventually turning out all right.

The second reason for my encouragement comes from a pair of remarkable women who studied and wrote about the lives of normal couples who managed to stay together for thirty to fifty years. The observations and interviews made by Ronna Romney and Beppie Harrison with a wide variety of couples are candid, revealing, and inspiring. They looked at couples who were different socially and financially and in their living styles, yet who all considered themselves happy, and had the conviction that the work of making the relationship grow was worth it. These couples had good times and bad times. They had made mistakes and hurt the person they loved. They had had their own feelings hurt, argued, and had taken furious walks alone. But after these crises, they stopped, went back, and tried again.

These people learned to say they were sorry before they felt sorry, because regaining peace was more important than the thing they had argued about. They had learned how to fight, how to block out areas that were too sensitive, and had relationships that were still growing, changing, and becoming. They had learned that not all of their problems had to be solved overnight. They had learned that the fantastic night might not be the night of their anniversary, but a few days later when for some reason everything clicked. They had worked out a unique pattern for living together that suited them. These long-term marriages had all endured times when it seemed easier to just walk out; but nobody walked. Each partner had been able to put aside their original expectations in the interest of marital harmony and try again when the first attempt or method failed. Many of the marriages were rooted solidly in at least one partner's determination that this marriage, unlike the one he or she knew as a child, was going to work and thrive. To summarize, they had all learned that you have to make your own marriage.

Not every marriage can work; some should not. But if you find yourself in a marriage that has glimpses of being right in between the frustrating patches, Romney and Harrison would encourage you to fight for it.[11]

THINKING—AND ACTING—TOGETHER

Marriage is not two people who are perfect at living, but two very imperfect people who become expert at forgiving. It is the spirit evoked in a quotation on the wall in our bedroom at home: "The purpose of marriage is not to think alike, but to think together." Conscientious, concerned, caring parents must also learn to love each other. Then they will have a growing capacity to love, teach, and honorably lead their own children. When a young couple married, after a somewhat stormy courtship, a friend suggested that perhaps they were at the end of their troubles. After two years, and a continuing struggle for control, acceptance, and partnership, the young husband remarked, "We may have been at the end of our troubles, but they didn't say *which* end."

When Shawny and I married, an older friend counseled us, "You will probably have children. But they are not the center of your marriage. You say you are 'in love.' But do you like each other? Are you friends? You need to know that the best thing you can ever do for your children is to love each other." In other words, the children don't come first. The marriage must come first. Both of you can bend yourselves to that larger entity, and then the marriage provides stability that sustains each of you individually as well as the children. That has turned out to be very wise counsel.

Do you husbands and wives love each other? Truly love each other? How do you know? In any dictionary, the word "love" is found as a verb as well as a noun. Love must be demonstrated. Are you like the old gentleman who, standing at the graveside of his wife of forty years, was heard to remark, "She was a dear woman. I really loved her . . . and I nearly told her once." Or are you like the woman who reminded her husband, "I told you, the day we married, that I loved you. If that ever changes, you will be the first to know!" Another woman asked of her husband of ten years, "Do you love me or do you not? You told me once, but I forgot."

We all forget what is not rekindled anew. If we do not rebuild it, the love in our lives starts to deteriorate. We need to give and receive a handful of hugs each day to sustain our sense of acceptance, trust, and esteem. If those hugs are accompanied by a word of appreciation, a compliment, or an affirmation that is sincere, we will thrive. One psychologist suggests a ratio of ten compliments to every statement of constructive criticism. What is the norm in your home? What is the current balance in the emotional bank account you have with your spouse and children? You can change the environment you live in by changing how you treat those you live with. It isn't what they do for us that causes us to love them; it is what we do for them. The habits of caring that become a lifestyle for us become the basis for longevity as well as influence, and will lead to relationships that last.

John Gottman, a psychologist at the University of Washington, studied more than two thousand married couples over two decades, in an attempt to discover the key to sustained marriages. The couples he studied had been married from twenty to forty years to the same partners. He learned that how couples communicate reveals whether or not their marriage will survive. Couples who argue vigorously can have a successful, lasting marriage and so can couples who avoid confrontations altogether. But when criticism, contempt, defensiveness, or stonewalling (refusing to communicate) become habitual, the marriage is in jeopardy.

Communication can become difficult in marriage when you are overwhelmed by negativity and your natural talents for resolving differences are lost. Validation and healthy approaches to resolving conflict need to become second nature so they won't abandon you when you need them most. Gottman concluded that even with wide differences in occupations, lifestyles, and styles of marriage, strong undercurrents of love and respect were the continuing, reliable antidote for criticism, defensiveness, and stonewalling.[12]

Parents can make an enormous difference in the lives of their children. Parenting can be fun. It is worthwhile. It is perhaps more important than we know. It may be true that one of the primary benefits of having children is that as parents we learn so much from the experience. Our children won't really learn until they have children of their own. Whatever your current relationship with your children, you can influence them and create improved relationships that will be fulfilling and enriching for the rest of your life as you learn to influence with honor.

QUESTIONS AND ACTIVITIES TO HELP YOU ASSESS WHAT YOU WANT AND HOW YOU ARE DOING

1. What was the primary teaching/disciplining style in your home when you were a child—doubt, fear, fairness, or honor?

2. When you are under emotional pressure, what is your first response to a crisis in your own home today?

3. When you or your spouse have handled a problem particularly well, pause and analyze what happened. What were you feeling? Did your emotions help or hinder? What was the source of the ideas and actions that worked? Congratulate and reinforce each other. If it happened at all, it can happen again.

4. When are you most vulnerable? When are you likely to do something to your children that you regret? Review the lists in Chapter 4 and begin to catalogue what goes on when you are not successful. Building awareness is often a sensitizing process that marks the beginning of a real change.

5. How would you characterize your dominant approach to influencing your children today—powerlessness, coercive power, utility power, or principle-centered power? Establish a personal goal and commitment to move from whichever level you tend to function at to the next higher level. You might want to conduct a family council, listening to your children's concerns, making your children

aware of each type of power and of your commitment to improve. Enlist their aid.

6. Establish a set of agreed-upon signals that will allow your spouse to intervene when you are too emotionally involved to objectively discipline a child. Support each other in the middle of the problem, and debrief later to brainstorm better alternatives for next time.

7. If your children are still young, visit with an older couple you respect whose children are raised or have left home. Ask them what worked best for them, what they regret having done, what really mattered in the long run, and what they feel good about. A shift in perspective often accompanies such an open dialogue.

8. Remember that family life is a living laboratory. No one has all the answers. No one has it all together. We can improve if we keep working at it. Do your best, then do better the next time. You *can* do it.

CHAPTER 10

TEACHING WITH POWER—HOW TO HONOR THOSE YOU TEACH

> The highest function of the teacher consists not so much in imparting knowledge as in stimulating the pupil in its love and pursuit. To know how to suggest is the art of teaching.
>
> HENRI AMIEL

PRINCIPLE-CENTERED TEACHER POWER

The most significant person in your life may have been a teacher. Perhaps you are a teacher today. Teachers profoundly affect us. Education and the teaching profession are part of an important foundation for our competencies and capabilities, our values and beliefs, our society, and our way of life. I have a deep, personal commitment to education, having taught high school and college, having been a principal in a private residential school for troubled teenagers, and having taught for church, scouting, and civic organizations all of my life. But schools, students, and educators are in trouble.

Consider the following three scenes:

Scene A. A five-year-old returning frustrated from his first day at school told his mother: "I'm not going back." "Why? Didn't you like school?" she wanted to know. "No," the boy replied. "I can't read, I can't write and they won't let me talk."

Scene B. Mother to son: "You have to get up and get ready for school now." Angry son's response, "*No!*" "Why not?" the mother asked, trying to be understanding. "I'll give you three reasons. The kids don't like me. The teachers don't like me. And it is no fun." The mother responded, "I'll give you three reasons why you must go. They are expecting you. You are forty-two. And you are the principal."

Scene C. Administrator: "I create resources for learning." Principal: "I build supportive learning environments." Teacher: "I help children discover the beauty of the world." Child: "I hate school!"

Humorous or serious? The challenges facing teachers who care and want to make a difference are many. But who is in control? Who has the power? Some teachers may say, "The problem is with the parents. They don't care. They blame us, but they don't come see what goes on every day. They don't support our activities and programs. They don't follow up on homework and assignments. They don't hold their own children accountable. They won't turn off the television. How do they expect us to undo the damage from many years of inadequate parenting? We can't do it alone."

Some parents may feel that the teachers are the ones who do not care, who worry only about their time off, their pay increase, their programs, their second job, and not about the children they are paid to teach. In addition, in the midst of an information explosion, we have what John Naisbitt described as a "world drowning in detail but starving for knowledge."[1] According to one report, in a single edition of the *New York Times* there is more information than a person had to process in their entire lifetime a few hundred years ago. Today, available information is reported to double every few years. The president of the New York Public Library, Vartan Gregorian, has observed that one way of paralyzing people is by inundating them with trivia.[2] The explosion of information is not equivalent to the explosion of knowledge. When information becomes a commodity, wisdom and judgment are at a premium. Teachers hold the key to unlocking the timeless wisdom of principles rooted in the natural capacities of our children. Principles do not change; but if we honor them, they can change us.

WHERE IS THE POWER IN SCHOOLS?

Is the power in our schools today to teach these principles? The nationally recognized educator James Comer describes the overwhelming problems that surface when power is lacking:

> When children do not learn or behave well in school many on a school staff experience a sense of failure and feel powerless. . . . Out of a sense of frustration, disappointment, and anger, parents and consumer groups often mobilize to attack schools. Administrators and teachers often mobilize power to acquire new resources to protect themselves. These efforts often lead to a chaotic and episodic movement of power to the groups most able to mobilize at a given moment. Teaching, learning, and school behavior do not significantly improve. Rather, apathy, anger, and conflict are often the final product. People often lash out at one another. The fighting is often subtle. . . . Being late to an assembly when a highly controlling principal wants a teacher to be on time is one of the ways to get back at or undermine the higher authority person who demands performance but does not provide adequate leadership and support. Not participating in school programs is one way that parents express alienation, anger, and objection to the operation of the school program. Children who receive the "school is the enemy" message often go after the enemy—act up, undermine the teacher, undermine the school program, or otherwise exercise their veto power. In a school where parents, teachers, and administrators are struggling for power, the principal most likely has little. But while the parents and teachers have more power, it usually cannot be used effectively. The power of all involved is amorphous, fragmented, and tenuous. Thus nobody is able to address the school mission in a cooperative, systematic, sustained way, and the conditions contributing to student veto power grow and, in some schools, prevail. Administrators, teachers, and parents are paralyzed and powerless.[3]

Powerless or powerful? What is possible today in the classroom? The truth is that all these parties—parents, students, teachers, administrators, citizens—influence what happens in the classroom. But we have entered a phase in our society where education is valued for what it will give you rather than what it will make out of you. The result is that because teachers don't have that which society considers important in terms of wealth and status, the teaching profession is looked down upon, and teachers are disempowered.[4]

When I was a high school principal, I regularly invited each of my teachers to be "principal for a day." In that role, they did what I normally did, handling the flow of problems that came up during the day, making decisions, dealing with student and parent concerns, and so on, while I took their classes for the day. We both learned from this experience. I certainly gained an important perspective that enabled me to listen to the teachers' concerns with greater empathy. And they better understood why I made many of the requests I did during a normal school day. This exchange gave us each a better understanding, because the process allowed each of us to enter the world of the other, to get to know the demands placed upon the other, and to be more sensitive to the rationale behind the decisions and actions we each had to make.

The art of teaching, and the act of learning, primarily take place because a teacher creates the environment, orchestrates available resources, capitalizes on teaching moments, sometimes pushes back the desks, and does what it takes to help children. A country doctor's motto suggests, "Cure occasionally; help frequently; comfort always."[5] There is a parallel for teachers. We cannot reach or teach everyone. Every new teacher starts with a dream to reach the world—every person, every student, every class. Some teachers become cynical after a while, after being put down and ignored and opposed. They end up thinking, feeling, and sometimes even believing that no one can be reached. They convince themselves the battle is not worth it anyway. But teachers can help this one student . . . that one . . . the lonely one . . . the forgotten one. And teachers can influence many. When that influence is based on fear, it is coercive. It doesn't work for long and there are many unexpected and disruptive side effects.

AVOIDING THE PROBLEMS WITH PUNISHMENT BY CREATING ORDER, INSPIRATION, AND HOPE

Teachers who influence with honor avoid the shortcut mentality projected by other teachers who buy into a philosophy of force and fear. "Give 'em hell; be a tyrant the first week; put the fear in 'em for a few days and they won't give you any trouble all year." Every new teacher hears this conventional wisdom. This mantra is chanted each fall by teachers who do not know there is another, better way. Research has consistently shown that teachers who get after students for leaving their seats will predictably observe an increase in seat leaving. Teachers who criticize students as a first line of defense end up criticizing more. This criticism trap is created by teachers who do not realize that what they give attention to increases. Like an old song suggests, if you accentuate the positive and eliminate the negative, you will create a memorable, powerful place and way of learning.

There will always be teachers who revert to bribes and payoffs, because they are things teachers can control. But such reinforcement systems are usually teacher-controlled systems, not learner-controlled, and over time students learn to perform only when the reward systems are in place.[6] Other teachers may feel compliant but helpless, hanging on for one more semester until retirement or a changed assignment will allow them to escape unhealthy and unrewarding days in the classroom. Helplessness in the classroom is tragic. Students learn what the teacher is living; and if the teacher defines himself as a victim, he models powerlessness. The teacher who lives with fear will likely elicit it in students. All of these approaches are dead ends. There is so much more that is possible. The atypical teacher is the one who influences with honor, and does not merely exist in the world, but changes the world by how she lives her life.

The goal of discipline in the classroom is to solve the problem while maintaining a relationship with the student.[7] Those two ends are not mutually exclusive. The second, relationship maintenance, determines how you achieve the first, problem solving. As Richard Curwin and Allen Mendler advocate, you *can* "discipline with dignity."[8] You can rely less on guilt and blame and spend more time planning future behavior change. The best teachers don't see themselves or their students as victims. Because they are not filled with fear, they do not elicit fear in their students. With dignity, humor, creativity, and honor, they consistently make a difference for good in their students' lives.

TEACHERS WHO MAKE A DIFFERENCE

I remember reflecting on this point a few years ago while driving to the funeral of a dear friend. Dr. Lyal Holder had been a professor at the university throughout the 1970s and 1980s. A tragic accident had taken his life and, to honor him, I had made arrangements to attend the memorial service that was to be held at a local church. I thought about our years together, first in a student-teacher relationship and then as colleagues.

Lyal and I had often taken prospective schoolteachers to a primitive desert area to teach survival skills, team building, and trust building. The most difficult challenge for most of these students was the rappelling. After instruction and practice, each of the students would be hooked to a rope and asked to go over the edge of a cliff, down a seventy-five-foot vertical embankment to safety below. It was a challenge for even the most macho student, and though some described later the rush of exhilaration that came with accomplishment, many openly admitted the anxiety bordering on terror that accompanied going over the ledge.

Lyal was an expert climber and a master at calming the students when they were afraid. He had an easy, gentle way about him that inspired relaxation even in the face of the seventy-five-foot drop. On one occasion, he had gone with a group of students to a popular climbing spot and had spent the day helping each student over the edge. He stayed on top, instructing and encouraging, until the last student had made it safely down. Then he retied the ropes, with the special knot that would hold as long as pressure was on it, and started over the edge himself. But something went wrong. The procedures were the same. Lyal had done this many times before, in the same spot. But for some inexplicable reason, this time the knot slipped, and Lyal fell to his death.

All the memories of our teaching times together flooded back as I located the church and entered the parking lot. I began wondering who else might attend the services that morning. Lyal had been a teacher who was more popular with some students than with others. He had a way of making students think, by answering a question with a question, and of pushing students to go beyond the superficial, to learn how to learn. Some were annoyed by his approach, because they were looking for the quick fix of easy answers and memorized responses. Lyal was patient and didn't mind making students squirm a little, if in the process they learned more. After a long teaching career, helping undergraduates and graduates prepare for service in public schools, his life was over. Who cared? I wondered. Who would want to remember him? What difference did he make with his sometimes eccentric, often annoying, but always genuine teaching style?

I soon had my answer. The little church was filled to overflowing. People were standing at the back and in the foyers as the music, initiating the memorial service, began. The eulogy was simple and straightforward. His widow and children softly wept. But then an amazing thing happened. One of his former students walked to the podium and began speaking. It was only for a moment, but the tribute told of how Lyal had touched a life by asking more and causing this person to dig a little deeper. Another former student stood before the microphone and told how Lyal had inspired her to become a school administrator. She spoke for seconds, but her words described the making of a legacy. Another spoke of choosing his profession based on the inspiration Lyal provided. Another spoke similarly. And another. There was a veritable avalanche of praise and recognition, unrehearsed accolade after unrehearsed accolade, praise for a man who had not sought praise, by former students who had seldom appreciated, at the time, the influence this quiet man had on them.

In my mind's eye, I imagined the pebble that was Lyal Holder, the small smooth stone that had been polished until it shined, being dropped into the ocean of humanity, and each student that had passed through his classroom was a ripple, small too at first, then swelling as it moved from its source well beyond its starting place to other classrooms, other schools, other communities far removed from the university town where Lyal lived and taught.

I have not forgotten that scene, and the lesson I learned that morning. I have not forgotten the power of Lyal Holder, who patiently and consistently invited students to grow, nor have I forgotten the students he taught, who became master teachers, principals, and school administrators in hundreds of schools, affecting tens of thousands of children and teenagers. What is the power of a teacher? How long does the influence last? Where will the ripples stop? The potential impact is great.

THE POWER OF YOUR WORDS

Sometimes it is the accumulated lessons taught and learned over a lifetime that impact us forever. Sometimes it is a phrase or word spoken, deliberately or thoughtlessly, in a critical moment of openness or vulnerability, that precipitates an action, adds a nudge of encouragement or the hesitation accompanying wisdom, that we remember and that affects us in enduring ways. An inspiring teacher shared her philosophy with me. "I believe that we can accelerate learning for all students, especially at-risk students, by building relationships. There is great power in the words we use. Using powerful, positive words is a great way to begin to build trust in relationships. I have been moved and forever changed by such words."

Sometimes we are influenced in happy, pleasant ways. Sometimes the words sting in ugly, hurtful ways. When students are acting up, acting out, testing limits of policies and personal patience, the real message is actually a question about worth, about acceptance, about okay-ness. "Do you love me, even though I can't read as well as Mary?" "Do you think I am important even though my clothes are not as nice as John's?" "Am I a nice person even though my father has an embarrassing drinking problem?" Such questions are rarely asked directly. With young children, the behavior is the question. Yelling at them, punishing them, and ignoring them without addressing the underlying questions can be a statement: "I don't like you, you stupid, poor, person from a troubled family!"[9]

The words we speak are powerful. They can become a bridge to beginning relationships, by inviting students and others to change their feelings, their ideas, and their behavior, toward themselves and toward us. Teaching causes a relatively permanent change in behavior. Principle-centered power invites us to use words that will build up, not tear down, so that the changes in behavior are positive. A wise and inspiring educator suggested that if you want to lift someone, to inspire them to live better, you don't have to tear down their house, but merely show them a better house in which to live.

A VISION OF TEACHING

It is instructive to consider the root of the word "education." To educate is, literally, to draw forth or bring out something latent, hidden, or unexpressed; to assume or work out from given facts; to summon or call forth; to call to mind by naming or suggesting; and to create anew, especially by means of the imagination. What a visionary notion of teaching! Most schools have some excellent teachers, some mediocre teachers, and some who do not belong in the profession. Master teachers can set the tone and pace of a school. Since many people are not proactive, these teachers can inspire others to lift their sights and adapt to the environment they create. If your fundamental belief is that you know and others don't, then your job is to *tell* them, *control* them, *force* them—whatever it takes to *fix* them. If, however, your fundamental belief is that the students already have greatness and capacity within them, and your job is to help them learn to appreciate anew what they already intuitively know, your approach will be entirely different. You don't have to force. In fact, you can't. You will find other ways to elicit and evoke, rather than announce, inform, and instill. You will grow it and not try to install it. You will create the conditions that allow children to flourish, like master gardeners weeding and fertilizing and pruning but reverently acknowledging that the power, and the life, is in the children already. We cannot plug them in; we cannot give life to our students. We can, however, kill the spontaneity, creativity, and joy of learning, or we can create the conditions that help that life to grow and flourish and become.

Great teachers don't merely give the answers, nor do they merely share their own treasures, as valuable as that may be. Great teachers help students discover the greatness and possibilities within themselves. It may require a different kind of preparation, and more gentleness in your methods, but you can make a profound difference for good in the lives of those you teach. This sensitivity can't be forced. One of my young children brought home from school a short poem about a turtle. The poem told how a group of children found a small box turtle one day and wanted it to "play." But the turtle, frightened and bewildered, quickly pulled in its head. Then one of the children got a stick and tried to force the turtle to "come out and play." In spite of good intentions, the children killed the turtle.

Sometimes we are the turtle; sometimes we are the well-meaning but misguided child with the stick. Teachers must have the wisdom and skill to manifest the tough love described in Chapter 7. By carefully balancing firmness and gentleness, courage and consideration, structure and playful spontaneity, powerful teachers cause us to believe in ourselves. We begin to believe in ourselves because we believe in them. We celebrate all of our lives the relationships that result.

PROGRAMS DON'T CHANGE PEOPLE

Bill Milliken, a former school administrator, likes to say, "Programs don't change people; relationships change people." The careful cultivation of relationships remains one of the most powerful, profound things a teacher can do to impact students. A survey of managers of Fortune 500 companies concluded that managers need to get closer to their employees if they want to be good coaches. Openness, trust, and friendship were cited by the majority of respondents as key factors to a successful relationship.[10] Could it be that what good teachers have always known and done is finally being discovered by the corporate world? Relationships matter most. Socrates had remarkable insight when he proclaimed, "Who can I teach but my friends?"

Teachers who honor their students, who build relationships characterized by openness, patience, love, and discipline are rare and wonderful. Sara Lightfoot, professor of education at Harvard, describes both the plight of the powerless and the possibilities of transformational teachers as follows:

All good teachers have in common is that they regard themselves as thinkers, as existing in the world of ideas. This is true for a nursery teacher and a professor in the most distinguished university. The currency is ideas—but ideas as conveyed through relationships.

It requires extraordinary courage, nurturance, attention, energy, commitment, empathy, a sense of orchestration.

Most teachers feel excluded from the most critical decisions on school policy; they feel like front row spectators in a reform movement in which the signals are being called by governors, legislators, state education figures—everybody except them. When you're not participating in making the decisions about what it is you do every day, you feel powerless.

In our schools, students are mostly trained to get to the answer quickly. Part of teaching is helping students learn how to tolerate ambiguity, consider possibilities, and ask questions that are unanswerable. Adolescents listen for the truth. They can tell when adults are not authentic—so if you're asking them to take on adventure through a hard set of ideas, and you're not willing to go along, it's unlikely that they will be.[11]

What is the effect on ordinary schools with ordinary students and extraordinary problems when such teachers are empowered and mobilized? Lightfoot calls these new schools "good schools," with the belief that any school, regardless of its setting or its available funding, can become such a school. These good schools:

—are places where people set goals and standards and hold each other accountable.

—have leaders who talk about listening, building a sense of community, sustaining relationships, and supporting people through failure.

—have a sense of mission that kids and adults can all articulate. They have an identity. They have a character, a quality that's their own, that feels quite sturdy. They have a set of values. If you walk down the hall, kids will say, in their own language, "This is what this school is about. This is who we are." And adults will echo those same kinds of values. There is a kind of ideological stance that brings coherence to the school.

—support individual teachers in their personal, idiosyncratic expression. They allow them, as one principal puts it, to "disturb the inertia." These wonderful people are rewarded for being wonderful rather than denigrated for being wonderful, other good people are encouraged to be good, and relatively mediocre folks are inspired or nudged and supported in becoming better.[12]

Teachers in such schools have a voice in decision making, are recognized for their subject matter expertise, and are protected to share, love, serve, and give what they have to give. What must society do to attract and sustain such competent, high-character individuals back into a profession that needs them? What can teachers proactively do in the interim?

THE TEACHER AS LEADER, SHOWING THE WAY AND INVITING OTHERS TO FOLLOW

Every schoolchild knows the name of Helen Keller, the remarkable woman who has lifted our ideas about the limits of limitations. It was Helen Keller who said, "I am grateful for my handicaps, for through them I found my self, my work, and my God." But the story behind the story is the lifetime of sacrifice, vision, and service of another remarkable woman, Anne Sullivan, her teacher.[13] Helen Keller described herself as a ship lost at sea, in dense fog, groping her way to shore, without compass or sounding light or even an idea of where the harbor was. The light that came into her life was Anne Sullivan, and the day she arrived was later described as her "soul's birthday."

Anne had an extremely difficult life. Her mother died when she was young; her father disappeared. She lived with an aunt and uncle who didn't want her. She ended up with a sick brother in an almshouse—a public place of death and disease—all but abandoned by family, friendless, and nearly blind herself.

But something inside her refused to die, refused to give up. No matter how terrible the conditions of her life became, she never let go of hope or of her own humanity. She knew the pain that was born of ignorance, and she determined to not be ignorant anymore. School became the tool she used to shed herself of ignorance. In just six years, having had no other formal education, she graduated valedictorian of her class from the Perkins Institute for the Blind. Anne Sullivan's life had prepared her to become a teacher. Her first student—her only student—was Helen Keller. Helen Keller described her teacher's impact this way:

> Anyone can take children to the classroom, but only a teacher can lead them to learn. They must feel that liberty is theirs. They must feel the flush of the victory and they must also feel the heart sinking of disappointment. They must feel these things. . . . This was the very center of Teacher's work with me: to lessen my physical dependence on her and make it possible for me to someday continue my work without her. Teacher believed in me and I have resolved not to betray her faith. Conscious of her always, I have sought for new ways to give life to men and women whom darkness, silence, sickness, and sorrow are wearing away. It seems my teacher who touched my night flame is still about her work, using me to kindle other fires for good.[14]

Teachers who lead, rather than merely dispense information and manage classrooms, develop students who may choose to follow them, as Helen Keller followed Anne Sullivan, and extended her work beyond what Anne had imagined. To lead is to create opportunities that open up possibilities in others. To lead is to know where you want to go and to make the journey so interesting and enticing that your students will want to go with you. To lead is to create a legacy that may live in the students you influenced with honor.

I will be forever grateful for some wise, principle-centered teachers whose influence is still with me after many years. Although I was not the only one who was powerfully affected by them, I am well aware of their impact at sensitive turning points in my life. These teachers reached me because they cared, because they were willing to go where I was, and because their desire, as manifested by the way they taught as well as how they lived their lives, was to influence honorably. I remember Mr. Hill in seventh grade who invited me to draw and play the ukulele for a school program, which began an interest in music that is an important part of my life today. Mr. Kaeselou, in the eighth grade, asked me to help in a tutoring project and I discovered how rewarding teaching can be. Dr. Hugh Baird was a college mentor who helped me stretch by giving me opportunities beyond my experience level, and then helped me be successful. When I was uncertain about what I had to contribute, he said he needed me. I cannot think of these men without feeling gratitude and appreciation for their investment in me.

My wife, Shawny, recently met a woman who remembered being with her in elementary school in a small logging town in Oregon during a wonderful time of learning and growing. They laughed and sighed together as they recalled wonder-filled years with ordinary teachers who freely shared their interests year-round with the children. These teachers cared about kids. There was no theater guild, but every summer a full dramatic production came to life, run by one fifth-grade teacher and a group of unskilled but enthusiastic neighborhood children. They learned to love poetry and literature because they had listened for hours to this dedicated teacher. Another teacher asked Shawny to direct *The Mikado,* and somehow, with his belief and enthusiasm, she did it. There was magic and mystery in those years and Shawny often talks about the teachers and that special time. These expanding experiences accelerated her achievement test scores and caused such enthusiasm for learning that when her family moved to another state, teachers from the old school contacted the teachers from the new school, and mutually agreed that she should be moved ahead one grade.

Telling isn't teaching—beyond the words, it is what we experienced and what we felt that profoundly affected us. Teachers who influence with honor see beyond the moment; they know they are building for the future. They are neither reluctant nor afraid to invite partnerships with students and parents, citizens and administrators. They know that many eyes are watching them, so they judge less and guide more. They see themselves as mentors, not walking encyclopedias. They know they will not reach every student, but they also have learned that it is not always possible to know ahead of time which lives will be affected by what they do. So they spend more time opening than closing doors. They spend time creating options and do what they can within systems and hierarchies that are less than perfect and sometimes toxic for learning and for children. They do good. Because they care and because they keep trying, the Power Principle lives in them. Their message is heard.

WHAT IS YOUR MESSAGE?

Eknath Easwaran, a lifetime follower of Mahatma Gandhi and teacher of meditation, relates the following incident:

> Gandhi spent every moment of his adult life living the cause of Indian freedom. It was a congruent, spontaneous response for him, and it had a sustained effect on the British people because Gandhi identified so completely with his message. Once, while Gandhi's train was pulling slowly out of a station, a reporter ran up to him and asked him breathlessly for a message to take back to his people. Gandhi's reply was a hurried line scrawled on a scrap of paper: "My life is my message." This message did not require the vast stage of world politics, but could be put into practice here and now, in the midst of daily life. Gandhi was not only a political and spiritual leader—he was a great teacher. He did not have to plan speeches or stage events because everything he did embodied what he believed.[15]

We are all teachers as well as learners. There have been important people in your life who have impacted your life in ways you will never forget. When you have tough decisions to make, when you want to teach with honor, remember these people. Ask yourself what their message was. Ask yourself what they would do.

The answers are in you, often because someone else planted them there. You are a leader. If you lead with principle-centered power whenever and wherever you teach, you will teach what you are. Your life will become your message. And your teaching will live on, in those you honor.

WHAT DO I DO NOW?

1. In your primary teaching role, how powerful are you?

2. Under what circumstances are you likely to feel powerless?

3. When do you resort to coercive power? What results do you typically get?

4. How could you enhance your utility power as you teach?

5. With whom are you willing to make the investment needed for
   principle-centered power? Will it be worth it?

6. Are there others who share your desire who could help you improve the teaching atmosphere? Get together regularly. Listening to
   their concerns might be a good place to start. Focus the discussion
   on what you can do together, not on how awful or discouraging
   things may be.

CHAPTER 11

SELLING WITH POWER— HOW TO HONOR YOUR CUSTOMERS

> Character is the salesman's stock-in-trade. It is he who must
> first sell himself. Truthfulness, enthusiasm, and patience are
> great assets. The product itself is secondary.
>
> GEORGE MATTHEW ADAMS

EVERYBODY SELLS. IN THIS WORLD, LITTLE HAPPENS UNTIL SOME-
one sells and someone buys, whether it is an idea, a dream, a product,
a service, or a solution. When you sell, you influence someone to take
action—to buy what you are offering.

THE SELLING DILEMMA

Selling has for too long been adversarial. Jokes and stereotypes are
common about selling and those who sell, as well as about customers.
Some see customers or prospects as naive, gullible, a "laydown" or
dupes ("there is a sucker born every minute"); others see them as
hard-nosed, tough, difficult to deal with, and impossible to please.
Salesmen, on the other hand, are seen as ignorant, rude, inconsiderate,

and unavailable; or pushy, obnoxious, overbearing, and manipulative. What an unfortunate situation! Every day, people with problems and people with solutions can't get together because of how they see each other, and the beliefs they have about selling. Ron Willingham, in his book *Integrity Selling*, notes that "traditionally, salespeople have been taught . . . that selling is something you do to someone, not for and with someone."[1]

There is another alternative that is not adversarial (hardball) or impotent and weak (softball). It is selling with honor.

Selling with honor lasts a lifetime. To sell with honor requires both skill and integrity, product knowledge and people knowledge, a desire to serve and a desire to genuinely help. Selling with honor means that you assume your customer or prospect can always overhear you talking about them and you govern yourself accordingly. Selling with honor leads to a transformation in the relationship, because conviction passes from the seller to the buyer. You sell differently than others might because you see your purpose differently. Your tools are different. Your power is greater. You sell more. You are not afraid to walk away from a sale that is not right—not right for the customer, not right for the need, not right for your organization, not right for their organization. If it is not right for them, it is not right for you. You know that doing the right thing is always right. You believe that a win for the customer is ultimately a win for you, so you work harder to deeply understand their needs, because only then can you pinpoint your efforts on their behalf. You can sell with honor.

FOUR SALES APPROACHES

There are four kinds of responses you can make when you are faced with a selling opportunity. Every salesperson has choices. The first choice you make is to be powerful or powerless, to be victimized or to volunteer to make a difference.

If you choose to be powerful, you have three additional choices, three paths to power in selling—coercion, utility, or principle-centered power. As we examine each, I suggest you think about when you tend to operate with each type of power and when you act powerless. The choices you make will empower or disempower you and will lead to success, mediocrity, or failure in selling.

If you choose to be powerless, you become a victim who believes there is nothing he can do. Fate has determined his future. He believes that bad things happen, primarily to him. They happen predictably, all of the time and are not preventable. The powerless salesperson repeats the following self-talk many times a day:

> There is nothing I can do.
> Others get all the breaks.
> This area is sold out.
> They'll never buy from me.
> The other areas (or products or markets) are hot right now.
> If only . . . (I was taller, shorter, smarter, a woman, a man, younger)
> If only . . . (my product/service was cheaper, better, newer)

To be powerless in a selling situation is to let the inevitable occur. The norm most of the time is that few people buy until they are sold. The powerless person believes that everyone who can be sold lives somewhere else. To those who are powerless, selling is a mystery, with the uncertainty and unpredictability of a roulette wheel. To be powerless is to believe that nothing will make any difference anyway, because of_____(you fill in the blank—the excuse doesn't matter because if you really want an excuse, any one will do). Powerless salespeople do not perform and do not stay in the business very long.

Many who are powerless can be reclaimed. The ignorance and doubt that lead to immobility can be remedied. An old Eastern expression suggests "Blessed is he who knows not, and knows not that he knows not; awaken and teach him." Through example, seminars, books (nearly three thousand books have been written on sales and selling!), audio- and videotapes, mentoring and self-guided learning, formal or informal training, any motivated salesperson, and even a salesperson who only thinks that a different approach *might* be possible, can learn and grow and change. Most good books on how to sell are loaded with rags-to-riches examples of the tongue-tied beginner, ill at ease in his clothes and his calling, who caught fire and bootstrapped his way to fame and fortune by becoming the top salesperson in his office. Indeed, it seems like most sales books are written by people who lived that very life, and in the process of overcoming their own weaknesses, shortcomings, and deficiencies they became great salespeople.

One observation—the powerless among us are not just the sales wimps and nonperformers. Most of us can imagine a situation or being with a particular prospect (the president of the United States? The pope? CEO of the largest organization in our industry? Our father-in-law?) when we might be hesitant or reluctant to sell as well as we know how. To choose power over powerlessness in these situations is a dynamic choice that we all can make. As we increase our power in more situations, we become more powerful in all situations. We do not have to remain powerless.

SALESPEOPLE WHO MANIPULATE AND CONTROL— COERCIVE POWER

How attractive is this proposition? I heard a national sales manager introduce a new contest by announcing, "We are going to begin our quarterly sales contest Monday, and the winners get to keep their jobs." An international sales director claimed, "Win/win means that you win at everyone else's expense and then win again." Hardly a week passes without the nightly news warning listeners about the latest scam, some unscrupulous con artist fleecing the elderly, the unsuspecting, or the naive with some purchase that is "too good to be true." Coercion in sales is when you force someone to purchase what *you* want them to purchase, without their informed, willing consent. Coercion causes people to buy things they would not have bought, under normal circumstances, and that they wish they had not bought.

Coercion can be manifested in the relationships between the salespeople and the sales manager, as well as between the salespeople and the customers (and even between children and parents, who may each be attempting to "sell" something to the other). Coercion in sales runs the gamut from deception to demeaning and belittling comments, to managing the data in a way that critical information is withheld or misrepresented, to creating a false sense of scarcity or urgency, to suppressing positive information about the competition. With customers or prospects, you may sometimes feel it is justified to do one of these things to make the sale. But coercion, manipulation, and bullying or terrorizing, even in their more subtle or covert forms, lead to the predictable outcomes described in Chapter 4—negative, external, oppressive, dependent, resistant, temporary results. It is ultimately counterproductive and destructive to pressure someone into buying before they are ready, if the product does not genuinely meet their needs, if

they do not understand or appreciate the value of what is being purchased, or because you have momentarily outwitted or outsmarted
them.

The fact that people can be forced to buy under pressure has been
recognized by most states and communities in the form of legislation
which allows consumers a "cooling off" period within a certain number of hours or days after a direct sale is made. In other circumstances,
customers end up buying something they do not have the money to
purchase, do not need, and do not want, only to impress someone they
do not like or to comply with a salesperson who employs aggressive
closing techniques. The stereotypical sales approach used by traveling
salesman Harold Hill in *The Music Man* was to provide the promise of
value, collect the money, and get out of town before being found out.
This blatant routine is so obvious as to be laughable. But often salespeople are in delicate or awkward situations when their dominant desire is to close the deal and "get out of there" before the prospect finds
out what has been glossed over, artfully summarized, or withheld, out
of fear that the deal might not be consummated.

Living with the anxiety of being found out, or with the fear that the
sale may not be made (with whatever attendant consequence might
appear; remember the sales "contest" referred to above?), a tremendous toll is taken on the salesperson. Some quietly leave the profession. Others coast into emotional and spiritual burnout.

MAKING DEALS WITH CUSTOMERS—
UTILITY POWER

"Give me qualified leads and I will check them out for you."
"You pretend you don't know your product's flaws and I will pretend I don't know there is a lower cost alternative."
"You give me most of your business and I will give you a good deal
most of the time."
"You throw a concession my way and I will throw some business
your way."

These statements characterize the salesperson who sees selling as
deal making—transactional, transitory, and short-term. When we
make deals, we invite our customers to evaluate our service and our

offerings on a case-by-case basis. We are creating the ground rules for a relationship that is free, for the most part, of the pressure, fear, intimidation, and uncertainty of coercive power. The offer is constantly touted, "You want it? If you can pay for it, I've got it." Much commerce, many transactions, and a huge portion of selling activities would be listed here. "Caveat emptor," let the buyer beware, is the clarion warning to all who would make deals. Each party should be on guard. A little treachery may be tolerated, in the good-hearted "may the best man win" spirit of deal making.

Some order-takers are found among the deal makers. Order taking is a passive form of selling, relying on the implicit assumption that the customer wants it (or she wouldn't be asking) and we have it (or she wouldn't be asking us). It does not inspire extra-mile service, but it is not adversarial. It does not spur either party to look for synergistic, better third alternatives, but it does not leave human carnage in the aftermath of negotiating. It is a reasonable middle ground. It is aboveboard; there is no under-the-table dance of threat and acquiescence. Sometimes the salesperson comes out ahead; sometimes the customer comes out ahead. Both live to play another day. The reciprocity of these deals creates a sense of "I came through for you, so you owe me on the next round." Utility selling is based on old styles of equity creation and sharing, indebtedness and payoffs, tit for tat.

The downside of utility selling is that customers quickly learn the chant and intone it with impassioned fervor, "What have you done for me lately?" There is little security. You may lose the deal the moment someone outsells you, offers greater value, lower cost, quicker delivery, newer versions, or a wider assortment of accessories. Sales managers who make deals or use reward and reinforcement systems quickly learn that rewards teach salespeople to work—for rewards. There is a relatively brief half-life to any sales contest, competition, or program. Salespeople who resort to special deals, one-time discounts, mark-down pricing, or other unique considerations to maintain routine sales will find that customers not only come to expect such treatment, but will not buy without it. Everyone's behavior is shaped so that performance does not occur without some special arrangement in place.

There is another way to sustain selling, maintain a growing customer base, inspire increased sales, develop long-term relationships, and avoid burnout among salespeople. Let's review the third path to sales power.

HOW TO AVOID BURNOUT AND ACHIEVE SUCCESS—PRINCIPLE-CENTERED POWER

Burnout occurs for many who sell for a living because, they think, the hours are long, the travel is arduous, the day-to-day routine is filled with constant rejection, the competition is heavy. However, these factors are not the root source of burnout. Burnout occurs as a result of cognitive dissonance, the natural result of acting one way and thinking another, or speaking one way and feeling another, or doing one thing but believing another. Dissonance creates emotional and mental fatigue that is far harder to live with than the physical fatigue from a taxing road trip or intensive travel schedule.

We have all experienced this dissonance. When we feel like we have to withhold from a prospect some information that would keep them from buying, and we know it isn't right to do that, we feel the dissonance. When we feel like we have to misrepresent the facts or what we know about a competitor's product to make a sale, we feel the dissonance. When we are asked to do something that our gut tells us is wrong, yet if we don't do it we will lose an opportunity, look bad, or be embarrassed, we feel the dissonance.

We have different awareness levels and different thresholds for tolerating this dissonance. It requires tremendous energy to live with the dissonance. Yet we may live with it for one sales encounter, or one sales cycle, or one sales contest, or during a training period. But maintaining the energy is hard; it is a difficult juggling act. We get worn down. We get worn out. We get burned out. When the discomfort is great enough, we typically take one of three approaches. First, we may try to numb the pain, with increased activity, with distraction, with drugs, or with some indulgence. That helps us get by, for a while; it enables us to cope, without changing. Second, we may give up our values, beliefs, or the thoughts that are inconsistent with our actions. We may tell ourselves rational lies or half-truths that we temporarily want to believe. We may betray our values by supplanting what we really think and feel with what is popular or what others think and feel. Third, we may stop doing what we are doing or saying that is out of harmony with our thoughts and beliefs. In other words, we stop selling or we stop lying to our prospects and ourselves.

As I described in a different context, the key to motivation is motive. Our motives make a difference in how we sell. Our purpose, coupled with a congruent motive, determines the methods we use. If you want to avoid burnout, match your words with actions and your beliefs with behaviors. Believe in your product and know enough about your prospect to determine with full purpose of heart that the match is appropriate, and you will not only prevent burnout, you may have created a partner for life, a source of referrals, a center of influence that repeats your business and invites others to do the same. Courage comes easier because your motive is to benefit and to serve.

In summary, the best way to avoid burnout is to be what you appear to be, to use the knowledge you have, to speak from the experience that is yours, and to have ultimate confidence that the truth is enough.

HOW TO STAY MOTIVATED

One of the side benefits of selling with honor is that you avoid the burnout trap. Another is that if you do what you love, the money will often follow. People who love their work are energized by it. Sharing the excitement they have for their products or services in a way that solves people's problems is self-reinforcing. Success breeds success. Such salespeople have more positive "war stories" to tell more people, who in turn are inspired to buy and try, leading to additional war stories, and the whole cycle feeds on itself. The lines and boundaries between sellers and buyers blurs, customers become partners, partners become winners, stakeholders meet their objectives and the resulting enthusiasm and success are contagious. By many estimates, 80 percent of the commissions are usually made by the 20 percent of the sales force who are building for the future by serving their prospects and helping them become customers now.[2] What does this 20 percent know that the rest of those who sell the same products and have the same tools available don't seem to know?

Selling at its best *is* serving. Serving does not require you to be subservient; it requires you to be powerful. To serve is to offer what you have that will benefit another. It is not a weak image; it is one of the most potent images you can bring to mind. I like the thought-provoking idea of a salesman as a samurai warrior, not just a maniac with a shout and a sword, but a strong man with a mission who is respected by everyone. This old Japanese word literally means "one who serves." The samurai was trained for a lifetime of skilled service to his client lord, his family, friends, and the community at large. This service made him indispensable and brought him respect, honor, power, wealth, and happiness.[3]

A popular idea is that when someone wants what we have, we have the opportunity to "upsell" them, adding to the price of the purchase. I suggest another view: "upserve" them. Offer them more, because you know enough about them to sincerely recommend additional selections, more appropriate timing, accessories, or alternatives. To serve more is to offer added value, the key to maintaining relationships that are transformational, not merely transactional. Not just a samurai, but a super-samurai, a master, a salesperson who sells with honor. Anyone can make a sale or close a deal, because there are many prospects with many needs; but to make a sale that is the beginning of a lifelong satisfying relationship, with a new alliance created between buyers and sellers—that requires a deep commitment to service, inordinate developed skill, and an understanding of why people buy.

WHY DO PEOPLE BUY?

There are four universal human needs, which can be represented by the stomach, the heart, the head, and the spirit. The stomach represents our need for clothing, shelter, food, protection, and security. The heart represents our need to love and be loved, to be respected, to be treated kindly. The head represents our ability to think and problem-solve, to develop our talents and skills. The spirit is our whole person, with the capacity to find meaning, focus, and a sense of contribution through our work and our lives. We want to live well; we want to be treated well; we want to develop and grow; and we want to make a difference. Every selling opportunity should clearly focus on one or more of these needs. What can you offer to help your prospect live better, love more, learn more, and leave a legacy? What can you sell that will move them forward economically, socially, mentally, or spiritually? The more you have to offer that will help them do this, the better you will be able to serve them. The better you can serve them, the more effective you will become as a salesperson.

To prepare for a sales seminar I was developing for the account representatives at a popular national magazine, I did my homework by interviewing key people and studying the magazine itself. I learned that at the time the magazine was one of the most successful periodicals published in America and had been for many years. The appeal of the magazine was that it began in curiosity and ended with hope. Through the stories told each week, readers came to one of two conclusions. Either, "Whew, that is something that didn't happen to me, and I am grateful," or "Yeah! That is possible for me too and worth going for!" Hope was exemplified in the editorial direction which guided each issue. Through the lives and experiences of celebrities as well as ordinary people, the following messages were consistently and artfully presented:

I am not a victim.
I can choose what to do with my life.
I can organize my life to live my deepest values.
I can win with others.
I want to understand others, and in doing so I will be better understood.
I embrace the differences in others.
I can become better by working on myself.

You cannot sell with integrity unless you know where your prospect is in terms of each of these universal needs. You may not have all the answers and solutions they need, but unless you can demonstrate the line-of-sight connection between what you have and what they want, you cannot serve them at all. Knowing why people buy prepares you to establish credibility, present your case, and supply what they need. Everybody knows how to talk; few know how to listen. Excellent listeners generally sell more than good talkers. Listening deeply, establishing conditions of trust and safety, and demonstrating that you care in ways that matter to the prospect enable you to plant the seeds today that will bear rich fruit tomorrow.

Selling today is seldom a one-shot, short-term, quick-fix transaction. Selling cycles are longer. More people are involved at each phase of the process. Multiple factors must be considered at each potential point of connection. If you understand why people buy, then you have begun down the path that will result in your truly honoring your customers. Your goal is to help them succeed. So when you honor them, they will honor you. The result is a transformed relationship.

When the Macy's department store chain was put up for sale, it was to be the largest sale ever made by the group handling the transaction, according to its president, who was my client. Many complications necessitated a web of legal professionals meeting on both sides of this deal, which ground the whole process nearly to a halt. This was potentially a billion-dollar deal. Can you imagine the pressure on all parties to do well, not be taken advantage of, and to come out looking good? The president told me that there were many deadlines, much negotiation, many subcommittees handling specific aspects of each detail, with a never-ending parade of reports, offers, counter-offers, ploys, stalemates, facades, and frustrations. Gradually, issue after issue was resolved somewhat in utility power fashion, with compromise on both sides. Everyone stood to lose a lot if the deal did not go through, so there was some fear on each side as well. They finally agreed on the general amount and the percentage rate on the financing, but they had six additional critical areas left up in the air.

When the big day came for the "final showdown," the principals on each side arrived at the downtown hotel, with a string of attorneys in tow. The president approached the senior member of the opposing negotiating team and asked if he could talk with him privately for a few minutes. Warily, he agreed, but "only for a few minutes." The president told me that he had worked hard to develop trust among the senior members of the negotiating teams who were leading the project. He had come to respect the professionalism and integrity of the "opposition." So he decided to honor him in an unusual way.

He told the other man, "I trust you. I am going to write down the six areas on separate pieces of paper, give them to you, and invite you to select the three which are the most important to you, and I will give them to you. Whatever you want in those three areas, I will give it to you, and I will take the other three areas." He said the other party stopped in mid-speech, his jaw dropped, and he looked stunned. "No one has ever dealt with us that way. I can't believe you are serious." He was so surprised that he was literally undone. He found a chair and sat back, breathing heavily. After a long silence he looked up and continued, "If you are serious, I'll do it. Actually, I know what you want, and I was prepared to present an initial position, then a counterposition, etc., to finally end up at what I thought you would take. But why don't we just move ahead?" Then, after another quick breath, he confessed, "In reality, I only need two areas, not three. Let's do it!"

Fifteen minutes later, the two men, both grinning, walked back to the group, and gave the necessary instructions for the attorneys to work out the details and finalize the deal. Normally, it would have taken days, days of agonizing, anxiety-ridden, emotionally distressing arguing, bluffing, nibbling, and undercutting to get to a mutually acceptable position, and at best, that would have been a low-level compromise. This was literally a major win for both parties. There is no sales gimmick, technique, or ploy that would have achieved this remarkable result. Honor, earned by each and extended tentatively by one to the other, converted a defensive transaction to a delightful victory for all concerned.

There are many ways to describe or characterize this approach to selling. Collaborative selling, partner selling, new selling, samurai selling, power base selling, sales mastery, advanced selling, strategic selling—each has a different twist on how to sell by serving customers legitimately, and each approach attempts to get you to have a new view, a long-term view, a changed perspective about the process. When you see it differently, you will sell differently. Tremendous success awaits you when you learn to integrate character and competence by selling with honor.

I WANT TO IMPROVE—WHAT DO I DO NOW?

1. What is the foundation for the kind of selling you do most of the time—doubt, fear, fairness, honor?

2. Think of a valuable prospect you would like to influence. What could you do today that would increase their capacity to trust you next time?

3. With this prospect, what could you do, within your circle of influence, over the next week that would give them a reason to increase their trust in you?

4. Are you experiencing sales burnout? How often are you in situations when you feel pressure to compromise to get a sale or close a deal? What is another approach that is less stressful and more honorable?

5. Do you know why your customers buy? How can your understanding help you serve them better?

6. If your goal becomes "upserving" rather than "upselling," what would you do differently? How would your customers be able to tell the difference in your new approach?

CHAPTER 12

LEADING WITH POWER— HOW TO HONOR THOSE YOU LEAD

One person who really knows how to lead is worth more than a hundred who have merely studied leadership.

AUTHOR UNKNOWN

YOU ARE A LEADER. WHATEVER YOUR TITLE, POSITION, OR ROLE, IN some relationships with some people, you are looked to for direction, counsel, advice, decision making. Whether you are the formal leader or are informally recognized as a leader, you can lead with power. You are also a follower and sometimes it is important, even necessary, for you to listen to others, and follow them. Whatever your position or relationship, others may know more than you or because of ability or experience be in a better position to lead. As Will Rogers was fond of saying, "We are all ignorant, only on different subjects." So there are times when we will follow. In this chapter, I will help you understand many ways to describe and explain leadership and followership, so that when it is time for you to follow, you will be able to honor your leaders, and when it is time to lead, you can lead with power.

WHAT DO WE KNOW ABOUT LEADERSHIP?

There are many approaches we can take to understand leadership because many different paradigms of leadership exist. We can study historical figures, we can look at the traits and characteristics of historical or current leaders, and we can observe what recognized leaders actually do. But traditional approaches to understanding and teaching leadership have been limited in their application because they have focused only on the history, environment, traits, and behavior of the leader. However, leadership is an interpersonal process that involves choices by both leaders and followers. To have a more complete understanding of leadership, we must consider the role of followers as well. What combination of circumstances, traits, and behaviors provides optimum leadership? And perhaps more timely in this age of choice and opportunity is this critical question—given all the choices that people have today, why would someone choose to follow you?

Before we address this question, let's consider the approaches used in the past, see their contribution to our understanding of leadership, and clarify how they limit our perspective. As with most paradigms, each approach offers some insight—none of them is wrong, but each alone is incomplete.

THE HISTORICAL APPROACH

Often when we seek to understand leadership, we look to the leaders of the past for answers. We study the examples of kings, generals, presidents, and patriarchs. This approach may ignore the significant women who have led with honor and distinction and is often limited by an inherent flaw. As Shakespeare observed in *Twelfth Night*, "Some are born great, some achieve greatness, and some have greatness thrust upon them." That is, unless you achieve it on your own, greatness is something that happened to you by birth or by circumstance. It is the traditional heredity versus environment argument revisited. Many kings have been leaders only by birthright, not by action. Sometimes military leaders come by their authority through social standing or privilege. Often social leaders emerge only as a product of specific circumstances in a specific time.

If we are seeking to define qualities of greatness in past leaders so we can emulate them, the historical approach falls short. If leadership is something that happens to us, we are prevented from doing much about it. We cannot go back and change our parentage. Nor can we orchestrate world conditions to propel us to greatness. So, even though it is fascinating to learn about these people, the historical approach doesn't help us when deciding what *we* must do to be effective leaders.

THE PSYCHOLOGICAL APPROACH

Psychologists have argued that a better approach to understanding leadership is not to focus on what happens to you, but to study something about you. Perhaps leadership is determined by your personality. Leaders are charismatic. People want to follow them. Advocates of the psychological approach suggest that rather than looking to heredity and environment for signs of leadership potential, we should examine our character traits. The result is often a list: effective leaders are trustworthy, loyal, helpful, friendly, courteous, kind, obedient, cheerful, thrifty, brave, clean, reverent, and so on. This well-known list, from the Boy Scouts of America, sets an exemplary standard for its members, many of whom become leaders in business, political, and social life.[1] The Girl Scouts have a parallel list in their Scout law, part of which includes being honest, fair, friendly, helpful, considerate, caring, courageous, strong, and responsible.

While these traits are certainly admirable, there are others which, though characteristic of some leaders, are not. Books such as *Leadership Secrets of Attila the Hun* also offer alternative lists of traits we can emulate to gain power and leadership. How valuable are such lists though? As we study the traits of leaders, we soon realize that there is no single group of characteristics that determines leadership. Some leaders are extroverts, larger-than-life figures. Others are more thoughtful, reflective, introspective, and analytical. You've probably known leaders in both categories. So which personality traits do we cultivate? The answer is not obvious.

THE BEHAVIORAL APPROACH

In the 1940s behavioral psychologists presented a new argument. The behaviorists claimed that it is not personality that determines leadership, but behavior. If we can learn to reinforce certain behaviors and extinguish others, we can lead people with little resistance to do what we want them to do. Leadership is action, not position.

The behavioral approach has led to a change in management style in many organizations. Some managers have tried to increase their effectiveness by leaving offices and circulating more frequently among those they manage. "Management by walking around" is characteristic of a behavioral approach. It invites leaders to go where the action is, to observe firsthand, to deal with real people where the work actually takes place.

Though we can usually learn something by observing what leaders actually do, some have noted the limitations of this approach. One observer quipped, "Wandering around doesn't make you a good leader any more than sleeping in a garage makes you a car." You can go through the motions and not get the desired results; you can have the appearance without the substance. Another significant limitation with the behavioral approach is that we can observe and document what someone does, even videotaping them on the job, and supplementing the video record with a self-report; still, this does not tell the whole story. It does not identify feelings or history or levels of trust. It is possible, even likely, that someone can do the same things a leader does and get different results. Behavioral responses can become methods or techniques we attempt to use "on" others. When you focus primarily on imitating a leader's behavior, followers may feel manipulated or "done to." Few of us like to have someone use techniques or methods on us. Observation of an effective leader may not tell us why a particular behavior works for one person, yet when someone else repeats the behavior, they do not get the same results. Mechanical repetition of someone else's behavior or style by modeling another person without understanding may in fact cause others to choose not to follow us.

CONTINGENCY THEORIES

Aware of the limitations of previous approaches, investigators of leadership expanded their focus in the 1960s. At the time their new premise was that you could not understand leadership if you looked at only half the picture. The fact is that you do not have leaders unless you also have followers. What about the followers? Where are they in the equation? An effective leader is able not only to draw on her own strengths but also to sense their individual followers' strengths and needs and address them accordingly. This means that she may treat different followers in different ways. For example, some people need instruction, while others can participate with you in decision making. Some people need coaching, some need directing, some will do things on their own, and some will accept the responsibility that comes with delegation. Leadership then becomes the set of activities you would engage in to optimize the connections between the task, the followers, and the circumstances; what you do as a leader is contingent upon those you want to lead and what you are trying to accomplish.

There are a variety of contingency theories, each focusing on some aspect of the leadership equation. Perhaps the best known contingency theory is that of situational leadership. Ken Blanchard, author of *The One Minute Manager* series, along with his partner, Paul Hersey, first described situational leadership in their book *Management of Organizational Behavior.*[2] They explain how successful leaders come to understand their subordinates' task maturity, achievement motivation, and willingness to accept responsibility, and adapt their leadership styles to the situations they find themselves in. This is a useful approach. However, people are not static; when people change, what or who signals the corresponding change in leadership? How do you assess maturity? How do you acquire the needed flexibility to vary your leadership activities?

This approach has been popular, but I believe it falls one step short. I don't believe that leadership is only a matter of "figuring people out" so that you can get what you want out of them, or do to them what you need to do to get the results you want. All relationships are dynamic and two-sided. You may have choices when you decide how to lead others, but they also have choices when they decide to follow you.

Given all of the choices others have, why would someone choose to follow you?

It's about choice. It's about options, and people today have more than ever. It's not just what you do to them. Have you ever walked into a room where you're about to deal with some people who report to you and they're talking amongst themselves about you? While visiting a company I overheard this bit of dialogue:

"Do you think this is a good day to ask for a raise?"

"I don't know—did you see his tie? Whenever he wears that tie, he's having a bad day."

What was going on here? The same thing that happens wherever there are leaders and followers. When you are in a leadership role, you spend time thinking about what you can do to influence those you are responsible for. At the same time, while you are attempting to figure them out, what are *they* doing? That's right. They are trying to figure *you* out. They're thinking, growing, and planning too. And if you're not sure that's true, ask yourself what you do when your boss shows up unexpectedly. Would you attempt to guess what's going on?

I believe that people are, for the most part, self-directed; that all the time we spend figuring them out is matched by time they spend figuring us out. I believe that people want to make choices, and it is therefore valuable to think about the context of our leadership requests. No one likes to be summarized, labeled, or put in a box, even if the categorizing is so that we can serve them individually. The human spirit resists being ignored, or being treated like an automaton. Leadership is more than simply matching a way of leading with a preferred way of following, or matching leader style with follower preference.

Followers must be included in the formula. The contribution of contingency theories to our understanding of leadership is great, because under their premise, followers as well as leaders are factored into the formula, and the many possibilities facing a leader are highlighted. But if we are to better understand leadership, we must move further. If leadership is more than position, the result of world conditions, personality, behavior, or identifiable contingencies, what is it?

CONTEMPORARY PERSPECTIVES ON LEADERSHIP

Contemporary thinkers have added much insight in recent years to theories of leadership. Here is a composite of additional perspectives I have encountered in my attempt to understand and teach leadership:

Leadership is an attempt at interpersonal influence, directed through the communication process, toward the attainment of mutual goals.

BUSINESS SCHOOL INSTRUCTOR

Leadership is not about being famous.

LAURA TIMMIS

You can manage what you do not understand; but you cannot lead it.

MYRON TRIBUS

Some people think leadership is the art of getting other people to do all the work.

FORTUNE 500 EXECUTIVE

To be a leader, you have to be around.

COLGATE TECHNOLOGY EXECUTIVE

Leadership appears to be the art of getting others to want to do something you are convinced should be done.

VANCE PACKARD

The real leader has no need to lead—he is content to point the way.

HENRY MILLER

The final test of a leader is that he leaves behind in others the conviction and the will to carry on.

WALTER LIPPMANN

You've got to lead and not drive, inspire and not dominate, cause respect and not fear, win support and not opposition—that's leadership.

SEMINAR PARTICIPANT

The first responsibility of a leader is to define reality. The last is to say thank you. In between the two, the leader must become a servant and a debtor.

MAX DEPREE

Leadership is the ability to get men to do what they don't want to do, and like it.

HARRY TRUMAN

A leader almost always acts subconsciously and then later thinks of the reasons for his actions.

JAWAHARLAL NEHRU

Leadership is discovering the organization's destiny and having the courage to follow it.

JOE JAWORSKI

A leader is someone who translates intention into reality and sustains it.

WARREN BENNIS

What I observe from these statements and from my own years of research and study about leaders and leadership is that this is an intensely human enterprise, and it does not fit neatly into definitions and boxes. Leaders have all the spontaneity, unpredictability, frailty, vulnerability, and potential that is possible in the human race. If we are to lead with honor, we must start with the premise that flexibility, adaptability, and wisdom are possible, that we have the seeds of greatness in us, and that if we care deeply about the lives of others, we can work together to accomplish worthwhile things.

WHAT LEADERS HAVE TO DO; WHAT LEADERS HAVE TO BE

Caring deeply suggests a different kind of relationship between leader and follower than merely boss and subordinate. If a contrast can be made between the roles of master and slave, then an integration is found in the role of leader as servant. Robert K. Greenleaf, director of management research at AT&T for many years before founding the Center for Applied Ethics, has championed the idea that people will freely follow the leaders who have proven themselves as trusted servants. How do you prove yourself as a trusted servant? You have a dream, you show others the way. You have a sustaining spirit, you listen, you empathize. You believe that "the 'typical' peson—immature, stumbling, inept, lazy—is capable of great dedication and heroism if he is wisely led."[3] You cultivate awareness. You believe in the virtue of change by persuasion rather than coercion. In short, leaders serve, and in the serving become worthy of the trust of others.

Different kinds of leadership are required at different times; but at all times it is a combination of character and competence that is needed. Inspiring leadership must be coupled with the organizational skill born of seasoned technical expertise. This integrated blend of character and competence is often evident by its absence more than its presence. It is rare, and like most rare things, it is extremely valuable.

Much of this book has focused on what a leader must be, in order to influence with honor. There is also much that a leader can *do*. The leader *doing* is a pathfinder, a team builder, and a gardener. In a recent seminar, I asked leaders to analyze one of their successful leadership experiences by identifying what they had to do in each of these areas. This is a typical list:

As *pathfinders*, they had to recognize needs and accommodate the legitimate needs and wants of all stakeholders by clarifying:

Vision
Context
Direction
Location
Goals
Strategy
Purpose
Pace

As *team builders*, they helped others achieve together as they had to:

Create healthy, safe conditions for risk taking
Help others become leaders

Provide resources and be a resource themselves
Help some move from dependence to independence
Help others move from independence to interdependence
Help others get things done
Get out of the way

As *gardeners* they worked hard, often behind the scenes, to:

Create a culture and mores that embody core principles and values
Help determine how we work together
Help us agree on worthwhile purposes
Create enthusiasm and understanding in a critical mass of followers
Identify and remove obstacles
Provide support systems
Provide recognition and rewards
Organize and supply raw materials
Prune, when necessary
Plan for the harvest

The leader who exercises power with honor will work from the inside out, starting with himself. As you increase your capacity to path find, team build, and garden, your power base will enlarge, your ability to serve will increase, and your potential for leading with honor will escalate.

You may notice that these three primary roles of leadership incorporate some attributes that have traditionally been considered masculine and some which are frequently labeled feminine. The truth is that leadership requires both halves of our brains, both elements of our nature, and reliance on the best in both men and women. It is interesting that current studies of leadership are identifying various strengths, such as the ability to listen, nurture, care for, and be compassionate, that once were considered to not be an asset in a leader. Let us examine briefly what might be considered women's ways of leading, with the end result that we can create a model of leading with honor that incorporates the highest and best of both genders.

WOMEN'S WAYS OF LEADING

It is an interesting irony that what new thinkers are calling the new ways of leadership have actually been incorporated for years as so-called women's ways of leading. Of course there have always been women who were powerful leaders, politically and socially. But most historians seem to consider women as leaders to be anomalies. It is certainly true that many women of the last half-century have been taught that the only available road to leadership was to mimic the methods employed by members of the good-old-boy authoritarian network. My purpose here is not to be defensive nor divisive, but to look at the real needs and the real opportunities that lie before us as we work together in marriage, business, education, and government to have the best leadership we can develop. I deeply believe that we can serve better together, in all the arenas of life that need inspired leadership.

The books on power in the 1970s were male-oriented, telling women how to get ahead in the corporate world by being more like the men. The assumption was that women as women were not really leaders. Sensitive women at the time were jarred, because the advice contradicted everything they instinctually knew about influencing others. Successful women leaders of the day talked about being gardeners on the job, nurturing, watering, growing others. This was viewed as soft-headed talk by most male executives. Yet women knew that people who were trusted, valued, and respected always did better work. Even well-meaning women authors at the time suggested that aspiring women study football, poker, and the military to understand the proper, relevant models of business.

Some saw clearly through this muddy water and offered an alternative view. For example, John Naisbitt and Patricia Aburdene concluded that "women can transform the workplace by expressing, not by giving up, their personal values."[4]

Sally Helgesen, writer and researcher, observed a number of current female leaders, looking for and capturing patterns among the details of their daily work lives. In the process, she identified critical distinctions between the management actions and styles of men and women. Although both men and women had busy, full days, the women did not view unscheduled tasks and encounters and answering mail as interruptions; in fact, they made deliberate attempts to be accessible, to demonstrate caring, involvement, and helping. The interruptions during their day were seen as part of the flow of the day, not barriers or obstacles impeding their progress toward certain predetermined objectives.

Responding to mail was a way of maintaining and attending to relationships by being courteous, and respectful. The job of the secretary was not to protect the leader, but to function as a conduit to the rest of the workplace. For these women, activities not directly related to their work were part of their day. When the same behavior is exhibited by a man, notice is taken. For example, a well-known movie celebrity stopped the filming of his current film because he had promised his child that he would call him at a certain time. That such a big deal was made of the call underscores not how wonderful it was that he kept his commitment to his child, even though it was at some inconvenience and expense, but how rare it was. For many men it is not customary to put their children first during their workdays.

Helgesen also found that women tend to look more toward the long term; to see their work as only one element of their identity; to schedule regular times and places to share information; and to value being in the center of things, facilitating communication. In contrast, men more often focus on the short term; define themselves by their work; hoard information as a way to control power; and pursue being at the top of things, where the control is clear and lines of communication all flowed down. Helgesen notes the worldwide phenomenon of the cyclical nature of women's domestic work with enjoyment of the process rather than the reward of completing a task. She concludes, "Increasingly, motherhood is being recognized as an excellent school for managers, demanding many of the same skills: organization, pacing, the balancing of conflicting claims, teaching, guiding, leading, monitoring, handling disturbances and imparting information."[5]

Joline Godfrey notes in her research that, until very recently, woman-owned businesses were not studied, and most of the commentary on women leaders was based on generalizations from studies of man-owned businesses. She argues for more research on women, their businesses, and their business methods, and laments that the best practices in woman-owned businesses are virtually undocumented and unshared. She observes:

The very basic notions of what women defined as success seemed to make their businesses different. What female business owners called "normal" was now being tagged the "new paradigm" by business gurus worldwide. And the national effort to "reengineer" everything was an attempt to get to where women already were. The new psychology on women revealed that relationships are a source of power that women are comfortable nurturing. Success among women is less a matter of conquest than of collaboration, and priorities may be determined as much by family and community imperatives as by a desire to amass wealth of things.

As the '80's came to a close we could see that women relied less on authority and traditional power relationships with their employees than men did. The very qualities that had been devalued because they were female were now claimed by many male writers as integral to a new and radical approach to the business of management.[6]

So, it seems that those who would lead with honor must not only tolerate or accommodate nurturing leadership styles, they must adopt them in an integrated, people-valuing, yet accountability-demanding way that is a mix of the best that men and women do when they lead. To lead with honor and power challenges the best in us all; there is little room for the small-mindedness of parochial or gender-biased thinking and acting.

LEADING WITH HONOR

Let's see what leading with honor looks like. Here are two examples, one modern and one from earlier in the century; one from a virtual unknown and one from a world figure. Both happen to be male, but their natural incorporation of both gender-based strengths is clear. Both leaders worked in such a way that many lives were permanently changed. Whatever the activity, whatever the subject, whatever the issue, one thing is certain: leadership makes the distinctive difference. Leading with honor, whether in the concert hall, the boardroom, or the neighborhood, makes the critical difference.

TWO HUNDRED SINGERS AND ONE LEADER

At a large Western university, a miracle is taking place. Every day two hundred college students gather quickly before the bell rings and start vocalizing, warming up for an unusual rehearsal. It is a striking sight as the musical director, Dr. Mack Wilberg, sits at the piano and begins playing and leading at the same time, hands moving from the air to the keyboard and back with fluid motions, pulling from the young men harmonious sounds that surprise even them with their precision, tonal quality, and beauty.

Just a few years ago, there were only fifty men in this traditional male chorus. But that was before Mack arrived, and began begging on campus for singers to come, to lift their voices, to sing. Now, when they sing, it is an experience that audiences never forget; it is a magical event. And the choir is now widely recognized as one of the finest in the United States.

Although the size of the large group makes extensive travel diffi-cult, Mack works his singers hard, pushing them to learn new and dif-ficult pieces, as well as popular and standard pieces, so that they are ready for their performing season. His ensemble is in high demand so they often perform two complete concerts in one evening, a remark-able feat even for a professional musical group.

What is the source of this phenomenon, a college singing group that consistently plays to sold-out concert halls? It is partially that new overtones are created when men sing in harmony, and so crowds have congregated whenever quartets gathered near barbershops for at least a hundred years. It is also the crispness and fullness created by two hundred well-disciplined singers, united around a common purpose. But it is more. It is the drive and passion of a man with a mission, who honorably directs his life the way he directs this unusual chorus. His mission is to turn young people on to music and give them a great ex-perience that will stay with them throughout their lives.

To fulfill his mission, he still actively recruits. Competition for the chorus is keen. Those who pass an initial audition with a senior stu-dent must then audition with Mack himself. He seems to know and re-member every voice, and is protective of the sound his chorus creates while constantly looking for strong, experienced voices that will add to the strength of his group by increasing its vocal diversity. He does a significant amount of arranging and writing for the group as well, so that the pieces he performs match the skill of his singers while stretching their capacities. His rehearsals are rigorous, because he has high expectations for his singers. Although it would be a challenge for any music professional to handle this many singers—and these are exuberant college males, representing every major except music—he seems to have them in the palm of his hand as he moves smoothly from composition to composition. Their respect for him is obvious.

"It takes a lot of effort, and I am absolutely worn out at five o'clock every day," Mack reports. In his lament, he sounds like the students, who claim that this choral rehearsal is the toughest class they have. But evidence of learning occurs daily, and the frequent performance schedule keeps the young men pushing for musical excellence. They miss other classes, occasionally, but not this one. They wouldn't dare. Mack expects much more of them.

Another nationally known choral director comments, "His musicianship is overpowering to anyone who has anything to do with him. He has the style and charisma to challenge students so they feel like choir is a worthwhile activity. That's not easy when you look at the competition from other campus activities. He is a genuine human being. He doesn't put on any airs."[7]

Bad leaders make you feel bad about yourself. Good leaders make you feel good about them. The best leaders make you feel good about yourself. The great leaders are like the best conductors—they reach beyond the notes to reach the magic in the players.

HOW LONG CAN YOU GO WITHOUT EATING?

Mahatma Gandhi provides a second example of great and inspired leadership. I have mentioned him many times throughout this book, as he is perhaps one of the finest examples of an honorable, principle-centered leader this world has ever known. Richard Attenborough made a movie about his life in 1982 . One of the scenes in the movie captures the essence of leading with honor. It also illustrates what John Erskine meant when he said "In the simplest terms, a leader is one who knows where he wants to go, and gets up, and goes."

In the movie, Gandhi is attending a meeting. The prime minister and various other dignitaries sit with him to discuss affairs of state. All of a sudden, unannounced and without invitation, a runner bursts into the room. He is bloody, dirty, out of breath. He exclaims that fighting has broken out in one of the provinces, that people are dying in the streets, and something must be done. He stands, breathing hard, awaiting an official response.

The individual responses of the officials at the meeting provide an intriguing study in leadership. Gandhi says nothing, but quietly pushes back his chair and slips on his sandals. In contrast, the prime minister responds loudly, pounding his fist and informing everyone that he predicted this and that troops must be sent to the provinces. Someone from the military replies that there are not enough personnel to have troops in every province. Someone from the treasury adds that the government could never afford that number of troops anyway. The whole idea seems, to him, impractical.

Meanwhile Gandhi moves toward the man who has brought the terrible, tragic news and begins asking questions. What is happening in the province? How long has the fighting been going on?

The prime minister makes another declaration. Someone else responds defensively, reactively. In the background Gandhi and the messenger move toward the still-open door. When the prime minister realizes that Gandhi is about to leave, he jumps to his feet, informing Gandhi that the meeting is not over. "Where are you going?" he asks. "I am going to the province," Gandhi replies.

As I watched the film, I asked myself, "Who told him to go? Who gave him his marching orders? Who told him what to do when he got there?"

Gandhi travels the distance to the province and learns more along the way. Civil war has erupted in his own land. His beloved people—Hindu and Muslim—are fighting, killing one another. When he arrives, it is worse than he has been told. The fighting has escalated. Blood is literally flowing in the streets. Women, children, and entire families are being slaughtered. His great heart nearly breaks. He has invested so much in these people in an attempt to help them see things differently, to value their differences instead of being threatened by them. Yet despite his efforts, things are falling apart. Gandhi surveys the scene and determines that he will not eat until the fighting has stopped. He stays in the province and begins to fast.

The word begins to spread in the province that Gandhi, the great soul who is their teacher, their leader, their friend, has arrived and has embarked on a fast. The fighting rages on. Gandhi stays in the province. He goes a day without food. Then two days, three days, four days pass.

When considering Gandhi's sacrifice, it helps to imagine yourself in his position. Have you ever been really, really hungry? What would you give up for something you really believed in? Sacrifice occurs when you give up what you want now for what you want most. It's a very poignant moment in the movie, and as I watched, I found myself wondering aloud, "What good is that going to do? One skinny man stops eating. How is that going to affect anything? These people are at each other's throats; they're killing one another!" Gandhi grows weaker. He is slowly dying.

The fifth, sixth, seventh, and eighth days come and go. On the ninth day, somewhere in the province a surprising incident occurs. Somebody, weapon in hand, makes a decision. Knowing his beloved leader is dying, he makes a personal decision not to fight, and throws down his weapon.

On the tenth day, someone else makes a similar decision. A groundswell of resistance mounts among those who are sick of the bloodshed, sick of the fighting. Finally, thirteen days after Gandhi arrived in the province, someone comes to him with some grape juice and bread and asks if he will eat, because the fighting has finally stopped.

There is something that comes from inside a person, when words and actions, feelings and thoughts are integrated, when what you want and what you are overlap, that is incredibly powerful.

Years later, someone approached Gandhi, wanting to know how they could develop the kind of power that had enabled him to influence literally millions of his own countrymen. This was his reply:

> I claim to be no more than an average man with less than average ability. I am not a visionary. I claim to be a practical idealist. Nor can I claim any special merit for what I have been able to achieve with laborious research. I have not the shadow of a doubt that any man or woman can achieve what I have, if he or she would make the same effort and cultivate the same hope and faith.[8]

HOW DO I BEGIN LEADING WITH HONOR?

You begin leading with honor by believing that you will never be more effective as a leader than you are as a person. Leadership is a journey toward integrity, union, and wholeness. It is a journey that starts on the inside. As you align your values with your actions, you generate the personal power that enables you to help others do the same. This requires nothing less than a transformation. Warren Bennis said, "When we talk about growing leaders, we're inevitably involved in personal transformation. While I don't think you can 'teach' leadership, I am certain that leadership can be learned and that terrific coaches can create some experiential setups to facilitate learning."[9]

Joe Jaworski, at the Center for Creative Leadership, observed, "If you want a creative explosion to take place, if you want the kind of performance that leads to truly exceptional results, you have to be willing to embark on a journey that leads to an alignment between an individual's personal values and aspirations and the organization's values and aspirations."[10]

If you want to examine and enhance your leadership potential, ask yourself the question: "What would cause someone to follow me?" That is the most practical question a leader can ask today. What outcome you really want will determine what you do, how you live, and how well you lead. You can become more powerful by leading with honor.

APPLICATION ACTIVITIES

Personal

1. Think of the many roles you have in which you play a leadership role. Who do you lead? Why would they choose to follow you?

2. Keep a leadership journal, a personal diary of attempts to influence others, what you did, how it worked, your history with that person or group, and other pertinent matters. What patterns do you observe? Can you see the results of your sustained efforts?

3. Have someone you respect directly observe your leadership attempts and give you feedback. Listen to them. Being open is the beginning of wisdom and learning.

Organizational

Warren Bennis suggests four simple things organizations can do to facilitate and accelerate the competencies of its leaders.[11] What can *you* do to orchestrate these yourself?

1. PROVIDE TERRIFIC ROLE MODELS. Look at the leaders around you. "I never met a man I couldn't learn from," said Mark Twain. What practices and principles can you adapt/adopt? What do you want to conscientiously avoid doing and being? Modeling is one of the best ways to "teach" leadership. That goes for good and bad role models. Often, we learn the most from negative role models.

Action item: Keep a journal of effective and ineffective leaders you observe and work with.

2. IDENTIFY AND REWARD EFFECTIVE COACHES. Find someone who is supportive but not controlling. Most executives are not as open and honest in giving candid feedback as they could be. They fear recipients will perceive feedback as criticism, that they will be ignored, that it will damage their relationship, or that they will be seen as a "bad guy."

Action item: Find a willing, caring, courageous coach.

3. ROTATE INDIVIDUALS WHO HAVE THE POTENTIAL FOR LEADERSHIP TO A VARIETY OF ROLES AND JOBS. By changing positions, we can learn a lot about ourselves and others. Have a plan but be flexible. Take unusual assignments that force you to grow and develop new competencies.

Action item: Have a career plan that includes diverse experiences and find sponsors who will support you.

4. PROVIDE POTENTIAL LEADERS WITH EXPERIENCES THAT WILL BENEFIT THEM. Appoint them to chair task forces that consist of a wide range of people, in terms of both status and position. Leading such a group effectively relies on persuasion, not coercion; on supporting, not controlling.

Action item: Be willing to take assignments that require you to move out of your comfort zone, and that invite you to build synergistically with others.

CHAPTER 13

WHAT IF *THEY* ARE TRYING TO INFLUENCE *YOU*?

> Never give in! Never give in! Never, never, never, never—in nothing great and small—large and petty—Never give in except to convictions of honor and good sense. Never yield to force and the apparently overwhelming might of the enemy.[1]
>
> WINSTON CHURCHILL

MOST OF THIS BOOK HAS FOCUSED ON HOW YOU CAN BUILD POWER in your life to do the things that are worth doing. I have assumed that you want more power, and that it would be valuable for you to cultivate that power by learning how to influence with honor.

But when someone else is attempting to influence you, your options are different, depending on what you want. Projecting themselves, people who are powerless may believe you are also powerless. With a lose/lose mentality, they may look for someone to conspire with them; they think, "I'm not getting anything, you aren't getting anything—poor us, let's go out and eat worms." Those who come after you with coercive power may expect resistance. If their perspective is win/lose, they may expect compliance. If someone is trying to bargain with you, they have settled for a basic form of win/win, and they will likely bargain or negotiate with you. But if someone is striving to live with honor, they will probably expect honorable behavior from you.

YOUR CHOICES WHEN YOU HAVE NO CHOICES

When you are on the receiving end of a power play, you may not initially think you have any options. Invariably, though, you do. There is always something you can do; there is always something you can change. Stephen R. Covey describes circles of influence around each of us, surrounded by larger circles of concern, in his book *The Seven Habits of Highly Effective People.*[2] He suggests that when you feel trapped, you ask yourself, "Does this issue have mainly to do with me?" Then change your behavior. "Does it primarily have to do with other people who are nonetheless inside my circle of influence?" Then change your methods of influence. "Does it have to do with people and things that are only in my circle of concern?" Then you can change your attitude toward it. There is *always* something you can do.[3]

If you accept what is imposed on you without question, without creating a proactive response, will that take you where you want to go? Will it help you be what you want to be? Will it help you do what you want to do? If not, don't do it! There is another way.

IF THEY DO NOTHING AND EXPECT YOU TO DO THE SAME

Do something! Change the situation. Create alternatives. This is what Debbie Reynolds does in an inspiring scene in the movie *The Unsinkable Molly Brown*. Debbie plays the film's heroine, Molly, who is trapped aboard the *Titanic* as it strikes the huge iceberg that led to the mighty ship's demise. There are two breaks in the metal skin of the ship, one above and one below the water line, and water has begun to pour in. Only a few passengers manage to get to a lifeboat.

In the terror of the moment, many panic. Some are immobilized by fear. In one graphic scene, a woman who has made it to a lifeboat stands up and begins screaming that they are all going to die. She is literally rocking the boat, jeopardizing her life as well as the lives of the other passengers. Molly, who has been in Europe cultivating gentility and the understated manners of the aristocracy, suddenly raises her hand, slaps the woman, and holds her down. Molly shocks the woman out of her emotional rigidity and stops her dangerous behavior. The unknown woman neither invited nor appreciated being slapped, but it saved her life. If Molly had also become paralyzed, doubting that she could do anything and resigning herself to the fate of a watery, freezing grave, not only would she have died, but all the occupants of the lifeboat would have gone down with her.

If you are in an organization that is being "done to," whether the changes are coming through hostile takeover, leveraged buyout, friendly acquisition, reengineering, downsizing, or rightsizing, you do not have to be among the victims. You can be a survivor. If your boss or your boss's boss is just waiting for the next big bad thing to happen to him and you, you can choose a different response. David Noer, a management consultant, has documented the possibilities for being proactive when organizational life is passively oppressive. His book, *Healing the Wounds,* describes the insecurity, feelings of unfairness, depression, fatigue, reduced risk taking, lack of credibility, lack of commitment, distrust, betrayal, and lack of direction you may feel when your company is under siege. His practical and timely solution? Manage the layoff processes, facilitate the necessary grieving, break the co-dependency chain, and shift from toxic fidelity to healthy self-responsibility.[4]

Don't live your life like the violinist who always wanted to play but spent his practice hours merely stringing and unstringing his bow. Others around you may be doing just this, waiting for the inevitable and living with leftovers. Doing nothing is disempowering. The less you do, the less you feel you can do. Move on. When you know what you must do, dig deep and act.

Pulitzer Prize-winning poet Mary Oliver has captured the feelings you may have as you move on, leaving behind those who would hold you down with them. Her brilliant poem "The Journey" is one I often share with those who are struggling to break free from a family, company, or situation that is immobilizing because others doubt that any other choice is possible, and therefore cling to *you,* preventing you from moving on.

The Journey

One day you finally knew
what you had to do, and began,

though the voices around you
kept shouting
their bad advice—
though the whole house
began to tremble
and you felt the old tug
at your ankles.
"Mend my life!"
each voice cried.
But you didn't stop.
You knew what you had to do,
though the wind pried
with its stiff fingers
at the very foundations—
though their melancholy
was terrible.
It was already late
enough, and a wild night,
and the road full of fallen
branches and stones.
But little by little,
as you left their voices behind,
the stars began to burn
through the sheets of clouds,
and there was a new voice,
which you slowly
recognized as your own,
that kept you company
as you strode deeper and deeper
into the world,
determined to do
the only thing you could do—
determined to save
the only life you could save.[5]

A warning: if you choose action over inaction, when you are op-
pressed by others' belief that nothing can be done, your very response
may seem an indictment to them. Although it is hard, and you may
feel that you cannot do it, "leave their voices" behind—press on. Over
time, they may take heart as they see you move forward; they may
find hope for themselves as they observe the courage in you, as you
change.

IF THEY ARE BEING COERCIVE—GET ON, GET BY, GET HELP, GET OUT!

When someone else pushes their ideas, their expectations, their beliefs on you, and expects you to comply, you can endure or you can resist. You may not feel that you have any choices when someone who has authority over you directs you to act. But there are in actuality four strategies you can have: you can *get on*—with your life, as soon as you can; *get by*—hang in there, for now, patiently and creatively surviving as best you can; *get help*—join with others for support and possible resistance; or *get out*—leave the situation, by going for "no deal." In the military, these options are represented in the acronym SERE, which stands for survive, evade, resist, or escape. If you feel that whoever is forcing you is an enemy, each of these approaches is a coping strategy that has its merits.

TEN PRACTICAL SUGGESTIONS

Here are ten practical suggestions based on these strategies, which can help you cope with a coercive organization or person.

1. Do not take it lying down. If a stranger enters a theater, sits next to you in the darkness and places his hand on your leg, what is the message to him if you do nothing? Organizationally, there may come a time for you to do something, to stand up and be counted, to make the tough decisions, to find your way through corporate or private moral mazes, to even be a whistleblower.[6] You *can* revitalize your company without sacrificing your job. (See *Managerial Courage* by Harvey Hornstein, New York: Wiley & Sons, 1986.)

2. Spend your time creatively preparing for your moment, your act of power. Make a plan. Rally your strengths. Consider your options. When a crossroads is reached, when options eventually present themselves, you will be ready to take action.

3. Comply as best you can, as long as your actions do not violate your basic values and standards or hurt others.

4. Invest the time to understand what they want. Behind the demands, underneath the authoritarian, oppressive style, what are they actually trying to accomplish? If you can understand what they would

like to accomplish, you may then be in a good position to serve them by helping them. As your value to them increases over time, you may simultaneously create some breathing room for yourself. And becoming more valuable to them may mean more trust and less monitoring. Further, this not only buys you time, but you may become an essential resource to them. If they cannot succeed without you, you have increased your power and you may subsequently have influence with them. Eventually, helping them achieve their wants as they express them earns you the right to help them achieve their needs, as you understand them. This approach is the basis of Edwin Markham's poem:

Outwitted

> He drew a circle that shut me out—
> Heretic, rebel, a thing to flout.
> But love and I had the wit to win:
> We drew a circle that took him in.[7]

5. Talk to others; brainstorm possibilities; get help from family, friends, agencies. Form a network that extends your resources as well as your possibilities and you will enlarge your circle of influence.[8]

6. Go underground. Perhaps to protect yourself for a time, the best thing you can do is lie low. If the environment at work or home is abusive or destructive, you may need to become invisible or disappear for your own good. Sometimes, from a less visible underground position, you can take proactive steps that put you in a position to have new options. National and corporate history is filled with accounts of courageous men and women who disappeared for a while, as an interim step to changing location, perspective, circumstance, and destiny.

7. Do something to improve your circumstances; most of us can improve things where we are without quitting, and it feels great. Because many people are not proactive, you may find that others will adapt to the environment you create. Bloom where you are planted. Make a difference where you can. Where possible, protect and buffer your own people from unreasonable policies, procedures, and work demands so that they are able to do their work better.

8. Bide your time; outlive or outlast the tyrants and you may live to replace them.

9. If you work in a toxic waste dump, get out. Change jobs, lifestyles, friends, cities. In each week-long seminar I conduct, there is usually someone who decides that they cannot return to their old

work or family situation as it was. The boss is too much of a dictator, too resistant to change, or the conditions of work and culture are so toxic that departure is the only viable alternative. For them, the only path of congruence is to leave. As one woman told me, "I am willing to swim upstream, but I am not willing to swim up waterfalls!"

10. If you do not perceive that your oppressor is the enemy (for example, if this other person is your spouse, and there are some redeeming qualities in them, and you would like to go for win/win, if possible, with them), follow the advice Abraham Lincoln relied on. When asked how he handled the demands and pressures of those who wanted him to follow their competing agendas, he replied, "Often I have fallen to my knees for lack of any other place to go." He had good company. Tennyson suggested that "more things are wrought by prayer than this world dreams of." As many leaders have discovered, to pray for or wish good for someone else can soften your heart, change your feelings toward them, and can silently influence them for good. You can make a difference, if only by quietly influencing others as you live your life with faith, confidence, and conviction. To do so, you must leave your notions of powerlessness behind you and embrace your potential to impact, influence, and affect.

CHANGING YOUR PERSPECTIVE CHANGES YOUR STRATEGY

Sometimes the force from others can be viewed differently, and when seen from a different perspective, handled in positive ways. For example, Scott Peck, whose books have inspired and given hope to millions, admitted that he has received criticism as well as accolades. He noted:

> Sometimes I get profoundly negative reviews. One critic wrote, "If it's proven beyond any shadow of a doubt that this works, then I'll get on the bandwagon. Until then, I prefer to believe it's a dog-eat-dog world out there." In another review, I was described as a tourist at the abyss. I realized that [to be able to see me this way] the reviewer must have been at the bottom of the abyss. And how do you feel about tourists at the abyss when you're at the bottom looking up at these people with their cameras. You're either going to hate them, or you're going to say, "I've got to get out of the abyss."[9]

If it is primarily a person rather than an organization that is pressuring you because they must be in control, you may be able to help them with a shift in their paradigm. If they could come to see themselves more clearly, their behavior might change. Giving honest, high-fidelity feedback to such people is often the starting point for their awareness building. People who control too much, at the wrong time, who feel that they must always be in control or who can't let go, are constantly wreaking havoc in the lives of those they work or live with.[10] They can learn to hold, but with an open hand. Would such a change improve your life?

Your strategy is to increase your options by increasing your sources of internal security. My goal is to help you become more flexible, less needy, more open, and less vulnerable.

To become less vulnerable, you must work on both what you can do, and what you are, your character and skills, so that you have much to offer as well as the will to go for what you want. Consider Warren's experience. He was president of a $7 billion company, the second largest in his industry in the United States. He described to me how he was shaking as he walked out of a strategic planning meeting with his board. He had "managed the data," withholding information and not fully disclosing what he knew. Why? Fear. He was afraid that if the board had certain information, they would recommend actions in a direction he did not want to go. He had done nothing immoral or illegal. But he had violated his own best judgment. He was the only person who knew what he had done, but that knowledge began to eat at him.

He was so shocked at his own behavior that he obtained a copy of the *National Business Employment Weekly*, found five jobs he qualified for, and applied for them all. He wasn't actually looking for a new job; he just needed the reassurance that he had marketable skills and didn't need to operate with the fear that he might lose his job if he did what he felt was right. The experience was so exhilarating that the following Monday, he took copies of the classifieds to his staff meeting and told all his senior staff to find new jobs! He then walked out, without an explanation, and left them for an hour. When he returned, he was grinning but they were in a state of panic. He laughed and shared his experience with them. His message? If you are afraid, if this job represents your security and your identity, you will be of diminished or limited value to me. You must know that you have other options in your pocket or I will not be able to rely on what you tell me. I want you here as volunteers, not as victims.

What did Warren finally do? He chose to stay, relishing the power of his newly discovered freedom.

GETTING WHAT YOU WANT BY INCREASING YOUR CAPACITY TO CONTRIBUTE

If someone wants to deal with you, count yourself fortunate. You are already perceived to be in a position of power. You must have something they want. As an ad for a popular negotiating seminar suggests, you may not get what you deserve in this life, but you can probably get what you negotiate. The techniques of deal making are readily available.[11] I offer below some specific pointers for increasing what it is you have to offer, so that when you are approached, your power will be greater.

1. Today's standard for career planning is zero base. Assume you start over each year, requalifying for your job or the new job you would like to have. If you were to reapply for your position, would you get the job? Determine to be the best candidate by putting yourself in the position of president or owner. As owner, what kind of hours would you put in? How could you save money? How could you become more profitable? If you are adding value each year, each assignment, each project, and each opportunity, you will become indispensable to your company. You will get the same results in any relationship. Think not in terms of what you are getting but what you have to contribute. Would you choose to do business with you?

2. Read, listen, watch, and study as a pathway to increased capacity. Take on continuous improvement as a personal goal. "But," you might protest, "if I go back to school, it might take ten years and by then I will be fifty!" Yes, and how old will you be in ten years if you don't get that advanced degree? At ninety Leonardo da Vinci said, "I am still learning." Most of the great thinkers of our day are accessible on PBS, in libraries, through books and video- and audiotapes as well as live seminars. Recorded information will stretch you. As Oliver Wendell Holmes said, "The mind, stretched by a new idea, never returns to its former shape." To read and listen to current thinkers as well as the classics will stretch and enlarge your thinking. Live education and

training gives you an opportunity to test your thinking, to get feedback, and to explore nuances of ideas.

3. Figure that the half-life of your knowledge and information base is two years, and all knowledge is doubling every five years. Take action now to stay on the crest of the information wave. Access the Internet. Subscribe to and read a variety of newspapers and periodicals. Learn what is going on in your field and who is doing what.

4. Enlarge your toolbag. While teaching college, I fielded all kinds of questions. The most frequently asked had to do with the future, with the selection of a major, and with preparation for uncertain times ahead. My consistent advice was to develop tool skills, writing skills, presentation skills, knowledge of the basics of accounting, the language of business, learn basic psychology since you will be dealing with people, become comfortable with available technology. To teachers, I would recommend continuing in-service instruction. To salespeople, take upgrade training and integrate it immediately. To parents, take parenting classes. Go to a couples' retreat or weekend seminar. Think of the tools you are acquiring that will help you do what you do more effectively. It is not your specific knowledge that will make you more competent; it is your skill with many interactive, interpersonal tools that will enable you to adjust to changing circumstances, capitalize on short-term opportunities, and accommodate new shifts. More tools will give you more to offer when you negotiate with others.

5. The Novations consulting group assists organizations with career-planning and succession-planning issues. They look at five possible stages for an employee. As you consider each of these, ask yourself what stage you are at most of the time:

apprentice—some skill, high potential
craftsman—high skill, predictable, high-quality work
artist—new creations, modifications, new products or systems
mentor—new product is another person you believe in; you are a
    model and you cultivate/allow a relationship
sponsor—can supply resources to create opportunities

You may be at any of these stages at any time with a certain person. Wherever you are, you can grow. For example, I don't believe you have to wait until you are fifty before you begin mentoring someone. My point is that if you have more to offer, you will have more power.

6. Enlist the aid of others. Look for and cultivate your own mentor relationship. Associate with a friend or associate who knows you and believes in you and can help you see your blind spots and areas to improve. Create a network or a mastermind group of supportive people who care about you and can provide some expertise you do not have. Make it worth their while to invest in you. Provide something in return, so that your value to them is sustained.

7. Plan for change. You will have many "jobs" in your life. This new reality takes us from the old paradigm of "having a job" to "doing a job." Count on it; plan on it; work to prepare for it; do not be caught off-guard by it.[12]

8. Get out of your comfort zone. Create/make/hire/have an experience that gets you out of your element at least once a year. Do something original, creative, or risky that shifts your perspective. Raft a river, write a book, become a volunteer, take a class, become an expert at something. A traveler in the Old West encountered a sign on one of the old washboard dirt roads which warned, "Choose your ruts carefully; you may be in them the next twenty miles!" Take a different route to work. Eat lunch in an unusual place. Get in a new place and look at your old life with new glasses.

9. Invite *them* to the bargaining table. Take the initiative by suggesting you will deal with them if they will deal with you.

Understand that when someone wants what you have, you are somewhat independent. You can choose to deal or not. Before you make your decision, however, you will want to know what they have to offer and under what conditions the offer is being made. Can you get what they have better, cheaper, or faster somewhere else? You are always free to consider your options. You are independent. When they see you differently than they did before, you will have increased power to negotiate, to bargain, to compromise, to get what you want.

INVITING BETTER RELATIONSHIPS BY HONORING CURRENT RELATIONSHIPS

If someone is attempting to influence you by being principle-centered, by honoring you, you are the recipient of a marvelous gift. You are about to have a life-shifting experience. You can be grateful. Express your gratitude. Share your gifts. Be courageous. Take appropriate risks.

Expand your circle to include others. Enjoy the synergy and sense of complementary partnership.

People are drawn to good ideas, to good people, to committed leaders who parent or teach or sell or serve in other roles. When I was a boy I heard a rousing song that captured this phenomenon. Although I have not heard it for many years, I still remember the inspiring music and the challenge to be a "stout-hearted man," to have character, to stand for what is right, to be noble. Part of the chorus reads:

> *Give me some men who are stout-hearted men,*
> *Who will fight for the rights they adore.*
> *Start me with ten who are stout-hearted men,*
> *And I'll soon give you ten thousand more.*[13]

You may falter; you may not have your own clear vision. But if you have the experience of partnering with someone who wants to build with you, that partnership will blossom if you have the willingness to examine your own motives. What are you contributing to the partnership? What is in your collective best interest? What matters the most now? What can you do together?

Lynn Andrews has studied Native American Indian traditions and suggests a process for creating what she refers to as an "act of power," a significant personal achievement which affirms our independent competence while opening us to interdependent possibilities.[14] If we can bring love (not discouragement) to this quest, we find the strength to do what we must do. This act of power must require much of us, or we won't dig deep enough to find the resources, perhaps dormant, that we already have. You must choose something real, something specific, something that will have symbolic and important meaning to you. If it is to be a real act of power, it must require extraordinary focus and will.

For me, the creation of this book was such an act of power. It was a challenge. It stretched me. It forced me out of my comfort zone. It required that I work with others in new ways. It pushed me to purify my motives. It helped me see myself in new ways. It caused me to develop new skills and competencies. It helped me to redefine myself, to examine the various roles I play as a father, husband, son, author, teacher, consultant, and student. It was not easy. I spent time with each of the power options, at various stages in the preparation of this book. At times I felt powerless—I doubted my ability, my understanding, my capacity to live up to what I wanted this book to be. At other times, I was afraid of what the whole project would mean. I was afraid that others would hold my life up against the standards represented by honor and that in my weakness I would not measure up to what I was teaching and my message would be diminished. At times I was tempted to bargain, with my associates, with my publisher, with my family, to settle for something less. But, in the end, I struggled through the doubts, the fears, the deals, to prepare a book that had in it the best that I wanted to have in me.

THE TRANSITION FROM FEAR TO PRINCIPLE-CENTERED POWER

One of my clients shared with me her experience moving through the various paths to power. I believe her story illustrates the proactive posture you can take when someone is "doing it" to you. This executive had attended a week-long seminar I was teaching. She had been the victim of a corporate upheaval, an organization freshly downsized after twelve years of stellar performance. She felt bitter and confused. As we spent time together, I suggested that two areas of focus might be helpful. First, I suggested that whatever else she did, she should be true to herself and her family. When the issues of work and work changes were safely behind, the safety net is clearly not a corporate one, but a personal one, consisting of family and friends. She had good friends and a loving family, which, according to her, became her "salvation" in those difficult times.

The second focus was much more subtle, having to do with respect for others. Her experience for twelve years had been in an organization that did not demonstrate concern for others. It was an unhealthy environment and it fostered unhealthy management styles in its leaders. She told me that she employed the same traits and practices that she despised. Even when she was approached by a headhunter who told her how bad things were, she found it hard to believe—she literally felt there was no other way to manage and deal with people on the job.

During our days together she found a different experience, building new relationships based on respect, regard, caring, and competence. I encouraged her to find the kind of work setting where her capacity to care would be an asset, not a liability. Her report to me, nearly a year later, was that she had now been "blessed" with an opportunity to work for a very large multinational company with a tremendous work ethic and unbelievable respect for their employees. The respect in this new organization was embedded in everything they did, including policies, plans, procedures, and strategies. She concluded, "Trust is a difficult trait to gain when organizations do not treat their employees with respect. I can now participate in the process of believing in both people and the organization. The growth process continues . . ."

A FINAL SUGGESTION

If they are trying to influence you, you have a chance to get what you want most. Whatever their approach, you have options. Most people have some relationships based on each type of power; but we also tend to have a predominant way of dealing with others and with life. Your options are real. If you are experiencing pain in certain relationships—the pain of immobility or the pain of discomfort or the pain of unrealized possibilities—you can make choices that will improve the quality of those relationships and the quality of your life. You have the power to make the change. It really does begin with you. There is *always* something you can do.

CHAPTER 14

HOW DO I CHANGE?

We cannot become what we need to be by remaining what we are.

MAX DEPREE

Y OU CAN CHANGE.

As I have illustrated, each of us chooses to be powerless or powerful. If you are feeling powerless, you can become powerful. If you tend to operate with coercive power, you can create new relationships and modify old ones so that the fairness of utility power predominates, rather than fear. And if you tend to make deals with people, you are about to experience a dramatic change in the quality of your most important relationships as you shift from utility to principle-centered power. We discover ourselves as we examine our power bases and check the balance of powers in our lives. How powerful are you now? You must start where you are. It will not be easy; but it will be worth it, because as you improve, your capacity to help others will also improve.

In this chapter you will learn how to increase your power to influence others for good by improving yourself first. Here is how you can improve yourself today. I will begin with one man's dilemma.

A DEATHBED CONFESSION

Let me tell you about Tom, a client who wanted to know about change during a week-long leadership program. Tom was a school superintendent for a large school district in California. He seemed detached at first, asking negative, critical questions about the principles we were teaching, yet he was also quick to backpedal, assuring us that he didn't see everything as bad. He went through the week this way. Friday morning, he asked if we could discuss an upcoming retreat he had scheduled for his staff. We talked through some possibilities for an inspiring and informative day-long session he could conduct for his people and I got up to leave. He asked if we might chat for one minute more.

"How do you change?" he asked. I was puzzled. Change what, I wondered? "How do I change *me?* I reviewed the written feedback from my co-workers yesterday and I heard what I have heard before—that I am cold and distant, that I have no feelings, that I am not sensitive to people. Every day this week I have observed people who were concerned, caring, sensitive to each other, and everyone seems to like them. I am sensitive, and I care a lot, but . . ." His words faded as he began to sob, tears filling his eyes.

When he finally began to compose himself, he was a different man. He was hurt. He was vulnerable. He was angry and frustrated and fierce. "All my life my mother taught me to hide my feelings. Don't let them out, she would say. Don't let people know what you feel. Keep your feelings to yourself. Be a stoic. Don't get excited about things; you will only be disappointed in the end. And never let others know what you are feeling.

"Well," he continued, "I did exactly what she said. I lived my life the way I was taught. I turned people away all of the time. If they had problems, I told them to work it out themselves. I was tough, and they could be too. Then this last spring my mother became very ill. I was called to her bedside. She took my hand and looked into my eyes for a long time before saying, 'I was wrong. I was dead wrong. Feelings are important. You've got to change.' And then she died.

"Now what do I do? How do I change? Why did she lie to me? Can I change?" His questions came as an angry barrage, fueled by years of pent-up frustration.

I wasn't sure what to say. I thought of the years this man had tried to do what he had been told, to live the way he had been told to live, to deny himself, to cut off his feelings, his humanity, his spirit, his soul. And now, the shriveled, denied part of himself was creeping from the dark closet into the light, tentatively, timidly, fearfully.

"Can I change?"

I hugged him and asked how old he was.

"Fifty-two."

"And your mother, how old was she when she died?"

"Seventy-nine."

"So," I said, "you learned in fifty-two years what it took your mother seventy-nine years to learn?" He slowly nodded, with a new realization beginning to dawn.

"Do you have children?"

"Yes," he replied, "I have a son—he's twenty-four."

"What if he learned at twenty-four what you are learning at fifty-two? Can you create this important legacy for your son? Can you help him as you work together to be something different now, and give him the gift of your experience, a gift that may add thirty changed years to his life?"

For the first time in all those years Tom saw a new possibility, which would come from his own capacity to change. We made a plan; together we mapped out some action steps that would constitute a new beginning for Tom and for his son. I would love to see the feedback from his associates a year later. Tom was beginning to see that a new life, a different life might be possible. As he stood up to leave, his countenance had changed. The anger had a way to go to dissipate. He looked like Scrooge must have looked when he awakened on Christmas morning in Dickens's *The Christmas Carol*, having survived the long night of despair and regret and newly filled with gratitude. Tom left the mountains in Utah filled with hope, but a mountain of change lay before him. He wanted to change, but he hadn't known how.

IF YOU WANT TO CHANGE, BUT DON'T KNOW HOW

Personal change is a three-part process that requires giving up old views and behaviors, considering new possibilities, and then stabilizing new ways. It consists of challenging old ideas, gaining awareness, experiencing hope, trying new ways by doing something new that is congruent with what we really want. But it is not neatly linear. In the real world it is messy and there are detours and sometimes your heart breaks and you get lost. It takes time. It can be discouraging. It takes persistence and commitment. It will require patience. And it's like cultivating a beautiful flower; you can't plug one in, you have to grow it and tend to it, and protect it and nurture it. For a while it is fragile. But it is a work of art, and it will benefit all who see it. It can be the same with your life. This chapter will help you change.

Most self-help books fall into one of three categories.[1] The first is the "recipe book," which promises that if you just follow the neatly packaged steps, you can't go wrong. I don't believe honor comes in such a neat package—the quest will last all your life. The second is the "nice friend book," which is inspirational and provides a quick psych-up, but is too simplistic and has no staying power. I hope you have derived inspiration from what you read here; but I also want to provide encouragement and hope for the difficult times when you are trying and the results you long for are not there yet.

This book has taken a third approach, with the idea that we can all use a guidebook which is genuinely helpful in dealing with the realities of daily living. Mere motivation is insufficient to sustain you in the truly tough times. This book has provided no simple formulas. I have acknowledged that life is difficult, that we learn a little, make some mistakes, learn some more, try a little harder, over and over and over again. The learning never stops. We continually learn as we live, then learn more as we share with others, which moves us to a new place, where we encounter old issues with new meanings. Our eyes are open a little wider. Our hearts are a little softer. We are a little wiser. We become more honorable and more powerful as we change and grow.

Let us examine these three phases of personal change.

AWAKENING STARTS THE PROCESS

The first phase of personal change, awakening, begins when something disturbs the status quo. The unexpected happens and the emotional impact on us is great. We cannot ignore this wake-up call. The disruption and its attendant pain are too intense. We are thrown far out of our comfort zone. Disequilibrium occurs. Old ideas are undone. Old habits are challenged. We are forced to release old ways of thinking. The illusion that we have it together is broken. We are gradually or suddenly aware that things are not the way we had supposed. *All significant change begins with this awareness.* Such wake-up calls may be planned or they may be unplanned. Through our desire, our will, our character, we may deliberately subject ourselves to unsettling circumstances. Things may be going well, but we "raise the bar" ourselves. Debbie Fields, of Mrs. Fields Cookies, suggests that "good enough never is." That corporate value keeps her employees constantly looking for ways to improve. It keeps everyone open to change, and, as a result, unflinching when a customer offers criticism. We can be that way, open to the observations and feedback from others. We can build a habit of looking at ourselves often, studying what we see and comparing it with what we want to find there. The force of conscience can be a powerful motivator.

More often, however, we are jolted by external events, sudden unexpected developments, surprise attacks, or accidents which, like a whack on the side of the head, refuse to be ignored. They demand action. We may reflect, we may become serious and introspective. We may consider changes and transitions. It is said that Lincoln grew the beard that became his trademark because a little girl wrote to him, appalled that her leader was not a handsome man. There may be things about us that are unworthy, incongruent, dysfunctional, or just don't work. We may have mannerisms or beliefs or relationships or habits that just do not work very well in helping us do or become what we want, and yet we have until now ignored the available feedback about ourselves or our results and as a consequence we end up living life below our possibilities. The net effect when we are jarred by the force of circumstance is a mobilization of our defenses and our capacity to cope; something new in our lives *must* be dealt with.

Suddenly we are aware that we are in trouble. Things may be worse than we thought. Things are not the way we thought them to be. We can delay action no longer. Now that we realize how bad things are, we have an awareness which up until now may have been masked or dulled by a frenetic activity level, by other pressures, by our fears, by our preoccupations, or even by substance abuse or the tyranny of addictions and compulsions.

Most of us live within a certain comfort zone, having adjusted to what life has been like for us thus far. If the temperature in a room is uncomfortable, you could adjust the thermostat on the wall and within a pleasant range you would then cease to notice the temperature; you would be oblivious to it. The temperature might fluctuate, but the highs and lows are tolerable. Similarly, most of us tend to live within a comfort zone emotionally, psychologically, and spiritually. In our relationships and with our chosen lifestyle we'll take risks but not too many because that makes us uncomfortable. We're not prepared to cope with discomfort. In fact, for the most part, many of us arrange our schedules and our work habits and our free time to avoid discomfort.

THE KNOWN PAIN EXCEEDS THE UNKNOWN PAIN OF CHANGE

Modern change agents have learned that in organizations, which are prone to bureaucracy and protection of the status quo, the pain of staying the same must be greater than the pain of changing before organizational change takes place. The same phenomenon applies in our personal lives. Will we manage the pain (schedule it) or wait for it to arrive (usually in the form of natural, inevitable consequences) and allow it to fester and escalate until it is unbearable? The pain and discomfort we have gotten used to is predictable; there is even a perverse kind of comfort in knowing what is coming, even if it is painful. The potential, new, unknown pain associated with doing something different is also real. But until the predictable pain is greater or harder to deal with than the unknown pain associated with change, we remain stuck.

Awareness breaks our reverie or immobility. Sometimes this comes when we encounter someone else who seems to be dealing with life differently than we are and their confidence and effectiveness creates a noticeable, attractive difference. A sense of competence radiates from them, and seeing them leads to believing in new possibilities. When we see it in someone else, even before we embrace the changes we must go through, we will consider the possibility that things could be different for us too. Without this awareness there will be no change.

Sometimes when I am working with couples, I start by giving them assignments that will build awareness. A husband, for example, may simply not be aware of what's happening in his marriage, and be ignorant of his wife's deepest feelings. So I ask him, in the first part of the exercise, to list the attributes in himself that are important to his wife, and the attributes that cause grief for her because they interfere in hurtful or demeaning ways. I ask his wife to make a similar list, reporting traits and behaviors in her that work or don't work for him. Then they exchange lists. There is usually an immediate reaction. He may feel that things are not as they once were when they were newly married, or not as good as they might be, but he's typically unaware of what his wife's real feelings are. Men are usually surprised by what their wife has written. Wives often have a clearer picture of their husband's feelings, but they too gain insights they did not have before. Then, in the second part of the exercise, I ask each person to describe what their spouse actually does that hurts or strengthens them, so they can compare what their spouse feels with what they feel. This awareness-building exercise usually creates a lot of dialogue between husband and wife and begins a process of mutual adjustment that ultimately improves the quality of their relationship.

The disconnection that can happen between marriage partners, with the resulting lack of communication and understanding and distortion in perception, can happen between bosses and employees on the job. Until there is awareness, change is unlikely.

ASSESSING THE BALANCE BETWEEN DESIRE AND PAIN

I know you can increase your awareness of yourself and the effects you have on others if that is what you desire. Here are some questions that will help you as you thoughtfully and introspectively look within. It could be valuable for you to take the time to write responses to these questions in a personal journal. Over a period of time, reflect on your responses. What patterns do you see? Transformation takes time; acknowledge the power of the process. Be patient with yourself as awareness comes, desire grows, and your capacity increases.

1. Now that you see more clearly the various paths to power, do you want to change? It's not as though someone else is judging you and found you lacking. But you may have an awareness that there is something available to you that could increase your power and influence and at the same time improve your key relationships.

2. How are your relationships with the people that matter the most to you? What is it like in the private moments with your husband or your wife or your children or your parents or your boss? What's the quality level in your routine interactions with these people?

3. What are the patterns in your important relationships? Would you like them to be any different? In what ways?

4. Are you withholding yourself in some significant way from people you care about? If you have written off another person, or grown

complacent or indifferent, not believing that things can improve, you may say as a recent client told me, "We don't discuss religion, we don't discuss politics, we don't discuss his parents, and we don't do country-western music [or whatever your spouse lives for that annoys you]." There may be some degree of detachment or even emptiness between you. Or, one of you may have barricaded part of yourself, put up "no trespassing" and "keep out" signs all over the place, so the other knows to stay away from that part of you. If you have pockets in your relationship where the message is "Don't get into this area, it's too tender, it's too sensitive, it won't work, I can't explain it and I can't even talk about it," then that part of you is dead to the other person. When you cut off part of you, because you have been burned or hurt or unsuccessful there, even if the reasons have nothing to do with this particular person, you simultaneously also cut off the possibility of their fully knowing you. Have you been given an ultimatum? You will both lose, unless you can make a new choice at this moment of opportunity.

5. Have you recently received feedback about yourself, through informal conversation or through a formal process of feedback surveys completed by those who work with you, that was surprising, shocking, or at least news to you? If you have been blindsided, consider this. If they know these weaknesses or patterns in you that keep you from being more effective, and now you know that they know, is this not a good time to take action to change? Unsolicited or even unwanted feedback about you that comes anonymously can be a real gift. Now you know. What are you going to do? What proactive steps can you take, now that your equilibrium has been disrupted? You are open; your views have been shaken; you have been awakened. It is time to move to the next phase.

RESHAPE YOUR THINKING AND YOUR BEHAVIOR

Okay, you say to life. You have got my attention, I want to do better. I believe or want to believe that things can be better. Winning with others is better than losing. Now what? How do I change, modify, adjust, improve, and reform my old ways? How do I consider new possibilities?

There are six different activities I have observed in the reshaping phase. These include:

1. Learning about alternatives
2. Getting help from others
3. Developing a desire for something different
4. Recognizing an opportunity to choose
5. Making the decision to change
6. Taking a leap of faith

I will describe how you can do each of these.

LEARN ABOUT ALTERNATIVES

First, the unsettling experience, whatever it was, may cause you to realize that you do have options, that there are possibilities for living and acting other than the ones you have chosen or settled into. You may see, for the first time in a long time, that there are tools to help you function differently. You may read, talk to friends, get professional help, pray, meditate, join a self-help group, all of which can help you acquire language to identify and clarify what you want.

Perhaps you have just met with a friend, or seen a movie, or read a book that you really identified with. Perhaps you lost a job and in your preliminary meeting with an outplacement firm you encountered job possibilities you had been totally unaware of. Perhaps you attended a support group for yourself or for partners of people with significant problems, and you heard for the first time from people who were handling the challenges you face, but in a way you did not think was possible. Perhaps a counselor or adviser at work has just gone over your peer reviews with you. However it happens, the end result is that you know you can choose to live differently, and now is a good time to pursue a change.

GET HELP FROM OTHERS

Second, in this newly open frame of mind, you reach out to others or someone reaches out to you. At a loss, uncertain, troubled, grieving, you reach out your hand and are surprised to find that someone is there for you. Someone else has faced this. Someone else has been there. Someone else is knowledgeable. They can help. They want to help. They will help.

Help usually comes from someone you respect, someone who has influence with *you*. You may feel some degree of unconditional acceptance from them. You may feel safe enough with them, or under their watchful care, to question your own experience, to consider the possibilities that were raised in step one, to challenge beliefs and perceptions. As a natural result of being cared for, you feel hope, an expectation that things can be better. This is not an artificial psych-up. The feelings are real, and essential for the next step to occur.

This significant helping person may be a professional, a family member, a stranger, a divine connection made through prayer, or a friend. Shakespeare describes such an encounter in *Julius Caesar* when Cassius offers to help Brutus:

> Therefore, good Brutus, be prepared to hear: And since you know you cannot see yourself, so well as by reflection, I, your glass will be, and will modestly discover things which you yourself know not of.

It may require humility to accept this for what it is—someone cares and can help. Accept the hand that is offered to you.

Develop the Desire for Something Different

Third, the hope that you feel creates a desire for things to be different, or at least a desire to believe that things could be different. I've dealt with some people who, when I describe the world of honor and trust, say that world doesn't exist. They say, "I've never experienced it, I can't remember ever feeling the way you describe people feeling in a deep relationship with each other. It's not a part of my world. I don't believe it exists."

When I'm confronted with this kind of a worldview, I assume they have a reason for their beliefs. But then I look for a crack in their emotional armor with this question: "Would you *like* to believe that it's possible?" Almost always they will say that they would like to believe, but that they don't.

Would you like to believe? Would you even *desire* to believe that it's possible? The potential for change stems from a desire on your part for things to be other than they are. Desire is so powerful. Desire is paramount. You have increasing awareness, you have a desire. Let that desire develop in you to the point that with some relationship you are willing to experiment, to try with enough of an open mind that you might have a different experience than you have had before.

RECOGNIZE YOU HAVE AN OPPORTUNITY TO CHOOSE

Fourth, you recognize that you have a choice. You can act. You are not a victim. Within your circle of influence, without asking anyone's permission, you can do something. This awareness gives you a reason to change as well as an opportunity to change. This is a liberating, almost exhilarating experience.

A woman told me that when she hit this stage as she was assessing a difficult marital relationship, she didn't know *what* she was going to choose, but it was a heady experience knowing that she *could* choose. New life, a surge of energy, the will to take action—all are the result of this recognition.

MAKE THE DECISION TO CHANGE

Fifth, you make a decision. You have recognized that you have a choice; now you exercise that choice. You commit. You will take action. You have determined a path and you will take that critical first step.

From the outside, it may not be noticeable to others, but you have already made a change when you decide to go for it. You may not have changed your location yet; but you are facing a new direction. You are headed somewhere else. This event is discrete, it is real, it actually occurs and you will be able to tell when it happens even as you experience it. It cannot happen against your will. In fact, it is your will that is being exercised.

Every single person I've ever worked with who has made a significant, positive change in their life can tell me when it happened. One man told me he was sitting in his kitchen with his wife across the table from him. He told her that their marriage wasn't going to go on the way it had been anymore. I asked him if he was trying to tell *her* what to do. He said, "No. I had decided that the way things were going was not what *I* wanted. And I began from that moment to change. I invited her to join me." I asked him if everything improved from that moment on. "Heavens, no! I fell down a thousand times. I had to make that decision again and again, to make the commitments I made to her on that day hold water. But that's when we started to have a marriage."

Warren Bennis calls this the "propitious moment," when something is said or done that has special resonance for us. A novel, play, poem, painting, or music selection can be a trigger that changes our life. Perhaps there is a special synchronicity between imagination and experience, between the possibilities of the future and the realities of the past that makes the decision possible.[2] I am not certain how it happens, I just know that it happens.

It's very difficult to change the way you are. But it starts with a decision. The decision's not easy to make, but it creates critical mass. Having made the decision, you have taken one step down a new path.

Richard Evans, past president of Rotary International, has asked this hard question:

> In what direction are you headed? If you don't change direction, you'll end up where you are going. . . . For life moves in one direction only—and each day we are faced with an actual set of circumstances, not with what might have been, not with what we might have done, but with what is, and with where we are now—and from this point we must proceed; not from where we were, not from where we wish we were—but from where we are.[3]

TAKE A LEAP OF FAITH

Sixth, a leap of faith occurs, in which the individual must choose to let go of the past, the old, the dysfunctional even as he embraces the new, the future, and the functional. Some people falter at this point, fearing the chasm is too wide to cross in one leap. But you cannot leap a chasm in two small steps. You must actually leave something behind, or you will merely carry it with you into your new circumstances. Nothing will have changed. It is a genuine act of faith to go from a place which is familiar (even if it is painful) and encounter something new. There is help at this point that is hard if not impossible to predict and plan for.

Elisabeth Kübler-Ross encourages us: "When you come to the edge of all the light you know and are about to step out into the darkness of the unknown, faith is knowing that one of two things will happen: There will be something solid to stand on, or you'll be taught to fly."

Will you take this risk? Being taught to fly means letting go of old ways. It is amazing how tightly we sometimes hang on to things that never really worked for us. Yet we routinely expect others to take scary leaps. It may seem relatively risk-free for us to tell our teenagers or our employees what to do or to verbalize expectations for a spouse. Consequently, we seldom find it necessary to go where they are, to be willing to experience what it is that they experience. It's very difficult to do that authentically. Are you willing to do that? How willing are you to take this leap of faith yourself?

STABILIZE NEW WAYS

It will take some time to stabilize new ways of thinking, feeling, and acting. It is normal to be timid, tentative, and to have old fears surface. Count on that happening. The decision you make will need to be re-made before each forward step is taken. But you can make that decision, and it does actually get easier to make with time. It will take determination, resolve, and a support system that can sustain you. And it will take a renewed commitment to be open to new awakenings, cycling through the change process, over and over again.

If you do not make the new behavior yours, the old behaviors will find a way of creeping back into your life. Under pressure you will respond the way you used to. Your emotions and moods will control you in moments of crisis. Wanting to succeed, you learn to fail. The kind and degree of change I am describing here is significant. Somebody might say, "I have changed. I am coasting in the same direction as before, but I am not sliding as fast." Slowing your speed does not help much if you are still headed in the wrong direction. The wrong direction is when you keep doing what you have always done, and, predictably, keep getting the same results.

WALKING IN SAND WHILE LENGTHENING YOUR STRIDE

I am inviting a 180 degree change. If you undertake this kind of change, you can count on slipping back from time to time. For most people, it is a common experience. It is a little like walking uphill in sand—it doesn't always feel like you are making progress, but you are, even when you take three steps and slip back two. It is hard to change, and it is sometimes hard to see the progress you are making because you are on the inside looking out.

I have been encouraged by the perspective of the American sculptor J.R. Rogers, "The successful man lengthens his stride when he discovers that the signpost has deceived him; the failure looks for a place to sit down."

As you lengthen your stride, you can recycle through this entire process, beginning with the pain of your failure, the awareness that accompanies that pain, which is another awakening, which can lead to action, help, another decision, and so on.

The decision making affirms your commitment to a better way. Each decision you make to continue the process strengthens you. Decisions must be made repeatedly until the new way of responding is habitual and characteristic. The great British prime minister Benjamin Disraeli once defined genius as "the power to make continuous effort." That will be required of you. But we are not talking about some cosmetic, superficial adjustment. We are talking about changing the quality of your life in ways that will affect you for the rest of your life.

Handling the Reactions of Others

You will be helped along the way because results are both immediate and long-term. The unburdening, the loss of old baggage, the new sense of freedom is instantaneous and somewhat heady. You may feel awkward with the new you in charge. Some people will like you better. They will be drawn to you although they may not have been before. Others will be made uncomfortable because they are not certain how to deal with you. Tell them what you are doing. Telling them makes a public issue of your struggles, but most people will be supportive and encouraging. You invite a renewal of your social contract with others as you describe what you are about. They need to have permission to release old ideas of who you are.

If your changes are in the direction I have invited, from powerlessness to coercive power, from utility power to principle-centered power, others will be the beneficiaries of your personal changes. They will be seeing you as more powerful, stronger, more determined and committed, while at the same time more susceptible to their ideas and desires. They will experience less coercive power and more reasonable deal making. Or fewer deals and more deep listening in a spirit of win/win. The point is, they will be getting something out of this too.

Some people may turn away from you completely as you move forward. They may feel threatened, or may not believe such change is possible, or may have doubts about their own possibilities, and your new behavior is a recurring reminder of what they are not doing. I was moved by a colleague who described to me what happened when a friend's father, who had been a heavy drinker for forty years, finally quit. It took a life- and marriage-threatening incident, but the father finally got help and changed. Changing saved his marriage and his life.

This success story has an interesting twist. The father had a drinking buddy for many of those years who did not have the impetus to change and who continued the habit which nearly destroyed his friend. One evening, after an extended period of sobriety, the two friends met. His drinking buddy challenged him. "You're no fun since you quit drinking!" The father's honest reply? *"You're* no fun since I quit drinking." A sobering thought. Ashleigh Brilliant has described this phenomenon when he observed, "I notice how much you have changed . . . since I changed."

SUSTAINED EFFORT PRODUCES SUSTAINED RESULTS

You must evaluate the results as you go. Is it worth it? Evaluate the consequences. Ask others for their perspective. Are you calmer? More influential? Happier? More serene? Exercise patience with yourself and with the process you are going through. You are also a work-in-progress. You are building something that has not existed before in you, and there are others, perhaps many others, who will not only be blessed and benefited by you, but will be inspired by you to take heart for their own journey. Persist in your new ways of thinking. If you can create new habits, over time they will create a new you.

You have made it this far. Congratulations. What questions do you have about the process of change? Most people want to know if it is really possible to change the things that ought to be changed. How hard will it be? Will I be able to see the new path? What will I need to let go of? I will address each of these issues before discussing where you go from here.

CAN I CHANGE ANYTHING? EVERYTHING?

When I say that there is always something you can change, I do not mean you can change everything. Obviously, you cannot. A colleague's grandfather frequently counseled his grandchildren, "You can do just about anything you want—but not everything." We all have limitations, and not everything may be possible. Martin Seligman has published a number of books and articles highlighting two decades of research on the things we can change and the things we cannot.[4] He documents that conditions such as anxiety and mood are within our realm of control, while some of the things we most often seek to change, such as body type, are unchangeable.

The Alcoholics Anonymous organization encourages its members with the serenity prayer, which reads, "God, grant me the serenity to accept the things I cannot change, courage to change the things I can, and wisdom to know the difference."[5] Seligman agrees with the organizers of AA that we can, even if genetically predisposed to alcoholism, overcome an addiction to alcohol. I have learned that this expression had been personalized to read, "Grant me the serenity to accept the *people* I cannot change, the courage to change the *person* I can, and the wisdom to know it's *me*."

We should not become discouraged, however, by things we cannot change, because there is always something we can do. For example, if I am frustrated by my weight but, after years of dieting and sustained lifestyle changes, seem to be stuck with it, I can change the way I feel and act about my weight. I can try to improve my strength, buy clothes that flatter my genetically inherited form, and accept the fact that I may never be a professional athlete. I can still be happy and empowered without being as thin as a supermodel.

BUT IT SEEMS SO HARD . . .

It is hard. As M. Scott Peck taught us in the first chapter of his insightful book *The Road Less Traveled*, "Life is difficult." But then he provided this encouragement, "Once we truly know that life is difficult—once we truly understand and accept it—then life is no longer difficult." As the oyster described in the following poem learns, *how we handle* what life gives us is much more important than *what* life gives us. And sometimes we can even turn our troubles into treasures.

> There once was an oyster
> Whose story I'll tell,
> Who found that some sand
> Had worked under his shell.
> Just one little grain
> But it gave him a pain
> (For oysters have feelings
> That are very plain).
> Now did he berate

This working of fate,
That left him in such a
Deplorable state?
Did he curse the government?
Call for an election?
Or gripe that the sea
Should have given protection?
No! He said to himself
As he sat on the shelf,
"Since I cannot remove it,
I think I'll improve it."
Well, years passed by,
As years always do,
Till he came to his destiny,
Oyster stew!
But the small grain of sand
That had bothered him so,
Was a beautiful pearl
All richly aglow.
Now this tale has a moral,
For isn't it grand,
What an oyster can do
With a small grain of sand?
And what couldn't we do
If we'd only begin
With all of the things
That get under our skin?

AUTHOR UNKNOWN

This simple thought, "Since I cannot remove it, I think I'll improve it," can be literally life-shifting. We don't have to change everything at once, and we may not even need to change everything at all. Here is an analogy. Hiking in the mountains above our home in the spring, my children and I came across a tangled mass of branches, rocks, leaves, logs, and debris in a ravine. A stream had backed up behind the logjam so that a pool had formed, restraining the natural downward flow of the water. It looked like it would take a well-placed stick of dynamite to remove the dam that had built up. But as we studied the mess, we could see that one particular log was in a critical position. It had fallen due to rot and decay, and had formed the main support for the dam. By dislodging that one log, we were able to release the water. There was enough potential power in the backed-up water that once the log was gone, all the remaining debris was swept away.

I call this the logjam principle. Sometimes the problems we face seem an impossible, intricate mess. We may not believe there is a way out. But if we can shift our perspective, if we can see more clearly, we may be able to identify a critical problem, one that is the result of decay or disuse of our capacities and strengths. This one issue may be the critical one, supporting depression, discouragement, or despair; this one needs to be removed and cast aside. By dealing with a few of these critical issues, we release the power in us to deal with the other issues or make them irrelevant.

WALK DOWN A DIFFERENT STREET

The following poem by Portia Nelson demonstrates the perspectives we might have when shifting from one kind of power to another.

Autobiography in Five Short Chapters

I
I walk down the street.
   There is a deep hole in the sidewalk.
   I fall in.
   I am lost . . . I am helpless.
      It isn't my fault.
   It takes forever to find a way out.
II
I walk down the same street.
   There is a deep hole in the sidewalk.
   I pretend I don't see it.
   I fall in again.
   I can't believe I am in the same place.
      But it isn't my fault.
   It still takes a long time to get out.
III
I walk down the same street.
   There is a deep hole in the sidewalk.
   I see it is there.
   I still fall in . . . it's a habit.
      My eyes are open.

I know where I am.
It is my fault.
I get out immediately.
IV
I walk down the same street.
There is a deep hole in the sidewalk.
I walk around it.
V
I walk down another street.

Which chapter are you in right now? Do you go into most situations expecting to fail, unprepared for what you might face, or do you consciously decide to succeed? We need to remember that even if we unexpectedly end up on the street with the hole, we can make the choice to take a detour, or to negotiate a new path. Perhaps the next time we will be able to take another street, avoiding the problem altogether, or maybe we unite with some friends, return to the street, and fill in the hole!

LEARNING TO LET GO

What does it take to move from Chapter I to Chapter III or IV or V? I like to tell a story about monkeys which illustrates the first step. On an island in the South Pacific, the natives had an unusual method for capturing monkeys. The potential captor would take a coconut, cut off one end, put in a few nuts, and attach the coconut to a vine. He would leave the coconut in a visible location and then wait. Before long, a monkey would come along, and being naturally inquisitive, start exploring the coconut. Invariably, the monkey would find the nuts, and reach in to grab them. The problem came when the monkey would try to pull its hand out of the coconut. It would screech and holler, bang the coconut on the ground or against a tree while its fist was still inside. It would do everything but open its fist and let go of the nuts. It was stuck.

Late in the day, the captors would move in and pull on the vine attached to the coconut. The monkey, exhausted from its struggle with the coconut, would draw on its little bit of remaining energy to fight, yet still would seldom let go of the nuts. It would lose at least its freedom and sometimes its life. For what? A handful of nuts.

Of course, we would never do anything so ridiculous. Or would we? Sometimes we "hang on," refusing to let go of experiences, feelings, grudges, or pet peeves. When we cling to them, we lose our ability to move on, to find power in the present and instead are stuck with powerlessness from the past. What emotional baggage do you carry that prevents you from being happy? What negative, disheartening feelings do you allow to dominate your thoughts and interfere with your freedom?

Michael McLean, a professional musician who attended one of our seminars, shared a beautiful song he and John Batdorf had written some years earlier that captured the spirit and power of letting go. Here are the words to his moving, inspirational song.

Let It Go

I can still recall the hour my father told me it was time
To let it go.
Though its mended wing had made it sing
He said the bird I cared for was not really mine.
"Let it go . . ."
"Letting go," he said, "seems to break your heart.
Though it will heal it feels slow to start."
Though the pain burned within me so
He held me tight, so I could let it go

Years have passed since then and so has he, but I still hear his words,
"Let it go . . ."
There's so much of life that can't be lived
When you're still holding on to hate and anger deep inside—
Let it go.
Letting go opens up the heart.
There is a new day hungry to start.
You can't change what has hurt you so,
But you will heal if you can let it go.

All that's wrong in your life . . .
Let it go.
All that is worth saving
Is love . . .
Love will hold you tight.
Love lifts the burden and love shines the light.
Only love nourishes us so;

If it's not love, then simply
Let it go.[6]

McLean's account of how this song came to be written is inspirational, because he lived what he wrote. Here is his experience as he told it to me:

> A few years ago, a wonderful songwriter named John Batdorf sent me a melody and asked if I'd consider writing the lyrics. Although I'd written songs for over twenty years I wasn't sure I could write a lyric to a melody that wasn't my own. I put John's tape on and listened. It was an extraordinary melody that I immediately felt connected to in ways I still can't fully explain. At eleven o'clock the night I received the tape I began working on the lyric and the next thing I knew it was six in the morning and the song was complete.
>
> I became emotional as I reviewed this new creation. The song seemed to be healing places inside of me I didn't even know were wounded. Although I didn't realize it at the time, the writing of the song was preparing me for a dramatic change in my life. A few months later I said good-bye to my full-time employer of fifteen years and began an adventure that would have been completely miserable if not downright impossible had I not learned to LET IT GO.[7]

"Letting go" has since come to have significant meaning for me as I teach. In our week-long executive seminars, we usually spend at least one afternoon in an outdoor, mountain setting solving simulated management problems and learning how to combine the strengths of management and leadership roles. At the beginning of our leadership laboratory we invite participants to "take something" from the mountain, a picture, a twig, a pebble, a dead leaf, or a mental image to keep as a reminder that will anchor their feelings, thoughts, and learnings from their afternoon on the mountain. Sometimes I play McLean's "Let It Go" for them and then invite them to "leave something" on the mountain as well—perhaps a habit that no longer serves them, an old belief system they have outgrown, or a grudge or ill feelings that they are holding about someone that continue to irritate them. Most of the participants linger at the end of the day, in deep reflection, choosing what they might let go of, and leave behind them on the mountain. I am told months and years later that one of the most significant activities of the entire week was the personal awareness and the help they received so they could muster the courage to let go of something that prevented them from moving on with their life.

As we let go of old things, we make room for new things. Letting go of dependence and fear, we have room for spontaneity, hope, and joy. By the end of the week, three or four of the executives in the group will visit with me privately, informing me that they are considering making major changes in their jobs. Some even quit their jobs in response to a growing awareness that the way they are living their professional lives is out of harmony with what they really value. Letting go of something in their life that is not working, they choose the path of power; they choose to live deliberately after perhaps an entire career of powerlessness; they choose to let go and move on, toward possibilities and unrealized potential.

One such executive, Mike, grew quieter and quieter as a week of leadership training progressed. He seemed all right, but was withdrawn from the group. By Thursday morning Mike said, "I think I owe everyone an explanation. I pulled away from everyone else on Monday evening when you asked us to go sit on a rock somewhere and think about our lives and begin to write a personal mission statement. All alone, I grew painfully aware that I'm not happy . . . and I haven't been happy for fifteen years."

Here is the story that unfolded. He was a senior executive in an international consumer electronics company. He felt successful—his income was in six figures, he had three homes, all the RVs and toys he wanted— but he was not happy. "I was happy fifteen years ago but I didn't realize it. I guess I just got numb and busy and allowed myself to drift away from what was important. Back then I was a band teacher for a junior high school. It was wonderful."

We were stunned. Band teacher? The most challenging job I could imagine would be the band teacher in a junior high school. Picture thirty or forty kids in a band room who are bowing and beating and blowing their rented instruments, with few of the instruments working properly and many out of tune. Although I love music, I think that would be a frustrating, irritating, thankless job.

"I know what you are thinking," he continued, "but do you know I was the best thing going on at that school and in that town. We worked together. One year we even went to the Rose Parade in Pasadena, California. I knew all of the kids and their families; they knew me and I made a difference. I had a hard time making a living, so I ended up changing careers. I got into electronics and wound up in management where I am today. I ended up going through a sad and painful divorce . . ."

His voice trailed off. I wondered out loud what he was going to do.

"I don't know what I am going to do next—but I can't go back to where I was Monday morning."

Mike was a different person than he had been just a few days before. The next day the seminar ended, and Mike, along with the other participants, headed home.

The rest of the story? A few months later I was in Dallas, Texas, doing a public seminar for several hundred people. On a break a stranger approached me smiling and said, "We know the same person . . . you remember Mike who was in your seminar at Sundance a couple of months ago? I used to work for him. He came back from your training and he was all excited—you know how people are. We were sure it would wear off in a couple of days, but it didn't. He was different. He was more purposeful, more deliberate, more committed. He negotiated for a different role in the company but senior management didn't want him to change, so he quit! It took a lot of courage, lots of determination, and he told me that he had to remake the decision to move forward over and over again. He felt support and understanding from the friends who knew him best. He realized that he was a volunteer, not a victim, in life and that he had the ability to match this opportunity, to choose what the rest of his life would be like.

"He left the company and relocated in a different state." I asked, half joking, if he was leading a band somewhere. "No—but he has remarried and has moved on with his life. He is working in a new career field and is very, very happy."

I have, with Mike's permission, shared his experience with a number of people who felt they were at a crossroads, trapped by mortgage payments or other people's expectations or their own doubts. If we are able to let go of the things that are holding us back, that are causing us to feel powerless, we can open doors to future power, success, and happiness. If we have the courage to change our perspective—to look at things from a new angle—we might find that we can have more legitimate power than we ever dreamed possible, the power that comes when we live courageous, honorable lives.

Consider what you need to let go of.

WHAT ARE YOU STILL CARRYING?

Learning to let go reminds me of an old Eastern story about two monks who had taken vows of poverty and celibacy and traveled about helping and serving others. On one journey, they arrived at a river swollen from torrential rains the night before. By the side of the river was a beautiful woman, nicely dressed, but perplexed because the bridge had washed out. Now, these monks had made vows not to look at women, think about women, or touch or talk with a woman. But one of the monks left his companion, went to the woman, and without a word lifted her up in his arms. He carried her out into the turbulent, waist-high water, and struggled to the other side. Setting her down, he bowed graciously and stepped aside to wait for his companion. The other monk was incensed. Their vows had been desecrated, in front of onlooking villagers! How could his companion treat their vows so casually! He not only had to be thinking about the woman, but he had touched her. The monk was enraged. He strode angrily through the stream and then continued his journey a few feet ahead of his companion. They traveled the rest of the day in silence. At night they stopped and shared a simple meal. They both retired for the night. But the first monk couldn't restrain himself any longer. He finally rolled over and angrily shoved his companion.

"How could you do that at the river today? I was so embarrassed. You have humiliated and disgraced our order."

"What are you talking about?"

"You know—that woman you touched today. You violated our vows!"

The second monk said, "Oh yes . . . the woman. Perhaps I did. But are *you* still carrying her? I set her down on the other side of the stream."

Sometimes we unnecessarily carry emotional baggage that prevents us from moving on. I know a woman who was married to an abusive man for many years. Her marriage ended, but her preoccupation with her husband—his weaknesses and his excesses—remained. She had built her emotional life around this man and to this day is trapped by his problems, continually replaying their old scripts even though the marriage is over. He has moved on with his life. He has remarried and lives in a nearby town. His new life only fuels this woman's fire. She spends much of her time talking about him, complaining about him, trying to find out the things he does and who he does them with and then telling anyone who will listen, envying the car he drives and the house he lives in. She refuses to let go of him, and as a result cannot go on with her life.

Perhaps there are things you need to let go of. Can you do it? Yes.

YOU CAN CHANGE TOO

Perhaps the appropriate measure of success is not whether you have a tough problem to deal with, but whether it's the same problem you had last year. What are you working on now? Are you in a different place with the same problems or in the same place, but with new problems? I know you can change.

Chad struggled but determined to take on a big issue, a problem he had been struggling with for years. Here is his experience. Reviewing the preassessment forms for a new group of participants registered for leadership training, I was struck by one entry. After listing his strengths and expectations, Chad made this entry: "I have low self-esteem . . ." I started looking for this executive, wondering how he would appear, interact, handle himself, and so on. Little did I know that this lone man, self-identified as someone who did not feel good about himself, would become the role model for courage and personal transformation to forty other leaders that week.

It started on the morning of the second day. Reviewing his written comments from the day before, I noticed an interesting comment: "for the first time in a long time, I did something last night besides watch TV." I felt like he was making a critical yet simple personal statement, noting a kind of personal breakthrough.

Tuesday we spent the morning talking about the many different kinds of power and asked the question why someone would want to follow us. He seemed to be thoughtful. That afternoon we headed for the mountainside in a foot of snow to learn some lessons in leadership. It was a great afternoon, with all I could hope for in bonding, awareness building, and a spirit of fun, learning, and mutual respect. As we concluded our session and sent everyone down the mountain and home for dinner, I noticed him lingering alone, with the fading rays of sunlight streaking across Mount Timpanogos behind him.

The next morning his feedback form reported a personal insight he had experienced on the mountain. Observing one of the group exercises from the fringes, he had noticed that a particular maneuver was about to fail. It occurred to him to intervene, but for a moment he paused, fearing rejection by the group if he was seen as an outsider, not participating but staying in the shadows finding fault and complaining. The moment for action passed, and the maneuver failed, as he assumed it would. He berated himself for taking the easy, quiet path, and determined to do better if he was given another opportunity.

Later Chad told me that the previous evening he had begun to sense a personal loss, and a resulting desire to connect with his wife. They had been married for a quarter of a century and did not have a "bad" marriage, just an indifferent one. His two children, one in college and one finishing high school, took some of their time and interest, and were the only thing they really shared anymore. But on the mountain, in the quiet majesty of snow and sky, he had yearned for something he had had a long time ago. Hurrying off the mountain, he hiked the hill to his room and called home. His wife answered.

"You want me to come to Utah? This weekend? Why? I can't—there is the trip into San Francisco, our daughter has a dance at the high school. It is out of the question."

"I would just like you to come up here . . ."

"Why?"

"Maybe we could go for a walk in the woods or something . . ."

"Why?"

"I would like you to . . ."

"Why?"

"I just want to be with you . . ." There was a very long pause . . . an eternity of silence . . . and then,

"Okay. I will come."

Another long pause . . . nervous laughter . . . and then. . . "Oh! I don't know if they can accommodate you. I'll call you right back." He called the front desk and the airline company and called his wife back. "It's all set. You are coming then? Great . . . that's great. I'll see you Friday afternoon at the airport."

What sort of victory is that? I have seen victory in the face of overwhelming odds. I have seen men choose the nobler path when it was easier to run or hide or shift the blame. But I think I have not seen greater, braver, or truer choices made than these simple determinations to reach out, reach back to a love that was lost from neglect and insensitivity. His simple courage brightened all our hopes and encouraged many of us who had expressed lofty public visions to look closer to home to apply our new commitments.

The next day, Chad was anxious to share the continuing evolution of this developing family drama. He had called home again the previous night, just to talk with his wife. He was greatly disappointed to find her gone. He wanted to talk, so when his fifteen-year-old daughter answered the phone, he thought, well, I *did* want to talk, why not . . . He attempted to use some new listening skills to empathize with his daughter, trying to understand her without judging. "You know what?" he said to me. "It is hard to be empathic with a fifteen-year-old girl!"

The next day in class, I asked Chad what phase he was in, or if he was "done." He said, "My college son is next—he is the toughest, and tonight I am talking to him." He was actually breathless as he described what he was going to do—his anticipation was greater than his fear.

I have not heard the next episode yet. But I sense it will not be a culmination as much as a beginning. What about his low self-esteem? I am not certain, but I felt that his new sense of self-worth might be as high and uplifting as the mountains towering over our seminar room at Sundance.

WHERE DO I GO FROM HERE?

A little doing dispels a lot of doubt. Start where you are, and do something now. Doing a little something may take you to new and different places emotionally and psychologically.

I learned many years ago while hiking in the mountains with the Boy Scouts that you often have to change your location before you will be able to change your perspective. Some things just can't be seen from where we stand today. To move from where we are requires the opposite of doubt—it requires faith. So if you will muster the courage to get in a different place psychologically, you may see some important things differently.

A story I first heard as a child told of a father and son who visited the train engineer while journeying on their first nighttime train ride. The engineer invited the little boy to sit up on his lap and watch out the front windows as the intense light went back and forth across the tracks in a figure-eight pattern, back and forth, back and forth. He noticed the boy was shivering. "Are you cold?" he asked. "No, I'm scared. What if something's out there and we hit it. You can't see very far." The engineer replied calmly, "You're right. So I just run to the end of the light. And when I get there, I can see further. I don't need to see further until I get there." That is really kind of a remarkable statement of faith. You can only see so far; but you're willing to go as far as you can see with the confidence that when you get there, you'll have light for the path ahead.

Bringing it all together requires introspection, awareness, courage, opportunity, wisdom, and persistence. You must continually be open to new data, new perspectives, the possibility that the way you do it or the way you see it is incomplete. The process of changing is never-ending. Perhaps we never "arrive." We will always be learning, changing, growing, reshaping, modifying, developing, becoming. The joy of living has more to do with the anticipation of what lies ahead and what lies within than with where we are today.

Consider the following questions before you read the final chapter of this book. Think about a specific relationship that is worth investing in, where the payoff would include being more effective in other relationships as well.

ASSESSING YOUR READINESS FOR CHANGE

1. Where are you now? Have you had a wake-up call? Is the pain intense enough or the desire great enough for you to take action?

2. What do you lean on now? What sustains you where you are?

3. Where do you want to be? What would a win look like for you and for the people you would like to influence?

4. Why do you want to change? What is your underlying motive?

5. Can you imagine yourself paying the price? In your mind's eye, can you see yourself doing what it will take to get started, to sustain the effort, to be tough in the hard times? What images will affirm your efforts?

6. Will it be worth it? Looking back months and years from now, what will you be glad you did?

CHAPTER 15

LIVING WITH HONOR—
THE LIFELONG QUEST

Success lies in doing not what others consider to be great, but what you consider to be right.

JOHN GRAY

WHERE WE STARTED

This book began with the following positive premises:

1. You already understand much about power because you have experienced its many forms as others have influenced you.
2. Power and influence can be acquired and developed.
3. You choose to be powerless or powerful every day.
4. Powerlessness and each of the three paths to power have different foundations.
5. Depending on the situation, you may attempt to influence others with honor, with fairness, with fear, or you may sometimes doubt your ability to influence at all.
6. The results you get with each approach are absolutely predictable.
7. Whatever your official title or position, ultimately your ability to influence others is a result of what you are, as well as what you do.

8. You can change.
9. You can make a difference for good, and the world needs what you can do.

The purpose of this chapter is to bring all of these ideas together, to provide direction and encouragement and hope so that you can share the Power Principle with others.

PEOPLE MAKE THE DIFFERENCE

Our greatest sorrows and our greatest joys come in our interactions with other people. If it takes a lifetime to bless one life, what joy that can bring. And if, along the way, we bless and are blessed in turn by many others, what a rich life we will have had.

We can encourage each other in our pursuits, difficult though life may be. No one really has any answers for anybody else. Perhaps the best we can do is pause on the sidelines from time to time, bandage each other's wounds, suggest an idea or two and some encouragement, then jump back into the game. Martin Luther observed that life is "like a besieged city surrounded on all sides. . . . Each of us has a place on the wall to defend and no one can stand where another stands, but nothing prevents us from calling encouragement to one another."[1] In a similar vein, George Eliot asked, "What do we live for, if it is not to make life less difficult for each other?"[2]

HOW WILL YOU SPEND THE REST OF YOUR LIFE?

At the end of your life, looking back, will you have lived in a way that is worthy of the best in you? Or will you spend your life learning and preparing to sing, without ever singing? I am inspired by people I have known in my work who are "singing."

Take a young boy, gazing at the stars and wondering if man will ever go there. Give him a challenging life, an engineering degree, a critical missed opportunity for promotion in the aerospace industry, eventual recognition by Congress and you have a Dan Goldin, director of NASA. Forming alliances with Russia, Italy, Japan, and Germany, he became responsible for space exploration for the entire human race.

Take a young girl, abused and introspective. Give her a dream that someday her life will amount to something. Have her grow up with the oppression that is life for many minorities. And you have an Oprah Winfrey, author, actress, philanthropist, and leader of the movement to revitalize and restore dignity to talk television. She inspires twenty million people every day.

Take an overweight, awkward, gangly boy. Have him live in poverty, with discouragement and disappointment as roommates. Give him financial success in his twenties, then financial ruin and betrayal by trusted friends, and you have a Tony Robbins, author, teacher, and mentor to millions who consider him their guide as they work to awaken the giant in themselves. In addition to his teaching and writing, Tony has sponsored numerous national projects to help children and adults across the nation gain skills and learn to believe in themselves.

My research on heroes has taught me that the typical hero is a normal person who had extraordinary demands placed on them, and they rose to the occasion. They did what had to be done. What we do determines what we become. Scholars publish; teachers teach; and as Joseph Campbell suggests, "A celebrity serves himself or herself; but a hero goes out and redeems society."[3] You have probably noticed that many of the people talked about in this book are not the typical "power" people. Even Mother Teresa, who has spent her life among the poor, considers herself only "a pencil in the hand of God. He has not called me to be successful; but to be faithful."[4]

What we choose to do is not nearly as important as what we become by the choices we make.

I was advised as I left college to "survey large fields, but cultivate small ones." Like large international companies, we need to think globally (save the planet—it is our home) but act locally (can I match my socks, deal with the neighbor's barking dog, get the holes filled in my street, take a hot meal to the widow nearby?). Does it take a parent or a village to raise a child? It takes *both*!

As Walter Anderson has written, "When we commit to high ideals, we succeed before the outcome is known."

As you go forward, start small. Accomplish the task at hand. Goethe said, "If everyone would just sweep their own front porch, the whole world would be clean."

THE POWER PROCESS REVISITED

You increase your principle-centered power when you stop trying to get it, and go on about your life, working on yourself, in humility and with diligence. Basically, you have to make decisions about means and ends. The power approach you take, as manifested by the tools you use, will determine the kinds of goals you will be able to achieve. Conversely, if you are certain about the outcomes you want in others' behavior, and the quality of relationships you want, then it is a relatively straightforward process to determine which power base to operate from. As you pursue principle-centered power, power as a focus paradoxically drops out of the formula. The less you concentrate on having it, and the more you work to be worthy of it, the more you increase your ability to influence the people you care about the most.

Consider the power process one more time. Examine the connections between the choices you make and the results you get.

POWER TOOLS AND PURPOSES

The following charts make clear that there is a direct connection between our tools and our purposes, our approaches and our results. I have summarized here a diagnostic tool which can help you decide where you are and what you want. Decide what you are trying to accomplish and I will tell you how to get it. Conversely, determine what tools you are using and I can accurately predict what results you will be able to achieve.

TOOLS/APPROACH	PURPOSES/POSSIBLE RESULTS
What you do . . .	*What you get*
Wait	
Disregard	
Delay	Uncertainty
Take no action	
Despair	
Neglect	
Become apathetic	

THE POWER PROCESS

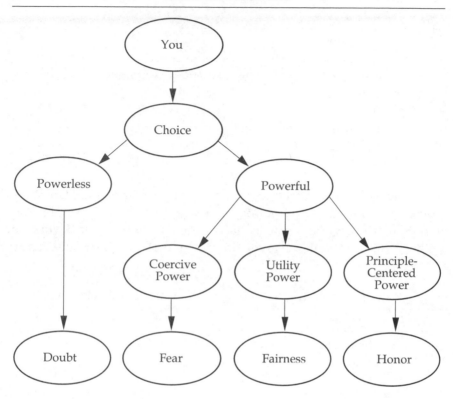

If you want compliance, I can guarantee how to get compliance—force someone, and if the threat is severe enough, you get them to comply. Bully them, threaten them, control them, and you will get the compliance you seek. Are there complications? Certainly. Do you have to continue to escalate the consequences and/or the threat to get the same level of compliance? Usually. Do others then generalize from the punishment to the punisher? Almost always. That is part of the price of control.

Tools/Approach	Purposes/Possible Results
What you do . . .	*What you get*
Bully	
Control	
Manipulate	

Tools/Approach	Purposes/Possible Results
What you do . . .	*What you get*
Intimidate Coerce Threaten Terrorize Force Use scare tactics Pressure Guilt load	Compliance

If, however, you want agreement, rather than compliance, you have to take a different approach. You have to negotiate with people. You may have to bargain. You may have to compromise. But if you are willing to live through the give-and-take of dialogue, you can usually get people to agree.

Tools/Approach	Purposes/Possible Results
What you do . . .	*What you get*
Negotiate Dicker Tit for tat Barter Deal Trade Volley Argue Exchange Arrange Haggle Contract Arrange Make deals Position	Agreement

But if you really want their deep commitment, if you want them to choose what is best for the majority, the majority of the time, whether you are there, whether or not circumstances change, then the Power

Principle holds the key. You must encourage their commitment. You must invite their participation. You must ask for their involvement. You must persuade, listen, unconditionally accept them, strive to live with integrity, make it safe for them to risk, be kind and consistent, and manifest tough love. If you are willing to pay this price, remarkable things are possible.

Tools/Approach	Purposes/Possible Results
What you do . . .	*What you get*
Persuade	
Be patient	
Be gentle	
Be teachable	
Be accepting	What's right and best for
Be kind	the majority most of the time
Gain knowledge	
Discipline	
Be consistent	
Live with integrity	

If you coerce people, they will make choices based on what they hope to avoid; if you negotiate with people, they will make choices based on what they want to get or obtain from you; if you live with the Power Principle, people will be inspired to make choices based on what they value or prize the most. It is all a matter of choice. We all have choices. The leadership choice is, What power base will I operate from? The followership choice is, What do I want? Who will I follow? Why will I follow them? Why will I listen to them?

I WANT TO INFLUENCE *YOU* . . . WITH HONOR

I hope to influence you. I want you to realize that you have already experienced principle-centered power in a key relationship in your life. I want you to believe that you can achieve what you want most by producing legitimate power with other people. I want you to develop hope that by conducting your life with honor, you can get the long-term results you want.

The world is full of worthy needs, causes which need champions, suffering which needs alleviating, good that needs doing. Leaders who operate from a base of principle-centered power can make a significant difference because of what happens to the people who choose to follow them. In addition, they can multiply the good that is done by leveraging the help they give others. When schoolteacher-turned-revolutionary-officer Nathan Hale was caught returning to his regiment with captured information about British troop movements, and arrested for treason against the British in the early days of our Revolution, he was taunted with the possibilities that would not come to pass since he was about to be executed.

He was only twenty-one—a rich and promising life lay before him. "Have you no regrets?" they reportedly asked him, mocking and demeaning his patriotic fervor. "Yes, he replied. "I regret I have but one life to lose for my country!" He lost his life, but it was given in pursuit of freedom for his children and grandchildren, ancestors of ours. Two generations later, a grandnephew, Edward Everett Hale, who was similarly challenged by the same pious, judgmental functionaries, answered the question this way, demonstrating the legacy that was in his blood: "I am only one, but I am one; I cannot do everything, but I can do something; what I can do I ought to do, and what I ought to do by the grace of God I shall do." As a clergyman and an author, the grandnephew carried on the tradition of faith and service. The legacy he had inherited was confirmed; his words were recorded and have been taught to schoolchildren for nearly two hundred years.

My purpose in writing this book was to give you hope, to encourage you in your work with other people. Napoleon suggested that a leader is a dealer in hope. I want you to believe that you know about power and leadership because you have experienced all three types of power, as a follower. I believe that you can be a leader who operates *with* others, who chooses principle-centered power as the primary way of influencing others in key relationships. I believe you can affect others for good in the way that you have been influenced for good in your own life. My belief that change is possible comes from my experience counseling, coaching, teaching, and learning from thousands of other people. My awareness of how difficult it is to change has been learned deeply through my own experience.

EARNING THE PRIVILEGE TO TALK ABOUT CHANGE

I struggle to live what I teach. But I want it badly. That desire drives me, humbles me, empowers me to get up, go back, apologize, try again, and never give up.

When trouble and opportunity come together, the result is often a crisis. In my own experience with crisis, the trouble came before the opportunity. After a series of business ventures and college teaching experiences in the 1970s and early 1980s, my clients and students encouraged me to begin a full-time speakers bureau and consulting company. I was a good coach, judged by the repeat business and referrals I continuously received. Success came quickly. Money came in faster and in greater amounts than I had ever experienced. I started to acquire the trappings of success. I started to look and act the part of the successful entrepreneur. I purchased some troubled but potentially high-paying investments. Cash flow was better than ever. But the balance sheet was ignored. My fledgling business was undercapitalized. It needed leadership at home and I was on the road. I brought in additional talent to manage our office and help grow the business, but it was the traditional case of too little too late. Like a nightmarish scene from Disney's *Sorcerer's Apprentice*, I had created a flood that had taken on a momentum and life of its own, and it was out of control.

The good people who joined me had a dragon to slay that was bigger than they were. It soon became apparent that I would be unable to fulfill my commitments, including extensive financial obligations. One resource after another dried up. I began the emotional decline I diagrammed in Chapter 2. Discouragement turned to mild depression, then severe depression. I became despondent. I started to flail in all directions, looking for someone or some institution to bail me out. I had a large unsecured loan from a local bank that had been extended twice and was finally due. Other bills, including business operating expenses, were two, then three, then six months behind and mounting as interest compounded on the unpaid bills. The inevitable telephone calls and letters came, polite at first and then increasingly menacing and threatening, not only to the office, but to my home. I began to retreat emotionally from my own wife, hoping for a miracle to pull me out of this fiscal and psychological whirlpool I had created. I felt I had few options and diminishing capacity to solve my problems.

As a last-ditch effort, I approached a former client, a self-made millionaire who I considered to be a friend, with my remaining shreds of dignity, hoping for any answer outside myself to solve my problems. He could easily have written a check, provided a personal loan, intervened with the bank (we had the same banker), or created a solution that would have solved my problem. But he refused. He gave me a story, instead, about someone he had helped financially, in which the help he provided only prolonged the inevitable. He was courteous but firm. I was angry. I was despairing. I needed money, not stories. I didn't know where to turn. I felt that I was in a maelstrom in which everything I had worked for, my profession, my friends, my reputation, my family, and my faith, were all being pulled under by a relentless undertow that I had set in motion and now couldn't handle.

Crisis? I did not have the presence of mind to label my predicament. I just knew the pain was intense, the sense of failure was immense, the size of the hole I had dug, not with bad intent, but with inexperience and poor judgment and feelings of neediness, was overwhelming, and my ability to deal with my problems was all but gone.

The months that followed were terrible. I found a lawyer who helped us inventory our assets, close our business, lay off our employees, and file for bankruptcy. I felt like I was a walking, living lie. My life had become a contradiction to everything I taught. I was supposed to be helping professional, successful men and women achieve more with their lives when mine was ruined. It was a dark day, a day I hit bottom, when Shawny accompanied me into court for the judge's decision on disposition of assets. She had done nothing to get us there. The actions had been mine. The unwise business decisions had been mine. The business failure had been mine. Yet she and my children and numerous other individuals and agencies were suffering because of me.

Out of that crisis, that failure, that horribly destructive day, a new life began. It took months, and the months became years, before I was fully productive again. I was helped along the way by many people who still believed in me, who wanted me to succeed, who felt that I had something worth offering. One by one I identified and worked on my problems. With the financial pressure simplified but still immense, I started working. I made a personal commitment to pay off every debt, to return to each creditor and make things right, somehow. I first paid the individuals, then the agencies, then institutions. It took sacrifice and planning, budgeting and deliberate living that had not been a part of my life. The mountain of debt gradually shrunk. I am not proud that I filed for bankruptcy and created the sequence of events that got me there. I take full responsibility for all the unwise decisions that led, inevitably, to that embarrassing, costly precipice. I am grateful that I have had the opportunity and means provided to pay back all the debts that had been dissolved in the bankruptcy.

As I began to work again, and to chip away at what seemed like impossible debt, my self-esteem and self-confidence started to flicker alive, with tiny, fragile wisps of possibility. I started to wonder if the rebuilding of a life, relationships, a career, a profession could really happen. I started to have hope.

It was during this time of personal reconstruction that Stephen Covey and I crossed paths. I had been impressed with his approach to proactive living while he was an executive assistant to the president of Brigham Young University years earlier and I was a graduate student. He had recently left the university with plans for affecting management in America. With only a handful of professionals, he was beginning an enterprise based on his vision. I made a proposal to train and coach these associates. This began a year-long contract, in which I got to know and respect the leaders of his new company, and he came to value the contribution I could make to what he was trying to accomplish. Out of our joint commitment, and the rapidly growing success of this new organization, I became one of the owners helping Stephen R. Covey and Associates transition to the Covey Leadership Center. My dream of teaching and bringing hope had a new home. I could return to doing what I wanted to do and the Covey Leadership Center became my home base for doing good in the world.

I am humbled by the opportunities I have today, to help create conditions that allow leaders to become better leaders, parents to become better parents, and executives in all kinds of associations to become more effective in their personal and professional lives. I am better off financially than I was before this crisis developed. I have a clearer focus to my professional life. I treasure my family relationships and work constantly to balance demands at work and at home so that I can live with few regrets. I have not arrived, but the path looks clear and our challenges are challenges of abundant opportunity, not survival. We have moved from survival through stability to success. Ultimately, we hope to make a significant worldwide contribution.

I am keenly aware that these opportunities might never have happened without the crisis that disrupted my life.

As I have revisited this whole experience with the friend who refused to give me the money that I thought would solve my problems, I have learned the wisdom of his actions. At that time I had begun to feel like a victim, powerless and helpless. He told me that it was hard for him not to bail me out, but he had confidence that if I was allowed to experience the full consequences of my actions, I would learn more, rebound more quickly, and bounce back faster because what I really needed to survive and then succeed, I had all the time. His vision and belief in my ultimate possibilities helped me move from powerlessness to power. I gratefully thank him for his decision, and for the crisis that enabled me to learn what I am trying to teach, to influence with honor.

WHERE ARE YOU GOING NOW?

What we can be, we can be together. A community of believers. Tolstoy once wrote, "The power of a group of people who live true to their convictions does more and more certain good than all writings. Let us, therefore, one and all, live true to our convictions." Our legacy will be that we served. The highest good we can do is to serve. We should serve first those we are with, and we should serve them with the needs they have right now. We can do it. A client who participated in our leadership training recently wrote me, "There is no doubt in my mind that I *can* do it. The only remaining question is, *will I?*"

A recent article noted the increasing interest in focusing on virtue as a virtue, in homes, in government, and in business. At the end of that article was this interesting statement: "The real risk of the virtue movement is that it will become just another example of what has become a leading American character trait. Talking a good game. There's no doubt that the pendulum was swinging back from self-expression to self-discipline. But if we're to be serious about all of this it means we will have to sacrifice some measure of the freedom we now have to do anything we want if it feels good. The true test of our character in other words will require more than applauding politicians and passing resolutions. In the end it's not the laws we pass, it's the lives that we lead."[5]

Can you make a difference? I think so. I could tell you many more stories, about dollars saved and lives changed. But fundamentally you already know because you have been blessed by someone who cared deeply about you and who lived true to their beliefs. Their memory lives on in the life that you live. And you could influence hundreds or perhaps thousands. No one knows where the influence will stop.

CARRYING THE FIRE WITH YOU

When I was growing up I thought that if I could just get one of these firebows the Indians used, I could start our campfire when our family went camping. I tried a few times with primitive, ineffective tools, but was never successful. Years later, when I was in college, I participated in a survival program conducted by Larry Dean Olsen. He was the technical specialist for the movie *Jeremiah Johnson*, with Robert Redford. Olsen helped the actor learn the skills of a real mountain man in preparation for his part. Once when I was on a survival trip with Larry, I had made a simple bow and I was pulling back and forth awkwardly with the bow, trying to start a fire. Larry came up to me and laughed, "No, we don't do that. You'll never start a fire that way. Let me tell you what the Indians really did—the nomads, at least.

"In the morning as we break camp, we fish down in the ashes and we find the hottest coal that we can find. By checking with your hand, you can tell which coals have a little life left in them.

"You take a live coal out and wrap it several times with long strips of bark. When it is almost sealed you end up with a fire bundle. We carry that all day long and at night when we're going to make camp again in a new place, we unwrap the coal and use it to start a new fire. We blow on it gently and soon there will be a tiny flame. If we feed it, pretty soon we have a roaring fire."

The Greek god Prometheus distinguished himself as one of the best friends mortals ever had, largely through his use of power. He was a fighter against injustice and unrighteous power. "Prometheus" means "forethought," and he was given credit for being very wise. But he is best known in the myths of the Greeks because he brought fire from the sun and gave it to men. The reason the ancients got into trouble was they lacked fire. Apparently they needed Prometheus to perform this fire-carrying service for them.

Good fire carriers are also a great need today. You don't need a fire where you are going because you can take it with you. Your fire is the knowledge and capacity you have that will be the key to your future.

It's not me, it's not what is in the books, it's not what's on you. Remember the Air Force lieutenant who survived without his survival gear? It's what's *in* you that makes the difference. If something ignited as you read this book, it was there all the time. If I helped you to discover or uncover or recover something, I assure you it was already in you. You already have what you need, and you have had it all the time.

Are you on fire? John Wesley, the founder of Methodism, said you set yourself on fire and the whole world will come and watch, and maybe they will read by the light that you give. The capacity you have is enormous. Your capacity to live, to grow, to share, to sacrifice. That is the fire within you. When you do the thing that only you can do, it not only inspires others, it invites their participation. Then they choose to follow you. There is a spark that ignites us that has its roots in the divine. The traditional Tibetan greeting "Namaste" acknowledges the god in others; and the root for the word "enthusiasm" is *en theos*, which means literally "god within us." When the best and highest in us engages openly and honestly with the best and the highest in others, there is fire.

You can reinstate the concept of honor as the source of power between people. You can treat your children, your neighbors, your students, your customers, your followers with honor. What if you treated friends as strangers, and got to know them all over again? You might ask what they have learned since you last met; you might ask where they are now; you might ask what you could do for them that would benefit them and increase the trust between you. Then you could turn the process around and treat the strangers you meet as new friends, which they may become. My mother tells about moving to a new town when I was a child. Mom was worried about my adjusting. I had lost my father in an accident just the year before. "Won't you miss your friends?" she asked, trying to be sensitive to my fears and concerns. But with the wisdom and insight only an innocent child might have, I replied with assurance, "Oh, I have some friends there, but I haven't met them yet."

WHAT ARE YOU MAKING?

Socrates said, "Let him who would move the world, first move himself." That reminds me of a story about a teacher who passed out crayons and blank paper and told the children they could draw any-thing they liked.

"What are you drawing?" he asked one child after awhile.

"A house."

"What are you making?" he asked another child.

"A snowman."

A third child was busy sketching, but the design was hard to figure out, so the teacher asked, "And what are you making?"

"Oh, I'm going to draw a picture of God," the child earnestly replied.

"How can you do that? No one knows what God looks like."

"They will when I'm done."

Perhaps when you're done, they'll know what influence with honor looks like. When you're done, they'll know what the Power Principle looks like. It may be that real character, with honor as its core, is not so much a magic list of admirable traits, savvy techniques, and memo-rable to-do's as it is an acknowledgment that the traits we most respect in others are tip-of-the-iceberg manifestations that character is already present. It is in you.

In summary, I would like to share an image and an invitation. Wal-ter Anderson, editor of *Parade* magazine, tells about touring in Russia and visiting Zagorsk, an hour's drive from Moscow. Entering the Church of the Trinity, part of a monastery described by his Russian guide as the center of Russian Christianity, he saw visitors in groups, queued up to kneel before a priest. In his words:

> I heard the notes of a hymn in the air—a haunting and penetrating melody, I thought, but one I did not recognize. And where, I wondered, is the choir? "The hymn is wonderful, but I don't see a choir." Our guide smiled. "As the people walk through," he explained, "they take up the hymn and it stays on their lips until they leave. The believers are the choir. This choir has new members every day; the singing never stops."[6]

We are here but a short time. Whatever our role—leader, parent, teacher, salesperson, friend, family member, CEO—we are the singers who become the choir. Are you singing? Are you teaching the song to others? You have one life to live. You live your life as you believe in living it and then it is gone and you are gone. Yet your legacy may live on in others. Your teaching and leading keeps the song alive. May the song stay on your lips long after you put this book down. May you sing full voice, loud and strong and clear and with power. May *your* singing never stop.

I end as I began, with my belief born of my experiences and yours. The principles we live by create the world we live in; when we change the principles we live by, we will change the world.

APPENDIX: AN INVITATION TO CONTINUE YOUR JOURNEY: NEXT STEPS IN YOUR QUEST

Y OU DON'T BECOME PRINCIPLE-CENTERED IN A DAY. PRINCIPLE-centered power, which enables you to influence others with honor, builds over a lifetime of deliberate living. In this book, I have invited you to consider a way of living the rest of your life. As David Starr Jordan has observed, "Wisdom is knowing what to do; virtue is doing it." Here are some possibilities for you to consider as you reevaluate your key relationships and the types of power bases you want to operate from. I recommend you implement one suggestion at a time. Give yourself permission and space to try and fail and try again. One course correction can put you on a path to a new and different place. One idea, realistically and patiently implemented, can change your life.

1. Share some key ideas with someone else within seventy-two hours. Who would you like to share with?

2. Review the references; obtain and read one of the books noted, to keep your learning alive. What book will you read next?

3. Call 1-888-7-POWER-9 to request a free permanent reference card listing the key principles of power and illustrating the power process. Keep the list where you can see it daily and where it can prompt you to assess your motives when interacting with others, especially in difficult situations. A daily reminder can help you achieve what you really want.

4. At the end of a week as you begin planning for the next week, recall incidents when you operated out of doubt, fear, fairness, or honor. What results did you get? How did you feel about them? Did each approach strengthen or weaken your important relationships? What does your behavior reveal about your real intentions?

5. Complete an analysis of your own power.* Invite someone who knows and understands you to review it with you. What insights does this give you about yourself? What changes would you like to make? How will you proceed?

---

*Covey Leadership Center provides forms to assist you in this process. Call 1-888-7-POWER-9 for a free sample.

6. Examine a key relationship that you would like to improve. What one thing would increase your principle-centered power? What restraining forces make this action difficult?

7. In a quiet place, ask yourself, "What can I do to live by the Power Principle?" Then be still and listen to the answers come from within you. Be true to what you hear; then, later, ask again.

8. What we nurture and pay attention to tends to change and improve. An action plan will help you focus on areas of your leadership which you would like to expand, clarify, improve, or strengthen. A few guidelines:

- First, acknowledge that the pursuit of honor is a lifetime task.
- Second, start by recognizing your desire to improve.
- Third, build on your strengths.
- Fourth, start where you are now.

How will you begin?

NOTES

Chapter 1: Power and Influence

1. Throughout this book, I include comments from participants and clients I have worked with. In nearly all cases, I have retained their actual wording, making only minor corrections for spelling or to clarify wording, tense, and so forth. Each statement has been taken from documents in my files. Specific references to people or places that might identify the individual have been generalized as necessary to protect their privacy. I am truly grateful for the hundreds of experiences that have been generously shared and which have helped me begin to understand the power of honor and the effects of its absence in our relationships. I share these actual accounts as they have been shared with me, with the hope that you might be encouraged to live with honor and have great power for good in the lives of the people you care about most deeply.

Chapter 2: Powerlessness

1. See Tony Schwartz, *What Really Matters: Searching for Wisdom in America* (New York: Bantam, 1995) for an insightful personal exploration and examination of various thought leaders in America in the 1990s.
2. See David Riesman's classic *The Lonely Crowd* (New Haven: Yale University Press, 1950) for an excellent prophetic analysis of the changing American character.
3. Sterling W. Sill, *Leadership* (Salt Lake City: Bookcraft, 1958), p. 48.
4. George Howe Colt, *The Enigma of Suicide* (New York: Summit, 1991).
5. Alan Loy McGinnis, *The Power of Optimism* (New York: Harper and Row, 1990), p. 127.
6. For an excellent summary and fascinating review of this theory by its authors, see Christopher Peterson, Steven Maier, and Martin Seligman, *Learned Helplessness: A Theory for the Age of Personal Control* (New York: Oxford University Press, 1993).
7. Ibid., p. 25.

Chapter 3: Power Shift

1. Unless specifically noted, all names in this book have been changed to protect the privacy and wishes of the actual parties.
2. See Christopher De Vinck, *The Power of the Powerless* (New York: Zondervan/HarperCollins, 1995) for background on how the essay came to be written, the effects on Chris's life after its publication, and other stirring, thoughtful essays by Chris.
3. Candy Lightner and Nancy Hathaway, *Giving Sorrow Words* (New York: Warner Books, 1990).
4. David Whyte, *The Heart Aroused: Poetry and the Preservation of the Soul in Corporate America* (New York: Doubleday, 1994).
5. David Whyte, *Where Many Rivers Meet* (Langley, Washington: Many Rivers Press, 1993).

Chapter 4: Coercive Power

1. *Annie*, Act 1, Scene 8, book by Thomas Meehan (New York: Music Theater International, 1977).
2. Warren Bennis, "Learning to Lead," *Executive Excellence*, January 1996, p. 7.
3. Murray Sidman, *Coercion and Its Fallout* (Boston: Authors Cooperative, 1989).
4. Dick Grote, *Discipline Without Punishment: The Proven Strategy That Turns Problem Employees into Superior Performers* (New York: Amacom, 1995).
5. Ibid., p. 18.
6. Kathleen D. Ryan and Daniel K. Oestreich, *Driving Fear Out of the Workplace* (San Francisco: Jossey-Bass, 1991).

Chapter 5: Utility Power

1. For more information on this approach, see Kenneth Blanchard, "Faster, Simpler, Better," *Executive Excellence*, January 1993.
2. Richard C. Huseman and John D. Hatfield, *Managing the Equity Factor* (Boston: Houghton-Mifflin, 1989).
3. Roger Fisher and William Ury, *Getting to Yes* (Boston: Houghton-Mifflin, 1981); and William Ury, *Getting Past No* (New York: Bantam Books, 1991).
4. David Nyberg, *The Varnished Truth* (Chicago: University of Chicago Press, 1993), p. 183.

Chapter 6: Principle-Centered Power

1. James C. Humes, *The Wit and Wisdom of Winston Churchill* (New York: HarperCollins, 1994), p. 75.

2. Stephen R. Covey, *Principle Centered Leadership* (New York: Simon and Schuster, 1991), p. 31.
3. 2 Timothy 1:7, King James.

Chapter 7: How to Honor

1. I am indebted to David Hanna, a Covey Leadership Center colleague, for the personal experience on which this illustration is based.
2. *The Forbes Scrapbook of Thoughts on the Business of Life* (New York: Forbes, 1976), p. 166.
3. A respected professor shared this with me while I was a student at Brigham Young University in the 1960s. I have been unable to identify an author.
4. *Beowulf*, translated by Robert Gordon (New York: Dover, 1992), p. 1.
5. *Minneapolis Star Tribune*, March 4, 1988.
6. Chungliang A. Huang and Jerry Lynch, *Mentoring: The Tao of Giving Wisdom* (San Francisco: HarperCollins), p. 43.
7. Ibid., p. 45.
8. Ibid., p. 44.
9. Harrison, *Spirit of Leadership*, p. 221.
10. Quoted by Vaughn Featherstone in "Charity Never Faileth," *1979 Devotional Speeches of the Year* (Provo, Utah: Brigham Young University).
11. Henry Wadsworth Longfellow, *Tales of a Wayside Inn*.
12. David McKay, speech given at Brigham Young University, Provo, Utah, April 27, 1948.
13. *Roger Dawson's Secrets of Power Negotiating* (Career Press, 1995; printed in the United States by Book-Mart Press), p. 229.
14. *Mahatma: Life of Mohandas K. Gandhi* (New Delhi: Ministry of Information, 1951).
15. Eknath Easwaran, *Gandhi the Man* (Petaluma, California: Nilgiri Press, 1978), p. 112.
16. Randy Pennington and Marc Bockmon, *On My Honor* (New York: Warner Books, 1992), p. 168.
17. For example, see Joseph Badaracco, Jr., and Richard R. Ellsworth, *Leadership and the Quest for Integrity* (Boston: Harvard Business School Press, 1989).
18. Pennington and Bockman, *On My Honor*, p. 169.
19. Adapted from Easwaran, *Gandhi the Man*, p. 112.
20. John 15:13, King James.
21. Quoted from Sill, *Leadership*.
22. Easwaran, *Gandhi the Man*, Preface.

Chapter 8: How to Increase Principle-Centered Power

1. Maxwell Anderson, *Joan of Lorraine* (New York: Dramatists Play Service, 1947).
2. Noah ben Shea, *Jacob the Baker: Gentle Wisdom for a Complicated World* (New York: Ballantine, 1989), pp. 29–31. Used with permission.
3. Sill, *Leadership,* p. 174.
4. Proverbs 29:18, King James.
5. Mary Scott, "Dilbert's Scott Adams," *Business Ethics,* July/August 1996, p. 27.
6. Andrew Powell, quoted in Seth Godin, *Wisdom, Inc.* (New York: Harper-Business, 1995), p. 49.
7. Walter B. Wriston, *Risk and Other Four Letter Words* (New York: Harper and Row, 1986), pp. 228–31.
8. Guillaume Appollinaire, "Le Larron," *Alcools et Calligrammes,* edited by Claude Debon (Paris: Imprimerie Nationale, 1991), pp. 108–13.
9. Susan Jeffers, *Feel the Fear and Do It Anyway. Dynamic Techniques for Turning Fear and Indecision into Power, Action, and Love* (New York: Fawcett Columbine, 1987). Excellent, readable, and practical suggestions.
10. Stephen R. Covey, *The Seven Habits of Highly Effective People* (New York: Simon and Schuster, 1989), p. 53.
11. Matthew 10:16, King James.
12. Anderson, *The Greatest Risk of All,* p. 77.
13. Marianne Williamson, *A Return to Love: Reflections on the Principles of a Course in Miracles* (New York: HarperCollins, 1992), p. 165.
14. See, for example, James Kouzes and Barry Posner, *Credibility* (San Francisco: Jossey-Bass, 1993).

Chapter 9: Parent Power

1. Victor Brown, Jr., *Human Intimacy* (Salt Lake City: Bookcraft, 1981), p. 14.
2. Carlfred Broderick, *My Parents Married on a Dare* (Salt Lake City: Deseret Book, 1995).
3. Barbara Bush, reported in *The Washington Post,* June 2, 1990, p. 2 (from a speech to graduates of Wellesley College).
4. Kathryn J. Kvols, *Redirecting Children's Behavior* (Gainesville: Incaf Publications, 1993).
5. Colt, *The Enigma of Suicide.*
6. Published by Brite Music Publishing, Salt Lake City, Utah, 1983.
7. Dr. Carter's book was published by Thomas Nelson in Nashville, Tennessee, 1991; Dr. Piaget's book was published by Doubleday (New York), also in 1991.
8. Published by Houghton Mifflin (Boston, 1993).
9. Published by Riverpark Publishing (Las Vegas, 1995).

10. John Rosemond, *Parent Power: A Common Sense Approach to Parenting in the '90s and Beyond* (Kansas City: Andrews and McMeel, 1990), p. 7.
11. Ronna Romney and Beppie Harrison, *Giving Time a Chance: The Secret of a Lasting Marriage* (New York: Bantam, 1983).
12. John Gottman, *Why Marriages Succeed or Fail* (New York: Simon and Schuster, 1994).

Chapter 10: Teaching with Power

1. John Naisbitt, *Megatrends* (New York: Warner Books, 1983).
2. Quoted by Bill Moyers, *A World of Ideas* (New York: Doubleday, 1989), p. 185.
3. James P. Comer, *School Power* (New York: Free Press, 1980), p. 29–30. This indictment is as timely today as when it was written in the 1970s. The book, a wonderful account of a successful educational intervention project led by a coalition of students, teachers, parents, and administrators, was reissued and updated in 1993. Their goal was to help the schools institutionalize a self-sustaining, self-improvement process. The project continues.
4. Moyers, *A World of Ideas*, p. 185.
5. Alan McGinnis, *The Power of Optimism* (New York: Harper and Row, 1990), p. 126.
6. Charles H. Madsen and Clifford K. Madsen, *Teaching/Discipline: Behavioral Principles Toward a Positive Approach* (Boston: Allyn and Bacon, 1970).
7. Grote, *Discipline Without Punishment*, p. 7.
8. Richard Curwin and Allen Mendler, *Discipline with Dignity* (Alexandria, Virginia: Association for Supervision and Curriculum Development), 1995.
9. Comer, *School Power*, p. 110.
10. "Don't Be Shy," *Business Ethics*, January, 1996, p. 15.
11. See Interview with Bill Moyers in Moyers, *A World of Ideas* (New York: Doubleday, 1989).
12. Ibid.
13. The Covey Leadership Center has produced a video vignette about the life of Anne Sullivan on which this description is based: *Teacher: The story of Anne Sullivan*. Contact the Center for viewing and purchasing information. Call 1-800-331-7716.
14. Ibid.
15. Easwaran, *Gandhi the Man*, p. 140.

Chapter 11: Selling with Power

1. Ron Willingham, *Integrity Selling* (New York: Doubleday, 1987).
2. Brian Tracy, *Advanced Selling Strategies* (New York: Simon and Schuster, 1995).
3. Chuck Laughlin and Karen Sage, with Marc Bockmon, *Samurai Selling, The Ancient Art of Service in Sales* (New York: St. Martin's, 1993).

Chapter 12: Leading with Power

1. Pennington and Bockmon's book *On My Honor* is a prescription for how the values represented by this list can lead to success in business.
2. Paul Hersey and Ken Blanchard, *Management of Organizational Behavior* (New Jersey: Prentice Hall, 1972).
3. Robert K. Greenleaf, "The Leader As Servant," in *The Company of Others: Making Community in the Modern World* (New York: Putnam, 1993). For a more complete explanation see Robert K. Greenleaf, *Servant Leadership: A Journey into the Nature of Legitimate Power and Greatness* (New York: Paulist Press, 1977).
4. John Naisbitt and Patricia Aburdene, *Reinventing the Corporation* (New York: Warner Books, 1986), p. 51.
5. Sally Helgesen, *The Female Advantage: Women's Ways of Leadership* (New York: Doubleday/Currency, 1990).
6. Joline Godfrey, "Been There, Doing That," *Inc. Magazine,* March 1996, p. 21.
7. The description of Mack Wilberg and his remarkable chorus is based on an article by Randal Shirley, "With Hearts Full of Song: The BYU Men's Chorus," *Brigham Young Magazine,* November 1994, pp. 43–46.
8. Easwaran, *Gandhi the Man,* p. i.
9. Bennis, "Learning to Lead," p. 7.
10. Interview with Joe Jaworski, reported in "Destiny and the Job of the Leader," *Fast Company,* June/July 1996, pp. 40–41.
11. Bennis, "Learning to Lead," p.7.

Chapter 13: What if They Are Trying to Influence You?

1. Humes, *The Wit and Wisdom of Winston Churchill,* p. 82.
2. See Covey, *The Seven Habits of Highly Effective People,* p. 86.
3. See Chapter 11, "Thirty Methods of Influence," *Principle Centered Leadership.*
4. David Noer, *Healing the Wounds: Overcoming the Trauma of Layoffs and Revitalizing Downsized Organizations* (San Francisco: Jossey-Bass, 1993).
5. Mary Oliver, *Dream Work* (New York: Atlantic Monthly Press, 1986). Used with permission.
6. The following titles address the issues thoroughly: Barbara Ley Toffler, *Tough Choices: Managers Talk Ethics* (New York: Wiley & Sons, 1986); Robert Jackall, *Moral Mazes: The World of Corporate Managers* (New York: Oxford University Press, 1988); Mark Pastin, *The Hard Problems of Management: Gaining the Ethics Edge* (San Francisco: Jossey-Bass, 1986); Myron Peretz Glazer and Penina Migdal Glazer, *The Whistle Blowers: Exposing Corruption in Government and Industry* (New York: Basic Books, 1989).
7. Edwin Markham, "Outwitted," *The Best Loved Poems of the American People,* edited by Hazel Fellman (New York: Doubleday, 1936).

8. See Barbara Sher's empowering approach to gaining your dreams by assembling others who have power in ways you do not and are willing to work with you as a support group because they have your best interests at heart, *Wishcraft* (New York: Ballantine, 1979).

9. M. Scott Peck, "Bringing Authentic Communication into the Workplace," *Business Ethics*, March/April 1994, pp. 17–19.

10. Excellent information on how to deal with controlling people can be found in Gerald W. Piaget, *Control Freaks: Who They Are and How to Stop Them from Running Your Life* (New York: Doubleday, 1991); and Les Carter, *Imperative People: Those Who Must Be in Control (Nashville: Thomas Nelson, 1991).*

11. *See Roger Dawson's Secrets of Power Negotiating* or Gerard Nierenberg, *The Art of Negotiating* and *The Complete Negotiator* (New York: Berkley, 1986).

12. For helpful suggestions, see Stephen R. Covey, "The New Contract," *Executive Excellence Newsletter,* January 1996 (Provo, Utah).

13. Oscar Hammerstein and Sigmund Romberg, "Stout-Hearted Men," (Los Angeles: Warner Publishing, 1925).

14. Detailed procedures are outlined in a gentle, wise way in *Teachings Around the Sacred Wheel: Meditations, Affirmations, and Exercises for Empowerment and Healing* (San Francisco: HarperCollins, 1990), Chapter 3.

Chapter 14: How Do I Change?

1. Tom Rusk and Randy Read, *I Want to Change but I Don't Know How!* (Los Angeles: Price/Stern/Sloan, 1984), p. 128.

2. Bennis, "Learning to Lead," p. 7.

3. *Richard Evans Quotebook* (Salt Lake City: Deseret Book, 1988).

4. Martin E.P. Seligman, *What You Can Change and What You Can't* (New York: Knopf, 1993); "What You Can Change . . . What You Cannot," *Psychology Today,* May/June 1994, pp. 34–41, 70–74, 84.

5. Attributed to Friedrich Oetinger (1702–1782), and to Reinhold Niebuhr as "The Serenity Prayer" (1934).

6. Michael McLean's song, Let It Go, with music by John Batdorf, © 1991 Shining Star Music ASCAP, is available on CD and cassette as a part of his album, *You've Always Been There for Me,* distributed through Deseret Book, Salt Lake City, Utah.

7. This event was described in correspondence from Michael McLean to the author. I am indebted to Michael for his generous encouragement and for sharing this insightful experience.

Chapter 15: Living with Honor

1. Glenn Richardson, "Why a Good Night's Sleep May Not Conquer Fatigue," *BYU Today*, July 1992, p. 15.
2. Harrison, *Spirit of Leadership*, p. 48.
3. Joseph Campbell, *The Hero with a Thousand Faces* (Princeton, N.J.: Princeton University Press, 1990).
4. José Luis González-Balado and Janet N. Playfoot, *My Life for the Poor: Mother Teresa of Calcutta* (San Francisco: editors, Harper & Row, 1985).
5. Howard Fineman, "The Virtuecrats," *Newsweek*, June 13, 1994, p. 36.
6. Anderson, *The Greatest Risk of All*.

INDEX

ABOUT COVEY LEADERSHIP CENTER

Dr. Blaine Lee is a founding vice president of Covey Leadership Center, a worldwide firm devoted to the development of principle-centered leadership based on many of the ideas described in this book. Their mission statement is:

To serve the worldwide community by empowering people and organizations to significantly increase their performance capability in order to achieve worthwhile purposes through understanding and living principle-centered leadership. In carrying out this mission, we continually strive to practice what we teach.

For more than a decade Covey Leadership Center has been recognized as one of the world's premier leadership development authorities, helping thousands of individuals and organizations solve personal, professional and organizational problems through Principle-Centered Leadership. Covey Leadership Center focuses on principles rooted in the unchanging natural laws that govern human and organizational effectiveness—laws that are timeless, universal, and intercultural.

This 700-member international firm is committed to empowering people and organizations to significantly increase their performance capability by building high-trust, high-performance cultures.

Covey Leadership Center's client portfolio includes eighty-two of the Fortune 100 companies, over two-thirds of the Fortune 500 companies, as well as thousands of small and mid-size companies, government entities, educational institutions, communities, families, and millions of individual consumers. The Center's work in Principle-Centered Leadership is considered by its clients to be an instrumental foundation to the effectiveness of quality, leadership, service, team building, organizational alignment, and many other strategic corporate initiatives.

Their vision is to teach people and organizations to teach themselves and become interdependent with the Center. To the timeless adage of Lao Tzu, "Give a man a fish and you feed him for a day; teach him how to fish and you feed him for a lifetime," they add, "Develop teachers of fishermen and you lift all society."

This empowerment process is carried out through programs conducted at facilities in the Rocky Mountains of Utah, custom corporate on-site programs and consulting, facilitator certification, as well as public workshops in over 100 cities in North America and over 40 countries worldwide.

Their unique contextual approach to building high-trust cultures by addressing all four leadership levels—personal, interpersonal, managerial, and organizational—has proven to have a sustainable long-term effect on individuals' or organizations' capability to thrive in a changing environment.

Covey Leadership Center
3507 North University Avenue, Suite 100, Provo, Utah 84604-4479

Toll Free: 1-888-7-POWER-9
Fax: 801-342-6236
International: 801-229-1333 or by fax 801-229-1233
Internet: http://www.covey.com

CLC's products and programs provide a wide range of resources for individuals, families, and business, government, nonprofit, and educational organizations, including:

Programs

Covey Leadership Week
Principle-Centered Leadership
The 7 Habits of Highly Effective People
First Things First Time-Management
The Power Principle
Facilitator Workshops for In-House Certification

Products

7 Habits Organizer time-management system
Microsoft Schedule+ with 7 Habits tools
7 Habits audiotapes
Living the 7 Habits audiotapes
Principle-Centered Leadership audiotapes
First Things First audiotapes

7 Habits of Highly Effective Families audiotapes
How to Write a Mission Statement audiotapes
The Power Principle audiotapes
7 Habits Effectiveness Profile
Stakeholder Information System (SIS) baseline report
Principle-Centered Living Video
Covey Reference Library on CD-ROM
Covey Leadership Library Video workshops
7 Habits poster series

Custom Consulting and Speeches

Custom Principle-Centered Leadership programs
Custom-On-Site programs
Consulting and speeches
Keynote addresses
Custom education programs

Publications

The 7 Habits Magazine
The 7 Habits of Highly Effective People
Principle-Centered Leadership
First Things First
First Things First Everyday
Daily Reflections of Highly Effective
    People
The Power Principle

Covey Leadership Center
    International Offices

CLC Australia
Ph: (61-7) 259-0222
Fx: (61-7) 369-7810

CLC Bermuda
Ph: (809) 236-0383
Fx: Same as Phone

CLC England
Ph: (44-121) 604-6999
Fx: (44-121) 604-6777

CLC Indonesia
Ph: (62-21) 572-0761
Fx: (62-21) 572-0762

CLC Ireland
Ph: (353-1) 280-0731
Fx: (353-1) 284-3697

CLC Japan
Ph: (81-3) 3264-7401
Fx: (81-3) 3264-7402

CLC Korea
Ph: (82-2) 3453-3361/4
Fx: (82-2) 3453-3365

CLC Latin America
Ph: (407) 644-4416
Fx: (407) 644-5919

CLC Malaysia & Brunei
Ph: (60-3) 758-6418
Fx: (60-3) 755-2589

CLC Nigeria
Ph: (234-1) 260-1760
Fx: (234-1) 261-6963

CLC Philippines
Ph: (63-2) 924-4490
Fx: (63-2) 924-1869

CLC Singapore, Hong Kong,
    Taiwan, China, Vietnam
Ph: (65) 838-8600 or 8629
Fx: (65) 838-8618/8628

CLC South Africa
Ph: (27-11) 442-4589/4596
Fx: (27-11) 442-4190

CLC Thailand
Ph: (662) 229-3911/20
Fx: (662) 229-3107

All other countries:
CLC International
Ph: (801) 229-1333
Fx: (801) 229-1233

ABOUT THE AUTHOR

Dr. Blaine Lee is a founding vice president of Covey Leadership Center, one of the world's premier leadership development authorities. Covey Leadership Center's client portfolio includes eighty-two of the Fortune 100 companies, and more than two-thirds of the Fortune 500 companies, as well as thousands of small and mid-sized companies, government entities, educational institutions, communities, families, and millions of individual consumers.

Blaine has created and delivered custom leadership development programs for many world-class organizations, including: Procter & Gamble, U.S. West, Intel, IBM, Pillsbury, General Motors, Conoco, Blue Cross/Blue Shield, Andersen Consulting, Arthur Andersen, NASA, Occidental Petroleum, MCI, Mass Mutual, Kimberly Clark, Prudential, Nabisco, Xerox, and many others.

Blaine has also been a contributing author to books by Stephen R. Covey and Norman Vincent Peale, and has written college texts on teaching and organizational behavior. His teaching takes him over a third of a million miles annually. His ability to deal perceptively with difficult organizational and people problems has made him a unique advisor to senior executives in many kinds of organizations. A trainer's trainer, he is called a "Life-Coach" by leaders who claim he helps them do with their lives what athletic coaches can do with their muscles.

Blaine has been studying, teaching, and coaching successful men and women for more than twenty-five years. He has been on the faculty of four colleges and universities and has twice been recognized as one of the Outstanding Young Men of America. He was the Director of Instructional Systems Development for the entire Air Force as a young captain. He cofounded and was Educational Director for two professional private residential schools for troubled teenagers. He created the National Speakers School, has mentored several past presidents of the National Speakers Association, and is listed in *International Leaders in Achievement* and *Who's Who in America*.

Blaine and his sweetheart, Shawny, live in a country home in the Rocky Mountains near Salt Lake City, Utah, where he relishes his time as a deliberate dad. He received his masters degree in instructional psychology from Brigham Young University in Utah and his Ph.D. in educational psychology from the University of Texas at Austin.